This Little Light Of Mine

This Little Light Of Mine

The Inspiring Story of Kevin Triplett … Carrying His Cross of Cancer

Wayne Triplett
Father of Kevin Triplett

THIS LITTLE LIGHT OF MINE
THE INSPIRING STORY OF KEVIN TRIPLETT
... CARRYING HIS CROSS OF CANCER

iUniverse books may be ordered through booksellers or by contacting:

iUniverse
1663 Liberty Drive
Bloomington, IN 47403
www.iuniverse.com
844-349-9409

Scripture quotations are from the Holy Bible, King James Version (KJV). Copyright 1989 by Thomas Nelson, Inc.

Cover graphic by Osbornes' Photo
Front cover/flap photos by Wayne Triplett
Back cover/flap photos by First Choice Resources, Inc.

ISBN: 978-0-5954-6174-5 (sc)
ISBN: 978-0-5957-0382-1 (hc)
ISBN: 978-0-5959-0475-4 (e)

Print information available on the last page.

iUniverse rev. date: 10/06/2022

This book is dedicated in loving memory to my son, Kevin,
whose faith, courage, and music continue to inspire and touch so many lives.

For Kevin
Love Dad

Kevin Wayne Triplett
December 7, 1986–November 27, 2006

Fighting cancer has been the roughest battle of my life, but I believe it has brought me closer to God and made me a better person. I think this is God's purpose for my life: to carry on in spite of what has happened to me, to make the best of difficult days, and to make lemonade from lemons.

—Kevin W. Triplett

CONTENTS

A friend that sticks closer than a brother—that was the relationship
that developed through the years between Kevin and Dr. Tom McLean.
Doctor, encourager, friend; Tom was all those and more.
Through good times and bad, he was always there for Kevin.

FOREWORD

On July 20, 2005, eighteen-year-old Kevin Triplett came to the emergency room with shortness of breath and chest pain. His oxygen level was very low, and a chest x-ray showed no air at all on the right side. We knew he had cancer that had spread to his chest, and the logical assumption was that it was growing. There was little doubt in my mind that Kevin was going to die soon, probably within a few days, maybe a few weeks at most. I had a heart-to-heart talk with Kevin and his father, Wayne, about my prediction. It was time to talk about a "Do Not Resuscitate" directive, get affairs in order, and plan a funeral.

Kevin lived for another sixteen months. He not only recovered from that episode, but was able to resume much of his normal daily activities for well over a year. It just goes to show how much mystery still remains in medicine. This episode also illustrates Kevin's fighting spirit and will to live.

What an honor and privilege for me to write this foreword for Wayne Triplett's book about his son, Kevin. As one of Kevin's oncologists, I obviously came to know him quite well. I will leave it to you, the reader, to judge the kind of young man he was, based on this book. Wayne's tribute to his only son is his expression of turning grief into joy. Despite having survived cancer twice himself, Wayne continues to share his faith, his earthly possessions, and his love and compassion for others. Kevin was definitely a chip off the old block.

Perhaps the greatest tribute I can give Kevin is this: In my career, I have known hundreds of patients who have died, many of whom have touched me deeply. Of all those patients, Kevin is one of only two whose pictures hang on my office wall.

Although progress is being made in the fight against cancer, we still have a long way to go. Kevin helped us inch closer to a cure by his willing participation in clinical trials. The knowledge we gain from these trials will help us cure patients in the future.

I implore you to apply the lessons from Kevin's life and this book. Live life to the fullest, show kindness and compassion, give generously, and turn your grief into joy. Finally, if the opportunity arises, enroll (or encourage a loved one) in a clinical trial. You'll be helping us inch closer to a cure. Kevin would've wanted it that way.

Thomas W. McLean, MD
Associate Professor of Pediatrics
Wake Forest University School of Medicine
Winston-Salem, North Carolina
June 2007

ACKNOWLEDGMENTS

The realization of this book is due in large part to the hundreds of friends and co-workers who cared enough to put their faith into action and offer encouraging words to Kevin and me. Their encouragements not only became the framework of this book but offered us additional strength to carry on. Only their given names are listed, but they know who they are.

The leadership and members of Millers Creek Baptist Church became our rocks in the time of storms with their unwavering support. Pastor Jim Gore and children's minister Shannon Critcher were stalwarts of prayer for us. Craig Church, student pastor, became Kevin's closest ally through his constant intercession with God on Kevin's behalf.

The *Wilkes Journal-Patriot* staff, including publisher Jule Hubbard, editor Charles Williams, and reporters Frances Hayes and Karin M. Clack, championed Kevin's battles with numerous articles heightening their readers' awareness of cancer. Many of those articles and excerpts are contained in this book.

We were blessed with a great medical team at the Brenner Children's Hospital at Wake Forest University Baptist Medical Center in Winston-Salem, North Carolina. This team was led by Dr. Allen Chauvenet, Dr. Tom McLean, and Dr. Marcia Wofford. Dr. McLean or "Tom," as you will come to know him through his e-mails, was with us all the way. He was more than just a caring, compassionate doctor. He became one of our dearest friends, willing to do whatever he could for Kevin any time and any hour of the day or night. My partner in research, his tenacity bought Kevin valuable time. Nurses Nancy Smith, Debby Cohen, Diane Samelak, Gina Idol, Billie, Dan, Terry, and Shea became our family, too. Liz Clark, his teacher, kept Kevin in the know while he was hospitalized. Jeff Ungetheim offered tremendous counsel.

Dr. William (Bill) Ward, an orthopedic surgeon, became a wonderful friend and inspiration to Kevin. His surgical expertise is legendary. Dr. Tom Pranikoff and Dr. Michael Hines were marvelous surgeons as well.

The M. D. Anderson Cancer Center team, along with God's grace, gave Kevin an additional fifteen months of life by providing the greatest of care. Dr. Pete Anderson, a pediatric oncologist and cancer researcher, endeared himself to us as a special friend, as did his chief nurse Peggy Pearson and nurses Maritza, Paula, Sandi, Nicole, and Toni. Pete's easy-going style and incredible knowledge base were truly inspirational. He and Kevin relished talking about the Civil War era, a passion for both of them. The entire nursing staff at M. D. Anderson constantly offered empathy and caring. Dr. Scott Evans was a reservoir of knowledge on Kevin's pulmonary issues.

Dr. Craig Bennett and Dr. John Pontzer offered great support locally. They were always inquiring about Kevin's progress and received notes from the specialists.

Physical therapy was a big part of Kevin's rehabilitation. In essence, he had to learn to use his right leg again. Randy Poteat, a physical therapist, came to our rescue and gave Kevin literally hours of therapy, good conversation, and encouragement and became a wonderful friend.

Tony Mancusi's special gift was his love of music, which he readily shared with Kevin as teacher and pupil. Music, especially the guitar, became a passion for Kevin as he turned to it for solace and inspiration.

Millers Creek Intermediate School, Mt. Pleasant Elementary School, Wilkes Career Education Center, North Wilkesboro Elementary School, C. C. Wright Elementary School, and the entire Wilkes County Schools system's staff and employees offered financial and familial support. West Wilkes High School students and staff were truly loved by Kevin and they loved him back. Fran Cantrell, the school nurse, was with us all the way as you will read in her e-mails.

Kenneth Crouse's advice in the area of alternative medicine gave us additional hope that healing can come in many forms. His words of encouragement meant so much to us.

The positive influence of Martha "Ms. Martha" McGee's nurturing and love laid a firm, Christian foundation for Kevin's life. She and her husband, "Mr. David," embodied the essence of a devoted, Christian family.

Terri, Steve, Andrew, and Lindsay Scott of Oceana, West Virginia, became friends for life as they faced their own ordeals as Steve and Terri's son, Aaron, one of Kevin's dearest friends, battled cancer. Reading Terri's poignant e-mails, you will glimpse the heartache and heroism shouldered by this remarkable lady and her family.

Aaron Scott and Matthew Earney, Kevin's close friends with cancer preceding him in death, were the cement bonding them in a common goal, to beat this disease. Each of them found solace in the presence of the other. Together they weathered many storms.

The boys in the bands, from the Edge (Gwyn McGlamery, Matthew Francis, Grant Miller, and Ricky Absher) to his beloved Taking Up Arms (Adam Minton, Charlie and Jim Coleman, and Joe Hutchinson), spent many hours together practicing and performing, which was the realization of a dream come true for Kevin. TUA's final appearance was a fundraiser benefiting Kevin's memorial scholarship fund.

Gwyn McGlamery, Kevin's closest friend, shared a special bond with a mutual love of the guitar and music in general. Both boys realized the formation of their own bands. Gwyn and Kevin were inseparable and together shared many trips to the movies, Alaska, the beach, concerts, and even the hospital. Kevin often said, "I never had a brother, but Gwyn seems like one to me." They loved each other like family.

My sisters, Jill Whitman and Naomi Triplett, supported him with frequent calls and cards. Kevin's grandparents, Ralph and Martha Shew (Pa and Granny), were always there for him, and he loved them dearly. Ruby Triplett, also his grandmother, prayed for Kevin constantly and loved it when he visited her. Kevin's mother, Kathy, loved him dearly and partnered with me during the course of his illness. His absence has created an emptiness in our lives which cannot be filled by another.

Kevin's life of sacrifice and humility offered the supreme motivation for this book. I continue to learn from the many things he taught me: patience, mercy, forgiveness, courage, and perseverance. Most of all, his faith has been the catalyst to catapult many lives from the mediocre to the superlative. His life served as a challenge to all of us, as Kevin said, to make lemonade from the lemons we oftentimes are given. It is a simple prescription, perhaps, for what troubles us. It is a simple prescription that Kevin proved works over and over, time after time.

PREFACE

"This little light of mine, I'm going to let it shine. I'm not going to make it shine, I'm just going to let it shine. Ev'ry day, ev'ry day, gonna let my little light shine." The words of this spiritual capture the essence of Kevin's life. The strength he needed to battle cancer beamed from the Light (Christ) and, in turn, shone to those around him.

Why did I write this book? Kevin touched so many lives, and the positive influence he had on people, young and old, endeared him to everyone. His story, his courageous battle against cancer, had to be told. His was a life well lived, grounded in an uncompromising faith in Christ that whatever happened, he would be fine. Driven by an initial obsession to find the magic bullet to cure his cancer and later to chronicle his struggles, I have relived the happiness and the heartache, which were his and mine, in the writing of this book.

Encouraged by many, this book is a collection of medical updates sent and e-mails received, chronologically arranged to allow you, as best as possible, to grasp the enormity of his struggle over the seven years of his affliction. You will go behind the scenes and witness the tremendous love and care extended to Kevin, his mother, and me, as you read the e-mails once known only to Kevin and me. It is peppered with recollections, and you will gain new insight into the battle that was his. Far from a glorification of Kevin, it is a testimony to the power of faith in one young man's life, as it catapulted him above his afflictions. Each chapter opens with verses of scripture Kevin had marked in his personal Bible which had special significance to him. Kevin's autobiography will offer you a glimpse of a life that mattered. The magic bullet eluded me, but Kevin's healing, nonetheless, is now complete, for he is at home with his heavenly Father.

My heart aches for him daily, and I miss so many of the things that were Kevin. The "bet I can make you smile and show your teeth" game we played when he was small; the "family hug" with which he often embraced his mom and me; the "give me five" he and I often exchanged spontaneously as we traveled down the road together; the sudden burst of laughter that he emitted when I grabbed his ticklish left knee: All of these are now precious memories. I can still see his infectious smile as I would raise my hand in praise to the lyrics of a Christian rock song that touched my heartstrings, while riding to and from chemotherapy sessions. Cradling his toboggan or his shirt to my face, I can breathe in the lingering essence which was Kevin. I am forever to relive in my mind's eye the way he would answer me with a slight left and right motion of his outstretched hand, and I can still see the inward turning of his lips as he made beautiful music with his guitar.

Indeed, Kevin and I often talked about "the book" I would write someday, and someday is now a reality. The writing of this book has been many things to me. Revisiting the harsh realities of his body ravaged with cancer, though painful, has helped me see just how monumental his accomplishments and dogged determination to stay alive were. My therapy lies in this writing. And by writing, I give you a piece of Kevin. He came to view his disease as his way of glorifying God. He lived by the creed "let others see Jesus in me," and that they did.

The irony that I developed cancer along the way is but a footnote to the suffering Kevin had to endure. By Kevin's stripes perhaps many will be healed, since he submitted to many cutting-edge, newly discovered therapies. Many lives have been enriched by their chance encounters with Kevin and with his story. The triumph of the human spirit over adversity became his mantle. The Word of God was his solace.

I offer this book to you with the hope that you will be strengthened and encouraged to persevere amid your personal struggles. My faith is stronger and my resolve to meet Kevin again someday is more determined. Until that day, I challenge each of us to live life to the fullest, as he did, and to find joy in the simple things. The trail Kevin blazed by the Christian life he lived guides my way, and our parting will be for just a season. Carrying his cross of cancer was difficult, but Kevin's little light (his faith in Jesus Christ) shone brightly. His inspiring story is my gift to you.

Wayne Triplett
Millers Creek, North Carolina
July 2007

CHAPTER 1

THOSE WERE THE DAYS

All smiles and in the buff!
Emerging from his secret hiding place, Kevin and "passie" were ready to rumble.

Kevin plants a kiss on Ernie, one of his favorite *Sesame Street* characters.
"Make that face, Kevin," said Dad.
And he readily obliged.

"Peep eye, Daddy," Kevin seems to be saying.
The outdoors beckoned as autumn leaves rustled under foot.

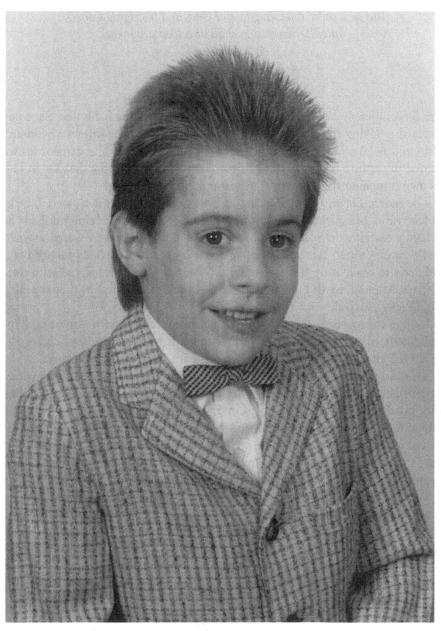

Kevin looked quite fetching wearing his dad's vintage bow tie and jacket.

But seek ye first the kingdom of God, and his righteousness;
and all these things shall be added unto you.
Matthew 6:33

The December 6, 1986, evening was a typical one. Much of that Saturday involved readying the nursery for Kevin's arrival. Everyone knows a woman's first child is late, never early, and we had weeks to spare. The camcorder we needed to capture his birth still eluded us. Little did we know that Kevin had his own timetable and his arrival was imminent.

The movie *Enemy Mine*, starring Dennis Quaid and Louis Gossett Jr., was on television and occupied us, but not for long. Kathy, while lying on the sofa, suddenly exclaimed, "Something is wet here. Oh no, I think my water has broken!" I recall yelling, "Are you sure? We better move fast!" We had practiced several drills to make it up the mountain to Watauga General Hospital with time to spare. After all, we did not want a repeat of Ricky and Lucy as they fumbled Little Ricky's arrival.

Kathy's composure soon faded as she began to tremble with fear, or perhaps excitement, at what was to come. I even dropped my "It's A Boy" cigars as I closed the kitchen door! Yes, our first venture into parenting had begun.

The early morning, December 7, 1986, labor seemed short lived, at least for me, because just over three hours later at 3:58 AM, high-pitched wailing resounded through the birthing room of Watauga General. Dr. Marchese had guided me all the way through Kevin's delivery, summoning me ever closer for his commentary. "Wayne, do you see him crowning? There is his head. I may need those forceps," he stated calmly. Yes, the Lamaze was a godsend. I think Kathy and I were both focusing on that spot on the wall.

What a boy, weighing in at eight pounds and seven and three-quarters ounces, and over twenty-one inches long! I remember Kevin turning his head toward me, recognizing my voice when I called his name. The days of his mom wearing the headset on her tummy as Kevin listened to the alphabet and symphonic music had made an indelible impression on him already. From that moment on, my life was never the same. What a momentous event, witnessing the birth of my son!

Kevin rapidly grew into his high chair gobbling up the latest flavor variations of Gerber and Beechnut products for each hearty meal. The Similac, a liquid formula, did not agree with him, so Infamil came to the rescue.

Soon, it was time for Kathy to return to work, and cutting the apron strings loomed before us. I had heard of a wonderful Christian woman who often kept mostly teachers' children in her home. Martha McGee (Ms. Martha) was all that and more. Kevin's time with her and her husband, David, helped mold him into a young boy with a good head on his shoulders and a Christian perspective. Each weekday morning, Kevin and I would arrive at her home arm in arm with a bag filled with baby bottles. Ms. Martha provided everything: a wonderful tree swing, plenty of space to play outside and in her basement, a row of high chairs in her kitchen equipped with a hearty breakfast for her toddlers, and the biggest heart ever. Martha remarked, "Kevin is the only child I ever kept that I never had to correct. He always wanted to please." She and Mr. David remain wonderful friends. Kevin and Aaron Bishop, his first best friend at Ms. Martha's, were inseparable, even when Aaron bit him. There was no need to worry, because they eventually worked it out.

As Kevin grew I kept reminding him that, "You've had your baby time. Now it's your toddler time." Each day I would rush home from Ms. Martha's with him just to play some of our favorite games. I never realized those build-a-blocks could reach so high! Kevin would laugh heartily when he watched me toss the roll of paper towels into the air, spin them around, and still manage to catch them. The "pampermobile" (an empty box which became Kevin's car) zoomed all over the house with me at the controls, either pushing or pulling. Our first home in the Ravenwood subdivision overlooked a hill. Kevin spent hours in his stroller with Dad pushing him up and down the hill, all the while racing a clear, plastic ball tossed on the pavement.

Kevin's toddler time was not without its moments of crisis. One afternoon, after picking him up at Ms. Martha's, he discovered his toboggan, or "bogger," was missing. I searched the car and house over to no avail. Finally, returning to Ms. Martha's, it turned up. Kevin needed it. The red bogger had a small ball on top, which he would rub over his eyelids or the palms of his hands until sleep overcame him.

A poignant moment I will always remember came one Saturday morning at Glenn's Tastee-Freez Restaurant. Kevin's mom and I had just pulled in to park with Kevin securely buckled in his car seat in back. We were trying to figure out our breakfast strategy before going inside. I questioned Kathy, "Who's going to feed the munchkin?" (That was a pet name I had given Kevin.) Suddenly from the car seat, Kevin chimed in, "Daddy's gonna feed the munchkin!" What a priceless gem from out of the mouth of a toddler.

Searching for that special action figure or toy became on occasion a futile adventure. Ninja Turtles, Star Trek figures, Star Wars death stars, and dinosaurs, were all up for grabs for parents like me making endless trips to Toys "R" Us.

A joy of a parent's celebration of childhood is the total immersion into a world of fun and games, where for a brief period of time the cares of adulthood are suspended. Kevin was quite ticklish and when I came at him for "belly sugar" (blowing on his tummy making a weird sound), he wriggled with delight. Sometimes we would mimic the Eskimos with a joyful nose kiss. Perhaps a throw back to my childhood, as Kevin would rush by, I would grab him with my legs, pinning him until he said the magic words "Dobie Gillis." He especially loved the times I read fairy tales to him. *Hansel and Gretel* was a favorite, but when I attached the plastic, green witch finger with the red fingernail to my index finger mumbling the words "nibble nibble" in my best witch voice, he would run for cover.

Kevin had a special way of making an outside chore so much fun. Raking leaves was not a mundane task. It was an adventure piling them into tight bundles with Kevin in the middle. He was my little "bird nest Kevin."

The lost-at-the-beach incident provided another moment of panic. Kevin and I had been floating on inflatable rafts in the waters just off the Myrtle Beach shoreline. Suddenly, on coming to shore, I could not find him. The current had carried me slightly down the shoreline and Kevin was not in sight. "Kevin, where are you?" I yelled. His voice did not return. After running up and down the beach several minutes, I saw his tiny figure approaching. We embraced and he said, "Dad, I was scared. I thought I lost you." "No, Kevin," I said, "you will never lose me." That was a promise I would honor the remainder of his life.

In September 1989, we moved to our second home in the Ravenwood subdivision, and Kevin made two more best friends, Frankie and Christopher Barger. What a time they had the nine years we lived there. So many firsts happened during this time. Kevin learned to ride a bike, played football, had sword fights, went on nature walks, pitched baseballs, rollerbladed, and shared in the incredible Ravenwood Olympics pitting parents against each other in some wacky events.

Kevin's first venture into pet ownership came when his Pa and Granny Shew allowed him to pick two kittens from a bountiful litter of little ones. He wasted no time in naming the black-and-white male Spunky, and the calico-colored female Bubble Gum. Today, my mother has adopted them, and they roam freely in the country some fourteen years after their births.

It was good-bye toddler time and hello boy time when Kevin joined a local tee-ball team. I could see that coach-pitch and regular baseball were looming in his future. I often kidded him about the movie *Angels in the Outfield*, since his team was the Angels. He said, "Dad, you better not do that angel wing flapping with your arms on the field." Basketball brought him much joy, too, as he played for Applefield Realty and later clinched the county basketball championship at Millers Creek Intermediate School. Coaches Dan Pardue and Mac Atwood recognized talent when they saw it!

An annual tradition was Christmas Eve at Granny and Pa Shew's home. Santa, a.k.a. Dad, always made an appearance bearing gifts to the delight of young and old alike. Kevin returned the warm nurturing they gave him with frequent visits to play, or to just sit and talk with them.

Kevin's mom, Kathy, and I separated in 1998, and I was ready to move again. I sold our house, and Kevin and I built a smaller one on Goddard Lane in Millers Creek. It was here that Kevin, Michael Parsons, and I became interested in WWF (now WWE) wrestling. I recorded almost every RAW program, which led later into our attending at least two live events. "Nonstop action" was the buzzword around our house.

It was also during this time that Kevin became concerned about the condition of his soul. He felt the tug of the Holy Spirit beckoning him to ask Christ for salvation. Kevin loved his Grandpa Shew greatly, so he became the perfect person for some private counsel. Kevin shared his feelings and knelt to pray. He gave his heart to Jesus! Later, he talked with Pastor Jim Gore of our home church, Millers Creek Baptist, to confirm his salvation experience. From this point forward, Kevin's great faith in God became a source of comfort and strength, especially in the difficult times which lay ahead. Kevin penned his salvation experience, which I framed with his photo and a lock of his hair.

Kevin wrote, "Back in 1999 I had been going to church. I believed in God and I believed that Jesus was His Son." Jesus said in John 3:16, "For God so loved the world that He gave his only begotten Son, that whosoever believeth in Him should not perish but have everlasting life." Ephesians 2: 8–9 states, "For by grace are ye saved through faith; and not of yourselves: it is the gift of God: Not of works, lest any man should boast."

Kevin wrote, "I knew I was a sinner. I wanted to get saved and go to heaven. I wanted to turn from my sin. I was at my grandparents house one day and we got to talking about Jesus. I told them that I believed and I wanted to get saved, and that I felt the conviction of the Holy Spirit drawing me to Christ. I told them I was afraid to go to the altar because of all the people in the congregation. I got real emotional talking to them and started crying. They told me not to be afraid. When I left their house that day I was not afraid any more. I think I might have been saved there."

Jesus said in Revelation 3:20, "Behold, I stand at the door and knock; if any man hear my voice and open the door, I will come in to him and will sup with him and he with me." Kevin continued, "About a week later my dad took me to see Pastor Gore. He shared the Gospel with me. We prayed a salvation prayer, and I invited Jesus into my life. I accepted Christ."

Jesus stated in John 14:6 and John 6:37 respectively, "I am the way, the truth and the life; no man cometh unto the Father but by me … and him that cometh to me I will in no wise cast out."

Kevin concluded with Romans 10:9, "That if thou shalt confess with thy mouth the Lord Jesus and shalt believe in thine heart that God hath raised Him from the dead, thou shalt be saved." Kevin stated, "I was baptized two weeks later."

On occasion, at home, I would venture upstairs to check on him. Sometimes he would be talking, but no one was physically in his bedroom with him. He would be praying, talking to his heavenly Father, much like you and I would converse. He would revisit his day of salvation many times in the future. Like many of us, as a new Christian, he struggled with doubt, but on repeated occasions, he fervently "drove down the stake of assurance" of his salvation. He loved his "quiet time" and he would steal away to his room almost daily to commune with his Lord. The strength he garnered from those intimate sessions was strength enough to see him through the major battles that lay ahead of him.

Kevin had no brothers or sisters, and of course received all the attention. That was no substitute for companionship though, and Kevin approached me for a puppy. Two puppies were located in a kennel near his grandparents' home and Kevin, on crutches, made the trip down the rain-soaked hill to take a look. Immediately, he fell in love with the tiny black-and-white rat terrier, which he would soon name Taco. Though difficult for Kevin to care for while on crutches, I picked up the gauntlet and nurtured the tiny pup to the full-fledged nineteen-pound dog he is today. Kevin loved him, and Taco brought Kevin many hours of companionship. Today, after seven years, Taco and I are still best friends.

At the time, those days seemed to never end. I relive the warmth of those wonder years before the dark specter of cancer made its appearance over and over in my mind. I take comfort in knowing that I can journey back to those carefree times in my memory. I have those memories forever with me.

CHAPTER 2

THE DIAGNOSIS

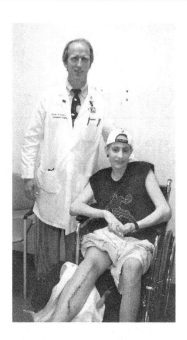

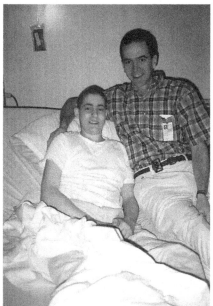

Dr. William (Bill) Ward removed Kevin's leg tumor then implanted a metal rod and allograft.
Dr. Tom McLean, Brenner Children's Hospital oncologist, treated Kevin's cancer for seven years, wrote the foreword for this book, and became a dear friend.

Dr. Allen Chauvenet and Dr. Marcia Wofford, oncologists at Brenner Children's Hospital, designed treatment protocols, and provided counsel and their friendship during Kevin's seven-year struggle with cancer.

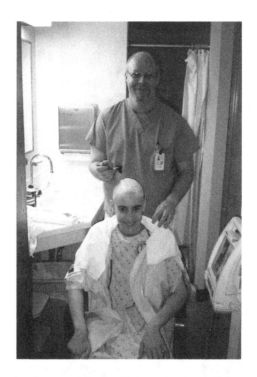

Terry Thomas was not only a great nurse, but a pretty good barber, too.
"A little off the top, Kevin?" he asked.

In appreciation of their dedication and care, Kevin and I presented his doctors at Brenner Children's Hospital with special thank-you plaques after his first year of chemotherapy.

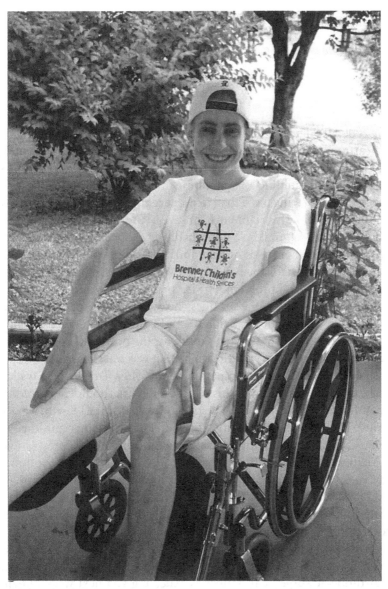

Kevin's new mode of travel was a wheelchair. He wore out two of them, along with three pairs of crutches, two leg braces, and a cane.

Have not I commanded thee?
Be strong and of a good courage; be not afraid, neither be thou dismayed:
for the Lord thy God is with thee whithersoever thou goest.
Joshua 1: 9

The year 2000 was dawning for Kevin and me. On New Year's Eve 1999, I purchased an attractive decanter of grape juice, and as midnight approached, Kevin and I toasted in the New Year. This new century offered so much promise, since we were thinking of building a larger home in the spring.

Kevin had been playing basketball in the seventh grade and had been experiencing some pain below his right knee for several months. Dr. Craig Bennett, an orthopedic surgeon, felt that he had probably developed tendonitis or a sprain, so he prescribed Kevin a series of heat and stretching sessions at the Wellness Center. Kevin was losing some weight, but with his basketball game schedule, this did not seem to be a problem. His leg pain was intermittent, but one day in late March 2000, I saw some puffiness below his right knee. I immediately set up an appointment with Dr. Bennett and Kevin was scheduled for an MRI. On April 7, we arrived at Dr. Bennett's office for the post-MRI consultation. We were not prepared for the devastating news that was only moments away.

As usual, we were in an examination room when Dr. Bennett walked in. After a few pleasantries and with his hand on Kevin's shoulder, he uttered the words that forever changed the course of our lives. He said, "Kevin, we need to get serious. The MRI showed a large, dark area below your right knee in the tibia bone. I am sending you to a specialist next week at Wake Forest University Baptist Medical Center. I think you may have osteogenic sarcoma or bone cancer. You can beat this, but it may mean a year or more of chemotherapy."

A cold chill and then a sickening feeling crept over me. I could feel tears welling up in my eyes and Kevin seemed stunned. "Are you sure, Craig? Could it be something else?" I asked. "No, Wayne, it looks definite and it has been growing for some time. This probably was the source of his earlier pain. In most cases, it is just growing pains. This is very rare. Dr. William Ward, a highly trained orthopedic surgeon at Baptist, is expecting you next week." Kevin, his voice shaking, questioned, "Will I be fine after my treatments? Will I be able to do normal things again?" Dr. Bennett tried to reassure us, but everything seemed a blur. If you had driven by Northwest Orthopedics that afternoon, you would have seen Kevin and me sitting there in the first parking space, crying, hugging each other, and trying to look for a silver lining somewhere on this dark, ominous cloud which enveloped us.

I called family members that weekend and, choking back the tears, tried to reassure them that Kevin would be fine. I recall Dr. Joseph Johnson, Wilkes County Schools' superintendent, calling me and asking how we were. I tearfully replied, "Yes, we are fine." "No," he replied, "you are not. Take whatever time you need, and we are here to help you in any way."

Michael Parsons, Kevin's close friend, posed a piercing question to me. "He's not going to die, is he?" Michael asked. I tried to reassure him that with proper treatment and surgery, Kevin would most likely be fine. Michael never knew, but that was a question I asked myself every day.

The following Friday, we were up early and on the road to Baptist Hospital in Winston-Salem, North Carolina. We were escorted to an examination room where Dr. Ward, fresh out of surgery wearing a green gown, surgical mask, and cap in place, came into the room and introduced himself. I later found out that he was a no-nonsense guy, who readily told it like it was. He did not mince words. He had the MRI of Kevin's scans on the viewer and called me over for a closer look stating, "This tumor is very close to a major artery. I may not be able to save his leg, but I'll do my best." Again, Kevin, his mother, and I were in tears, imagining the good health and happiness of Kevin last week, and now the horror of perhaps losing a leg. How could this happen to him? Why did it have to be Kevin, a young man with so much promise and plans for the future? Dr. Ward proceeded with a needle biopsy and it confirmed his suspicion. Kevin had osteosarcoma, a rare form of bone cancer affecting mostly young boys and girls. The odds of developing it are fewer than five cases per one million children.

Another oncologist, Dr. Marcia Wofford, walked in and filled us in on Kevin's chemotherapy sessions. Her calm demeanor was reassuring. We had to be back early Monday morning to begin treatments. The remainder of the day involved procedures and scans. I recall one poignant moment as I watched Kevin having a bone scan. The large machine loomed over his body and inched slowly down his torso. I had to turn my head for fear he would see me crying, not for myself, but for his many battles that lay ahead.

I managed to regain my composure enough to leave this note to my staff on the message board at the Career Center.

April 11, 2000

My son, Kevin, was diagnosed with osteogenic sarcoma (bone cancer) Friday. It is located in one tumor below his right knee. Scans show the remainder of his body is cancer free. Chemotherapy starts today (7:00 AM) at Baptist. He will have about three months of chemo then the operation (limb salvage hopefully). He will have at least five more months of chemo after surgery. Thanks for your thoughts and prayers. I hope to see you tomorrow.

CHAPTER 3

CHEMICAL WARFARE ...
2000–2001

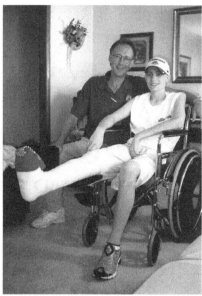

Tony Mancusi, Kevin's guitar teacher (top left), greatly influenced him.
Randy Poteat, a physical therapist, gave Kevin great stretching workouts for his ankle and leg.
Kevin looked forward to seeing both of his good friends.

The Walk for Friends at Kevin's school generated almost eleven thousand dollars for support materials for Brenner's pediatric patients. Judy Eller (Justin's mom), Fran Cantrell (school nurse), and Kathy Triplett (Kevin's mom) presented Nancy Smith (Brenner's nurse) with the very impressive check.

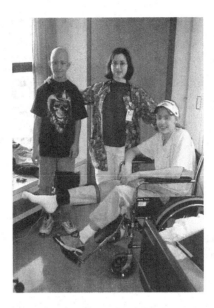

Matthew Earney (top) was one of Kevin's friends whom he met at Brenner's. Matthew's bubbly sense of humor kept Kevin laughing. Nurse Gina Idol had her hands full when both Matthew and Kevin were in the same room. She was great!

Aaron Scott and Kevin were best friends. Their friendship went beyond cancer therapy, all the way to Connecticut, where they had a great time in camp together. Our two families were interwoven and experienced all the ups and downs together.

We love and miss all three of "our boys."

One day, I played a joke on Ricky Absher, Kevin, and Gwyn.
I told them they were getting a tour bus, but it was really the Wilkes Career Education Center's van with the band's name, "The Edge," taped on the side.

The first public performance of the Edge with Kevin, Matthew Francis, and Gwyn was at their school's talent show.

Kevin's eighth grade prom was a night full of wonderful memories.
Kevin took Jenni Higgins (left) to the eighth grade prom, but his first dance was with Ashleigh Bauer.

*Come unto me, all ye that labour and are heavy laden,
and I will give you rest. Take my yoke upon you, and learn of me;
for I am meek and lowly in heart: and ye shall find rest unto your souls.
For my yoke is easy, and my burden is light.*
Matthew 11:28–30

After a worry-filled weekend, we returned to the Brenner Clinic at Baptist Hospital where we received a black, pediatric oncology handbook, or bible, as I called it. It contained the essentials that a newly diagnosed cancer patient needed to know: body image changes, coping suggestions, financial counseling, and dealing with hair and weight loss. Most of the handbook contained Kevin's treatment protocol. This calendar covering almost a year detailed the drugs and timetable for their administration. I recall the daily routine of checking off completed sessions thinking they seemed endless.

Two additional oncologists entered our lives. Dr. Allen Chauvenet, a veteran of many years of pediatric cancer research, was personable with a sharp wit to match. His booming voice in the hallways announced his coming. Dr. Thomas (Tom) McLean, highly skilled in his knowledge of oncological protocols, welcomed us with his soothing voice and caring demeanor. Tom ultimately would become almost part of our family, seeing Kevin through many years of cancer therapy. Kevin would be receiving chemotherapy two weeks each month. He would be hospitalized and receive ifosfamide, mesna, doxorubicin (adriamycin), cisplatin, and methotrexate. These drugs were the standard treatment for osteosarcoma then and offered him the best hope for a cure. He would receive two months of chemotherapy and then have surgery to remove the tumor. I recall Kevin's trips to Baptist at the beginning of each chemotherapy cycle. "Dad, pull over. I think I'm gonna be sick," he would say. We always carried a plastic bowl and a box of Kleenexes for these situations. Chemotherapy lasted hours and one particular drug, methotrexate, often caused him to develop nausea. He would insist I throw a towel over the intravenous line to conceal its orange color. The drug gave him many mouth sores. The miracle mouthwash, a special concoction, was never far away. Phlegm would often develop in his mouth, and he resorted to using a vacuum pump. The sound of the pump siphoning the secretions through the plastic tubing, with Kevin directing the wand in his mouth, still lingers in my mind. Cancer is hideous and forces even the strongest individuals to succumb to its daily assault on the body. Kevin's weight dwindled down to 108 pounds during the almost one year of chemotherapy, while his once-stout frame became fragile. After a month of chemotherapy, his hair became very thin and began falling out, slowly at first and then by the handfuls. Terry Thomas, one of Kevin's nurses at Brenner's, lathered and shaved his head to give him a more even look. Now, he looked like Terry on top. I bathed him when we returned home because he had become very weak. His frail, little skeletal frame was a stark contrast to the robust young man he had been just months earlier.

On the morning of June 26, we arrived at Baptist by 6:30 AM for his leg surgery. The family waiting area was teaming with Kevin's aunts, uncles, friends, and his parents. Our church's new student pastor, Rev. Craig Church, had arrived early, too. Craig offered much comfort to Kevin as he led us in a prayer. In fact, Craig was always present at each of Kevin's surgeries in North Carolina. As Kevin rolled into surgery, I fought back the tears and tried to be brave. "See you in a little while, little buddy. You will be fine," I said. He looked up at me calmly and smiled. I would get periodic phone calls from the operating room updating me on their progress. I found it difficult sharing this information with family members, often fighting back tears. Dr. Ward had presented us with some choices, including amputation of the leg if necessary, a total knee replacement, or a newer procedure called limb salvage that involved removing the diseased bone and implanting a donor bone in its place. It was obvious to Kevin that saving his leg was most important, so he chose the limb salvage procedure. There were no guarantees prior to surgery. Kevin remarked, "When I wake up, I'm going to look down and see if my leg is still there." It's hard to imagine a thirteen-year-old forced to deal with choices like these.

Finally, about twelve hours later, the news came that he was in recovery and that his right leg had been saved. Dr. Ward came out and said, "Kevin did well. He went in a boy but came out a man." Kevin would have many months in a full-leg cast, and a year and a half on crutches followed by physical therapy. He was alive and returning to me, and that was the greatest gift of all.

The measure of success of presurgical chemotherapy is not known until the tumor is removed, and the biopsy results are reported. That day came and an unsettling feeling resulted. Dr. Chauvenet came into the examination room where Kevin and I had been waiting, extending his usual courtesies. As the conversation continued he stated, "I need to share the results of Kevin's tumor pathology report with you guys." Kevin and I knew that for chemotherapy to be successful in the long term, a tumor kill (necrosis) should be around 98 percent. "Were the results good?" I asked. "Well," he said, "some parts of the tumor were killed at 100 percent, while other areas were not affected at all. The overall percentage is around 35 percent necrosis." I felt an ache in my chest and a lump in my throat. "What does that actually mean?" I asked. "It means," Dr.

Chauvenet said, "that there is a strong possibility that he will have a recurrence of metastatic disease, in other words, more tumors somewhere, sometime, most likely in his lungs." My heart sank. At that moment, I knew Kevin's fight could possibly be much longer than one year. Kevin's usual candor and positive spin on things salvaged the session. "At least, I have my leg and maybe the cancer won't come back," he beamed. We later learned that Kevin's tumor kill was the lowest of any patient they had ever treated for osteosarcoma at Baptist. Time would tell. We would have to wait.

After Kevin's surgery, time in the hospital often went by slowly. Friends sometimes called, but visitors from back home other than family, were rare. Steve Moree, principal of West Wilkes High School, brought some of Kevin's fellow basketball players down for a visit. Brenner's was located on 10 North in those days, several years before the new Brenner's was built. During the long days there, we would sit in the lobby overlooking the roadway and watch the construction of what would become the new Brenner's addition. The hospital rooms were small, especially for two patients. We learned quickly that if we did not get the side of the room with the closet, our quarters would become even more cramped. Parents slept in the fold down chair nightly, beside their child. Most nights, I was up every few minutes seeing to Kevin's needs, checking the IV pump or offering him the plastic urinal. The IV fluids, which flushed the chemo agents from his body, meant an almost nonstop use of the urinal. In short, this routine became established way of life, far from the outside world where peoples' lives in general were uninterrupted by cancer. I would not dare leave Kevin. Where he was became home enough for me. Some nights, I would switch the IV pump light to off and even crawl under his bed to reach the controls of the under bed light in trying to secure a dark room for sleeping. I remember vividly on many nights reaching my hand out between the railings of his bed and stroking his hair or rubbing his back, reassuring him that I was there as the constant click, click of the IV pump meshed with the voices in the hallway at the nurses desk.

Kevin and I often patrolled the halls during the day, he in his wheelchair and me pushing the medication pole heavily laden with bags beside him. Many children spent their holidays in the hospital, but the kind staff made it as festive as possible. One gentleman would occasionally come by in a clown costume doing magic tricks, and a lady would serenade us with a guitar or violin in hand. Kyle Petty visited once during his motorcycle ride to raise money for cancer research. A highlight for Kevin was a visit from two Carolina Panthers' players including Muhsin Muhammad and several Panthers' cheerleaders. A segment was filmed by WXII channel twelve, and Kevin appeared on television with Muhammad.

Before Kevin's cancer diagnosis, I had marketed my home for sale and had received a firm offer. I had bought a lot in the Cedar Ridge subdivision of Millers Creek, so Kevin and I decided to move ahead with our plans to build. During his treatments, his mother and I alternated staying with him in the hospital. I would race home, meet with the contractor, and handle the essentials of construction. Climbing stairs would be an impossible task for him initially, but Kevin found a way to reach his upstairs bedroom. He would sit on the bottom stair and inch upward, one step at a time, lifting himself with his arms, until he reached the top. I would bring up the rear (or bottom) by holding his outstretched leg brace. The upstairs would have a bonus room just for Kevin, and he would be spending more and more time there soon, changing its name to his music room.

Playing sports was out of the question for him but, unknown to me, Kevin was developing a brand-new interest. "Dad," he said one weekend, "I want a guitar. I promise if I can take lessons, I'll learn to play it. It would be fun and give me something to do. I can practice in my music room." I bought an electric Peavey guitar as a Christmas gift for him and he had big plans. Tony Mancusi, the music teacher at the North Wilkesboro Bible Book Store, had captivated Kevin with his musical ability, and Kevin immediately began taking weekly guitar lessons with him. Tony remarked, "Kevin has a natural ability with the guitar. I can tell he practices and really studies. He is a great student!" After completing a number of music books over several years, Tony cut him loose. "I've taught him all I know. Now, it's up to him," Tony said. The guitar and music offered Kevin an outlet, a break from the seemingly endless hours of cancer therapy. Although chemotherapy left him very tired, he looked forward to coming home on weekends to take lessons and practice. This musical gift would serve him well in the years that lay ahead. Kevin was soon to meet another budding guitarist during one of his weekly hospital stays.

One Monday, we entered Kevin's hospital room and, as luck would have it, the best bed was already taken. Greeting us with a big smile and Southern accent was Matthew Earney. Matthew had developed cancer as a young child and had already had many surgeries. That did not dampen his spirit one bit. He immediately made friends with Kevin. Both boys loved playing the guitar. Matthew's mom, Crystal, his dad, Vince, and sister Carrie were often there for the long stays, just like Kathy and me. An occasional walk to Hardee's became a welcome break for them. Matthew never minced words and when his favorite nurse, Gina Idol, was not assigned to his room, he became quite vocal about it. "Where's Gina? She's the best nurse. Get her in here, now! Get rid of these other morons." Of course, he was only kidding. Matthew was obsessed with gathering tokens which could be redeemed for soft drinks. He would always say, "Kevin, have they brought your token today? Do you want me to get one for you?" Nothing was impossible for Matthew. Even though his cancer had reoccurred, he was vibrant and full of energy. The handmade birthday card and popsicle stick gift were precious. Matthew even introduced us to a new soft drink which was commonplace to him in his hometown of Bessemer City, North Carolina, near Charlotte. Cherry Lemon Sundrop brought much joy to Matthew, but it left a bitter aftertaste in our mouths. He was a true friend to Kevin and they spent many hours together. That joy abruptly ended when we learned of Matthew's untimely death on March 18, 2001. Matthew and his dad were nearing their home by car when a group of horses from a neighbor's pasture bolted in front of them. One of the horses fell on Matthew's side of the car, crushing him. Kevin thought so much of Matthew that we attended his memorial service in Bessemer City. Matthew looked so handsome as his family had fulfilled his final wish of burying him in a white tuxedo and white casket. Matthew was clutching a white Bible in his hands. We will never forget Matthew and the strength Kevin and he drew from each other.

For months Kevin's leg remained in a cast. This presented an unusual problem for him with dry, itchy skin in places he could not reach inside the leg cast. Leave it to Kevin to solve the problem. A ruler can serve many purposes and it makes a fine leg scratcher when inserted inside the cast. Kevin and I were a sight to behold trying to negotiate the shower with his right leg in a twenty-gallon trash bag, fighting to keep the water from seeping into it. I recall Kevin's poignant comment as he dangled his feet in a water basin. "It feels like a bath almost," he said with excitement and a huge grin. I carried that statement with me on a notepad in my briefcase for the longest time.

Finally, the cast was removed revealing the sixty-nine staples resting just above the snakelike scar running from his right knee to his ankle. His first bath in months yielded a bumper crop of dried, scaly skin waiting to make its trip down the drain. Life's simple pleasures were revisited.

I knew other parents would benefit from having an awareness of what cancer therapy is like for an adolescent, especially if it happened to their child. I shared those thoughts as well as cancer warning signs in a newspaper article.

July 2000

Wilkes Journal-Patriot
"Childhood Cancer ... Up Close and Personal"

Summer is welcomed by everyone as we anticipate playing in the surf, enjoying a hot dog at the game, or packing a picnic lunch and heading for the mountains. It is often a time of bonding between parent and child as the cares of everyday living are brushed aside for a well-deserved vacation.

Parent bonding takes on a different form for the young cancer patient. Summer days and nights are typically spent recovering from the previous day's chemotherapy. The parent, as caregiver, becomes even more visible as the nights are spent at the child's bedside. Beach trips and biking are future events only imagined. Simple pleasures, running through the park or swimming with friends, become much more of a gift when relived in the cancer patient's memory. Life is put on hold for a minimum of one year. The choices of where to go on vacation are exchanged for choices of amputation or limb salvage. For a life to be saved, a year or more of chemotherapy and major surgery is the price to be paid. This gift of life becomes even more precious.

Thirteen-year-old Kevin Triplett's diagnosis of osteogenic sarcoma (bone cancer) of the tibia below the right knee in early April had been followed by ten weeks of chemotherapy. During this time, I had purchased a cross necklace as my special gift for my son, Kevin. He had worn it only a few days when on the morning of surgery, June 26, as we were leaving for the hospital, he opened his clenched fist to reveal the tiny necklace. "Here Dad, you can wear this for me today," he remarked. With a reassuring embrace, I slipped the necklace around my neck. As the twelve hours of surgery neared its end, Kevin's mom revealed that Kevin, the night before, had told her of his plan for me to wear the necklace, and that he had slept with it to be sure. "I suppose he forgot," she remarked. Tearfully and with pride, I gently pulled the necklace from beneath my shirt. "No," I beamed. "He remembered."

The surgery was successful with the removal of the tumor and implantation of a donor bone and metal rod. Months of physicals and chemotherapy lie ahead, but the road to recovery has begun.

Osteogenic sarcoma is rare and affects only four out of every one million children (usually adolescents). There is a seventy-five percent chance of long-term survival after having this form of cancer. We'll take those odds. Although amputation may have increased the odds of no reoccurrence, saving his leg was well worth an additional 5-10% risk factor. We'll take those odds, too.

Life is fragile, and we should handle it with care. Parents should pay close attention to those seemingly minor aches and pains of the adolescent years. Although odds are on your side the diagnosis will not be cancer, we never know for sure. Early detection is the key to survival.

Family, friends, and faith continue to sustain Kevin and his family. Ralph and Martha Shew and Ruby Triplett, Kevin's grandparents, continue to provide him with their time, love, and support. Rev. Jim Gore, pastor of Millers Creek Baptist Church, Rev. Shannon Critcher, children's pastor and Rev. Craig Church, youth pastor, remain sources of encouragement. Thanks so much to our home church of Millers Creek Baptist, Rock Spring Baptist, other area churches, Rev. Linwood Campbell, the WFU Baptist Medical Center group including Dr. William Ward (orthopedic surgeon), the Brenner Children's Hospital Oncology physicians (Dr. Allen Chauvenet, Dr. Tom McLean, Dr. Marcia Wofford) and Brenner's 10th floor nurses' team, Dr. Craig Bennett, Tyson Foods, Wilkes Career Education Center staff, Wilkes County Schools' personnel, the Make-A-Wish Foundation, Ron Hutchins, the Inspirations, and friends at large for your cards, gifts, steadfast support, and prayers during this ordeal. You have truly helped the healing process to begin.

For a child, your child, to develop cancer is every parent's nightmare. As emotionally draining and debilitating as it is, each day of treatment is one step nearer to becoming cancer free. A cure for cancer is a wish we all embrace, but until then we hold fast to the outpouring of concern each of you have expressed. The road ahead lies unmapped, but for Kevin and other cancer patients, may it be a smooth one.

By October of 2000, Kevin was well into his chemotherapy protocol. Kevin was now an eighth grader, although not attending his regular school, Millers Creek Intermediate. He had been under the tutorage of the Brenner Children's Hospital teacher, Elizabeth (Liz) Clark. She believed in a strong work ethic greeting her students each morning with a language or math text and several assignments. Kevin's friends at his home school had not forgotten him. His classmates had been suffering his absence as well as the loss of another classmate, Justin Eller, to cancer. Most students had known both Kevin and Justin for many years. Justin had developed leukemia at the age of four and was a fifth grader. Students had been deeply affected by the loss of one friend and the chronic illness of another.

Fran Cantrell, the school nurse, knew the students wanted to do something to express their love and support of both boys. Talking about cancer is never easy, but knowing that Justin and Kevin had a positive impact on their school and community, they were ready to take action. Fran stated, "The spirit of Justin and Kevin has inspired all of us to appreciate our lives, to enjoy the blessings we have, and to demonstrate a caring attitude toward each other."

The Millers Creek Primary and Intermediate schools' staff and students decided to hold a celebration honoring the lives of the two boys. The event to be held in October 2000 would be called the Walk for Friends. Donations would be collected during the last week of October with all the money raised going to Brenner Children's Hospital in Winston-Salem, North Carolina, in honor of Kevin and in memory of Justin. On that late October day, physical education classes would walk the track in celebration of their friends, Justin and Kevin.

Kevin's friends wanted him there if possible. He had been undergoing chemotherapy since April, and side effects had kept him home on most days. True to his word, Kevin arrived, and I wheeled him to the track in his wheelchair. His friends soon surrounded him saying, "Hey, there's Kevin. It's great to see you. We miss you. When are you coming back to school?" Kevin beamed with joy to see many friends he had been missing all year. Refreshments were even provided. Fran continued, "The students wanted to do something for their friends. They wanted to let Kevin and his family and the family of Justin know how important those boys are to them."

"Many of them are at the age where they question a lot," said Fran. "Still we take for granted that they are not going through the grief process, but they are. Kids need to talk about this and feel like they are doing something for their friends. Just like adults, they want desperately to help, but don't always know what to do."

Students were very positive about the walk. Many of them had talked at church about the walk. The entire month was spent with teachers emphasizing healthy living, but reminding students that cancer cannot be caught like a sore throat. There was no target amount set, no prizes for the top individual or class, and all would participate in the walk in the spirit of caring.

Justin's mother, Kevin's mom, and I were guests on the platform for a victory assembly. Principals Al Olson from Millers Creek Primary and Dr. Michael Matheny from Millers Creek Intermediate shared words of inspiration, and Fran, along with Nancy Smith, our wonderful nurse from Brenner's, came forward for the presentation of the check. "I'm happy to present a check to the Brenner Children's Hospital children's cancer fund for $10,614.87," exclaimed Fran. Immediately applause broke the silence as everyone stood honoring this great achievement. It was amazing that a group of students in one week's time had raised this amount of money. Nancy was overwhelmed, "I would never have believed this could be done. It is simply astounding what you have accomplished to honor Justin and Kevin and this check is greatly appreciated. I am so proud of you. This is wonderful!"

I recall watching students, staff members, and parents walking around the track with the sole purpose of honoring Kevin and Justin, by helping other unfortunate children with similar illnesses. As his friends filed by, I caught a glimpse of Kevin's frail, slender hand gently waving at them. Tears came to my eyes as the image of them walking contrasted starkly with Kevin sitting in the wheelchair. His cap protected his thinning hair from the sun but could not conceal his pride and joy at being there.

Before the check presentation was made, I had to share with the group what their spirit of giving meant to me. I had to tell them thank you.

October 19, 2000

Someone once said that friends are the most wonderful gifts we can give ourselves. We had no idea that Justin and Kevin had so many friends and had made such an impression on you, until you came through for them. You didn't have to make a donation, but many of you did. You didn't have to write cards and send e-mails, but many of you did. You didn't have to visit and call, but many of you did. You didn't have to walk, but I suppose all of you did. You, in a sense, have been there for Justin and Kevin.

What a surprise to open the local paper and see the article, "Walk For Friends Honors Classmates" along with pictures of our two boys, and to know that it started right here with you.

You, Millers Creek Primary and Millers Creek Intermediate Schools, along with the Millers Creek community at large, have made a positive statement by your gifts. You are saying that we feel some of the pain our two friends felt and in your own way are saying that this disease, the big "C," can and will be beaten someday.

Thank you, Dr. Matheny and Mr. Olson, who have made time for this cause, and a special thank you to the wonderful Mrs. Fran Cantrell, school nurse, who spearheaded this entire effort and kept us informed on what was going on. A very special thank you especially to you students and staff (for everyone that gave or wanted to and to everyone who walked), thanks for caring and for making a difference.

Until someone you know, like a family member or friend, develops cancer, it seems far away. All that changes when it strikes a family member or friend. You concentrate on just making it day by day, enjoying little victories. The battle isn't over. Kevin has completed seven months of chemotherapy and has at least three more months before completing this treatment course. If all goes well, he hopes to be back with you by early February.

The Brenner Children's Hospital does a wonderful work. Over the past seven months, we have seen up close and personal the caring and dedication from this wonderful team from the doctors to the nurses. Just press your room buzzer and they are there for you to answer your questions, give out some pain medication or just talk.

We are happy that Nancy Smith, Nurse Nancy, is here with us today. It is certainly a worthy cause that you have joined with Brenner Children's Hospital to champion and help others who are in need.

Thank you again for Justin and for Kevin. Through the gifts you have given, other kids will have their lives made easier. It's a wonderful tribute to your caring for them. Thank you so much.

As news of Kevin's battle with cancer spread, I continued to add names to my e-mail recipient list as a means of keeping Kevin's special friends informed on his condition. These mailings were simply called "Kevin's Medical Updates." People cared and wanted to be there for us. Many friends and co-workers responded with words of encouragement of their own.

December 15, 2000

So glad to hear that Kevin's treatments are going well. We still have you both on the prayer list, and we know that it really does help, even if we can't see the results we pray for come as easily as we might wish.

Forgive the slow reply. Hope you had wonderful holidays, and that you and Kevin will have the best New Year ever. Hang in there. Ron

Chemotherapy presents a whole set of new problems. Bleeding from low blood counts can occur anytime, as I shared with Fran. Kevin rarely became agitated with these episodes. He typically said, "Bring me my Kleenexes, hurry!" Usually, in a matter of minutes, the bleeding would stop.

December 27, 2000

Dear Fran,

I had a bit of a surprise this morning. Kevin was at his grand-mothers, when I received a call at 4:30 AM that his nose would not quit bleeding. I knew his platelets were low. After paging the doctor, I rushed him to Baptist arriving at 7:00 AM. He received one unit of platelets and two units of red blood cells. I just got him home to Millers Creek about 9:30 this evening. He is doing well, although I have to give him five Neupogen shots. Kevin is watching me type and says to tell you hello.

Keep us informed ... Wayne

As a principal, I needed to be at school as much as possible. However, everyone knew Kevin's needs came first with me. While Kevin recuperated from chemotherapy, he began staying at his grandparents' home. Ralph and Martha Shew were blessed with their new house guest. Kevin loved talking with them, and of course, they treated him like royalty.

Whatever Kevin wanted, or needed, he always received. After his weekly hospital discharges, he would immediately call them by cell phone on exiting the parking lot. "Granny, what did you fix me to eat? I'm leaving the hospital now, and I'll be there in about an hour. Fix my place on the couch with two pillows please. I'll see you soon. Love you and Pa." He was great company for them, and their deep affection for each other grew.

February 14, 2001

Dear Fran,

As you may know, I spend most every weeknight at home alone while Kevin is at his grandmothers. He has been with me on weekends.

I took Kevin Tuesday to see Dr. Ward. He wants Kevin to continue to wear the leg brace for another three months (mid-May) before he even considers him walking. His ligaments had to be totally reat-tached to the allograft; therefore, his leg is somewhat "free moving" from left to right. This is typical. If it were too tight, he would walk stiff-legged. His leg may tighten up some later. He may have to wear a support brace ultimately all the time. He will be getting physical therapy to increase his ankle movement which has been somewhat tight due to nonuse.

All in all, the visit was encouraging. His x-ray looked good. He should start healing faster now that he is off chemo. If his blood count looks good tomorrow, I may contact his teacher(s) and bring him to school some next week. It all depends on his counts.

He really needs to go shopping. He has really not had any social life since April last year, nor has he gone anywhere except our homes and the hospital. Talk about adjustment. I do want him involved in his course selection for next year.

I hope next week he can get back into circulation. He should be back soon. You will be the first to know, as long as you check your e-mail.

Thanks for your continued friendship and for all the hope and warmth you have given us. You are special! Wayne

March 20, 2001

Hi Ron,

Kevin finished his chemo treatment number twenty-one last month and has returned to school. He has spent 112 days in the hospital since last April. He lost weight to 108 pounds, but has now gained to 137 and his hair is growing back. He is still being checked monthly with scans, etc. and will be followed for a long time. He will have his portable catheter (in his chest) removed sometime in the future. All in all, he has handled it well. He will be in a leg brace for at least two more months before they will consider letting him bear any weight on it. Frankly, he may need a sports brace from now on. Anyway, he has his leg, and we are extremely grateful for that.

He lost his aunt to a stomach and heart condition last week, and a friend he met from Charlotte, Matthew Earney, was killed this week in a freak accident with horses toppling onto his car. Matthew was a cancer patient at Brenner Children's Hospital. They had become good friends. I am sending you the Charlotte Observer article covering that horrible accident. Matthew, always talkative and a country boy at heart, was a good friend to Kevin.

Hope all is well with you. Thanks for your prayers. Keep in touch … Wayne.

Kevin's life was about to change again. His small circle of best friends would enlarge with the meeting of Aaron Scott from Oceana, West Virginia. Entering the hospital room at Baptist, we noticed a young boy playing a video game aggressively. He was totally engrossed in the game, and we made our way to the bed near the window. It didn't take long for Kevin to catch the game fever too, and they went at it, together. They even shared common tastes. The boys sometimes ordered hot and spicy sandwiches from the local Wendy's. The boys' friendship blossomed. After all, both of them had cancer. Aaron had another form of bone cancer in his elbow, Ewing's sarcoma. He was in the midst of chemotherapy like Kevin. Aaron, his mother, Terri, his dad, Steve, Aaron's twin brother Andrew, and sister Lindsay became our new, adopted family. As Terri stated, "You guys seem more like family to us than most anyone. We are always here together, and our boys are such great friends." Later, Kevin and Aaron would spend an entire week together at Paul Newman's Hole in Wall Gang Camp in Connecticut. This camp gave young cancer patients a respite from their treatments, offering them fishing, horseback riding, rappelling, and even accommodations in a bunkhouse. Kevin had never flown before, and our boys were going it alone. "I'll be fine," Kevin said. "After all, Aaron and I will be together." And they were together, from that time on, as were our two families, through thick and thin. We, together, weathered the ups and downs of chemotherapy. Our love for them is immeasurable. Aaron lost his right arm to cancer, but that left him more determined than ever to play football on his school's team, and he did. After a bone marrow transfusion, Aaron developed a secondary cancer, a virulent form of leukemia (AML). On December 12, 2002, Aaron lost his battle with cancer. Kevin, his mom, and I traveled to West Virginia to pay our respects to Aaron and to his family. They did the same at Kevin's passing. Words cannot adequately express the depth of emotion our two families faced during our sons' illnesses. We will forever be joined to them, and we will see our sons again.

When Kevin was an infant, I purchased a Copy Tot kit with the intention of making a plaster impression of Kevin's hand or foot. As luck would have it, I had problems with the mold and the entire kit ended up in the trash. Years later, after his cancer diagnosis, I decided I had to have his hands molded as a keepsake. I found two young ladies in town who did this sort of thing and scheduled Kevin for a session. They were prepared with two two-liter bottles, one for each of his hands, which had almost outgrown the containers. His hands went into the doughlike material for a minute and on their removal, one impression was unusable. After repeating this procedure, we ended up with lifelike left and right hand models, each freestanding on its own pedestal with a glass covering. Today, they sit in my bedroom as a reminder of the creativity and musical giftedness Kevin possessed as a guitarist.

April 5, 2001

Dear Fran,

"It was a wonderful day. It was like a vacation. Thank God I am healed," said Kevin. He got to visit some old friends on the 10th floor at Baptist. His checkup went well with no problems. He will probably see you at school Friday. He is testifying at church on Sunday at 11:00 AM regarding his ordeal and faith in Christ. Thanks for keeping us in your thoughts ... Wayne.

Kevin had been talking with me for several weeks about something he felt led to do, to share his testimony at church and let the congregation know how important Jesus Christ was in his life. He was on crutches, but that did not dissuade him from standing in the pulpit with crutches nearby on that Sunday morning. Kevin was on fire for God, and it was apparent to everyone around him.

Pastor Jim Gore introduced Kevin, "For those of you who may not know Kevin, he is a young man who has been struggling and battling cancer for the last year and a half. He is going to share a word with us today."

April 8, 2001

Kevin's Testimony
Millers Creek Baptist Church

Good morning. Can everybody hear me? Okay. Is everybody glad to be at church this morning? Amen. I know I am. I just feel wonderful this morning. I've just had a wonderful week. I feel like the Holy Spirit has been with me all week. I've just felt great! First of all, I'd like to thank Jim, Shannon, and everybody in this whole church that have been praying for me and supporting me with all that I've been through. I know it has helped out. Earlier this week, the good Lord laid a testimony on my heart. I'd just like to share with you how I came to know Jesus.

Back in 1999, I had been going to church and I'd been listening to Pastor Jim preach, and I believed I was a sinner. I believed in God and that He sent Jesus to die on the cross for my sins. I wanted to get saved, but I was afraid to come to the altar because of all the people. I was kind of embarrassed. So, one day, I was at my grandparents' house and somehow we got to talking about religion and Jesus, and I told them how I felt, and how I wanted to get saved. My grandpa told me that you shouldn't be worried about what other people think. It's between you and the Lord. I was sitting on the couch, and I was feeling the Holy Spirit. I prayed a prayer, and I feel like the Lord saved me right there in that house. I can't tell you how I feel, but I just felt different that day. I just felt great. I was feeling the Holy Spirit.

Later on, the next week, my dad took me to see Pastor Jim. I went into his office and he showed me some scripture: John 3:16 and some other verses. We prayed the salvation prayer, and I asked Jesus to forgive me of my sins and to come into my life. I thanked Him for saving me. A couple of weeks later, on August 22, 1999, I was baptized, and I was trying to live a good, Christian life. Then, almost a year to the day, on April 2, 2000, I was diagnosed with osteogenic sarcoma, which is bone cancer. I was scared. I didn't know if I was going to die, or if I was going to lose my leg, or what was going to happen. I just kept praying. You all prayed for me, and I just kept my faith. I had a real good chance that I would lose my leg. I didn't know when I went into the surgery, if I was going to keep my leg. The night before, I did a bunch of serious praying. I had a cross necklace, and I held on to it all night.

The next day, I told my dad to wear it. When I went to the surgery, I was scared laying on the operating table. I didn't know what was going to happen. They put me to sleep, and when I woke up twelve hours later, I had my leg. I'm just so thankful for that. I kept feeling good and everything. I just kept believing, and the Lord came back to me. I kept praying, and my family did. I finished up in the beginning of February with all my treatments. I was real thankful for that. It seemed like I couldn't enjoy things. It seemed like if it was me just examining myself, or if it was possibly Satan putting all these doubts in my head about not being a Christian. All these things made me doubt my salvation really, really bad, seriously. It's scary as a Christian knowing I was doubting it bad. I was depressed. I wasn't eating good. I knew I had to do something. The last couple of months, I'd been counting on Pastor Jim and Shannon, and I saw some people in town. I'm still under doctors' care, and I'm taking some medicine and everything.

Last Sunday, I believe I had a spiritual awakening. I believe that when Pastor Jim was talking about this great revival he wanted to have, and everybody that wanted to be a part of it should come down to the altar. I came down on my crutches, and a tear almost came to my eye. I just bowed my head and prayed a little, silent prayer to myself, and I just felt the Holy Spirit. After that, it seemed like all these thoughts about doubt started to go away. He passed out a book, *Returning to Holiness.* I believe it, and I read the back about how you can know if you are saved. I read it. I was still having some lingering doubts. I went in my dad's bedroom and turned to that salvation prayer, and I bowed my head and said, "Lord, I believe I was saved back in 1999. I'm just making sure. I'm driving down the stake of assurance like it said in that book." I bowed my head, and I asked Jesus to forgive me of my sins and come into my life. Then it seemed like I still had some doubts. Now, I know for sure that I'm a Christian, and that I'm saved. I've never been more proud of my life for Him. I didn't want my pride to get in the way. I humbled myself. That's what we all should do. In the Bible in I Peter 5:5, it says God resists the proud, but gives His blessings to the humble. That's just what I'm trying to do, just let God use me. I'm prepared to do whatever he calls me to do. I wasn't afraid about coming up here. I've been talking about it all week. It just feels wonderful. I'm just so thankful I'm saved; I'm a Christian; I'm better; I'm healed; it's just wonderful.

I'd like to thank my two friends over here and my grandparents (Ralph and Martha Shew) back there. They've been real wonderful to me. They've helped me so much and prayed for me. You ought to meet them before the day is over. They're just wonderful people, my grandpa and grandma. Nobody could be better than her through my cancer. She took care of me and tended to me. They have been wonderful. I tell you, I could go on forever. Jim's got to preach. I'll be honest, I just feel wonderful. Praise the Lord! Praise God! If you're saved, just raise your hand. Yes, praise God! I'm feeling the Spirit! I just felt it all week. I've been taking some medicine, but I believe that the best medicine is the Holy Spirit! I believe that's what it is. I just feel wonderful. I'd just like to close by saying, that if you're not saved, and if you're having any doubts about it, just clear it up today. Just come down to the altar and talk to Jim or Shannon. They're just wonderful people. Just clear up your doubts or get saved. I urge you to. You'll never be the same. You'll start enjoying stuff better with the newness of life. You'll be so much friendlier. I've been so much friendlier. This week, I've been going around telling people about Jesus. I've just been feeling wonderful. Thank God for Jesus! Just thank him for everything! I'm happy! I'm happy! Praise the Lord! I believe I've said all I need to say. God bless.

Pastor Jim concluded, "When I get a blessing, I'm not much on raising my hand. I do that when I'm preaching. When I get a blessing, I get tickled. I have to be careful when other people are preaching. I don't want them to think that I'm laughing at them. That's just how I respond. I have laughed so much this week with Kevin, and thinking about Kevin, that my jaws are hurting. He mentioned to you that he had been so much friendlier. You can just see that in Kevin. He's a new man! I've just been excited. Thank you, Kevin, for sharing with us. That's great. God is good all the time. Amen."

"Father, thank you so much for yourself. May it be, God, that which Kevin is experiencing right now, that some of that joy and the overflow of what is taking place in his life would possess some of the rest of us. Lord, that we might experience that fire from heaven which he so much enjoys. Bless us as we continue our worship in Jesus' name. Amen."

Kevin's testimony had left an indelible mark on many who were in his hearing. It was a very special day for Kevin and me. I was so proud of him, and he knew that he had followed the direction of the Holy Spirit in sharing his testimony. There was a silver lining on the black cloud of cancer, and Kevin had a renewed purpose to do his Lord's bidding.

I took Kevin's testimony notes, a photo of him, and a lock of his hair and framed them. This display accompanies me when I speak at local churches and is a powerful statement to God's saving power in Kevin's life. Kevin continued to keep in touch with Pastor Jim.

May 9, 2001

How I'm Doing

Pastor Jim,

In last weeks *Open Door*, I saw your e-mail address, and I thought I would just send you a message to let you know how I am doing. People are still giving me compliments on my testimony, which I gave a few weeks ago. That was really a mountain top experience for me! I believe the Lord used me to bless other people. I still struggle some days with some thoughts or doubts, but I try not to worry so much, because I know I was saved back in 1999. Whether it was at my grandparents' house or in your office, I felt like I was being led to Christ by the Holy Spirit, and I believed in God, and knew I was a sinner. Then in my dad's bedroom, I prayed a salvation prayer to drive down the stake of assurance. I've not been doing the best job of going back to that stake of assurance like I should, but I'm working through this. I just need to trust God and believe, because I've done everything else. Love ... Kevin

May 10, 2001

Kevin,

Thanks for your e-mail. I just received it today because my new e-mail address was not set up on the PC in my office until this morning. When I got setup, it was forwarded in. You're on the right track; just stay the course and you'll be fine. I appreciate, love, and respect you very much. Jim

Kevin's mother, Kathy, an employee of Tyson Foods, and officials there had their own unique way of ministering to those in their family who were experiencing health problems. Tyson's generosity benefited many year after year as checks were awarded annually at the Gene Allen Lovette Memorial Ceremony. Kevin proudly offered words of thanks.

"Thank you for your gift to those of us who are fighting cancer. You do a great work, and the money is very helpful. Your time and effort show that you really care. I appreciate it very much," said Kevin.

May 2001

Excerpts from the *Wilkes-Journal Patriot*
"Ride Raises $17,000"

Almost $17,000 was raised and given to cancer patients in the third annual Gene Allen Lovette Memorial Ride on Thursday. About 20 motorcycles and 25 riders participated, going to Lynchburg, Virginia on Thursday for the Virginia State HOG (Harley Owners Group) Rally and to the North Carolina State HOG Rally in Burlington the next day. The group is returning to Wilkes County Saturday.

Chip Miller, vice president of Tyson's Chillpak division east, addressed the crowd gathered. Miller gave credit to Kirk Church (food service plant manager) and Gary Johnson (cooked products plant manager) for organizing the event.

It is held in memory of Gene Allen Lovette, a Wilkesboro man who was executive vice president of Tyson's Chillpak division when he died of cancer. The $17,000 was raised through each motorcycle rider paying $50.

Checks of $2,500 each were given to cancer patients. Another $2,500 was given to St. Jude's Children's Research Hospital.

Kevin continued to sharpen his guitar skills in his spare time when he was home recuperating from chemotherapy. He considered playing at his eighth grade graduation, but he wasn't sure if a tune by Metallica, a heavy metal band, would be appropriate.

May 24, 2001

Kevin expressed to us last week that he felt too much pressure to perform at awards day. We have always wanted him to play, but he told us he didn't want to, but felt that he would let us down if he didn't play. We told him whatever he decided would be fine. We have already auditioned and selected vocalists, but if he still wants to play, we could work that in. Metallica's fine with me. I'll check with the other teachers. Talk with him and Mrs. Cole this afternoon so we can make a plan. Our program must be finalized tomorrow. Mrs. Spears

Kevin's guitar prowess was continuing to progress, and he began looking for bandmates. Soon, my two-car garage became the focal point for numerous rehearsals in preparation for the school talent show. Matthew Francis from next door would cart over his drum set, while Kevin and I drove to pick up Gwyn McGlamery and guitar. Kevin pulled up a chair, rested his crutches on the concrete floor, and the Edge practiced what would become their anthem, "For Whom The Bell Tolls" by Metallica. Their talent show performance was met with thunderous applause. Kevin even ordered a special black shirt with flames embroidered up and down the front for this very special performance.

Kevin and his group delivered at the school's talent show in a big way. Although confined to a chair with crutches and a leg brace, and minus one shoe, nothing dampened his featured guitar solo in the least. The thunderous applause provided quite an adrenaline rush for the band. Kevin, always modest, played guitar for the love of playing. He had become quite a role model in his own, unassuming way.

June 13, 2001

Article from the *Wilkes Journal-Patriot*
"Most Respected ... Eighth Grader Kevin Triplett Overcomes Bone Cancer, Becomes a Role Model to Classmates and Friends"
by Frances Hayes

Illness Makes Triplett a Role Model to Friends

This year's superlatives at Millers Creek School were particularly meaningful. The eighth grade chose its classmate, Kevin Triplett, as most respected. What made Kevin most respected to his eighth grade class also has made everyone he knows respect him.

A year ago, Kevin was battling bone cancer of the tibia below his right knee. "The courage and strength he has shown in battling the cancer has made him a role model for his friends and classmates," said Fran Cantrell, the nurse at Millers Creek School.

Kevin stayed 110 days at Brenner Children's Hospital, missing two months of seventh grade and six months in eighth grade. His weight dropped from 148 pounds to 108, and all of his hair came out because of the chemotherapy.

Today, Kevin, with the tumor taken out of his leg, has gained back the weight and the hair he lost. He continues to be monitored with monthly visits to the children's oncology clinic at Baptist Hospital in Winston-Salem.

But the last year has added maturity to the young adolescent. His mother, Kathy Triplett, remembers the words of Kevin's doctor just before he went into surgery. "You will go into this a boy, but you will come out a man," she remembers. They appear to be true, although Kevin enjoys the normal pursuits of a fourteen-year-old looking forward to entering high school.

This spring, Kevin and his friends formed a band, "The Edge," which performed at a school talent show. Band members are Gwyn McGlamery, who plays rhythm guitar, along with Kevin, who plays lead guitar. Matthew Francis is the drummer.

Music has always been a love of Kevin's. It is one of the things that helped serve as an outlet for him during the long months of chemotherapy.

The other outlet for Kevin was his belief in God. Today, Kevin says faith has become particularly important to him. Attending Sunday school is now a priority for him, and he has talked about the importance of God to other teenagers. His father, Wayne Triplett, remembers Kevin coming home from treatments and turning to the music he loved when he was feeling the side effects of chemo.

Kevin received twenty-one chemo treatments causing his platelet count to drop to zero. This meant he could not go out into public. His father, Wayne Triplett, gave him more than 140 shots of Neupogen, a white blood cell stimulant, during the course of treatments. "But still, he stayed upbeat," remembers his dad. "He didn't complain even when the side effects hit particularly hard."

The Tripletts say the support of their friends and family was particularly important. Mrs. Triplett's parents, Ralph and Martha Shew, kept Kevin a great deal of the time. Wayne Triplett's mother, Ruby Triplett, was also very helpful in the healing process. The family remembers the continued help of their ministers, Rev. Jim Gore, Rev. Craig Church, and Rev. Shannon Critcher from Millers Creek Baptist Church.

Mr. and Mrs. Tripletts' employers were very supportive of the times the two were away from work as they took care of Kevin. Mrs. Triplett works in the transportation department at Tyson Foods, where money was raised for Kevin through the Gene Allen Lovette Memorial Fund. Mr. Triplett is the principal at the Wilkes Career Center.

The support of Kevin's friends from the Millers Creek Intermediate School was also vital. Their support could be seen in a celebration event held at the school last fall. The event was called Walk for Friends, and was designed as both a celebration and fundraiser. Students collected donations before walking around the Millers Creek track. The event was held in memory of Justin Eller, a sixth grade Millers Creek student, who died of cancer last spring.

"Both Kevin and Justin touched the lives of many students," said Fran Cantrell, school nurse and one of the organizers for the event. "These young men have had a positive influence on the school community. Their spirit has inspired all of us to appreciate our lives, to enjoy the blessings we have, and to demonstrate a caring attitude toward each other," she said. "The students wanted to help. They wanted to show these families how much they cared," she said. Students raised $10,895 which was donated to the Children's Cancer Fund at Brenner Children's Hospital. The fund is part of the cancer patient support program for children which provides counseling, a resource room, support groups, and more. The money raised by Millers Creek students will be used wherever needed, for Christmas or birthday presents, rewards after painful procedures from cancer treatment, meals, gas, and other things.

The Tripletts are supporters of local fundraisers held for the Relay for Life, sponsored by the American Cancer Society. This year, the Relay for Life will be held Friday, August 10 and Saturday, August 11 at the MerleFest grounds at Wilkes Community College. At last year's event over $100,000 was raised by teams involved in the Relay for Life. "The event will last all night long as teams walk laps, rejoice in life and honor those who have survived cancer," said Russell Golds, chairperson for the event. "Support Relay for Life in your area by donating your dollars, volunteering your time and cheering your community teams on," said Golds. All proceeds will benefit the American Cancer Society.

Kevin and I appreciated the opportunity to share with others the impact cancer had on his life, and cancer survivors everywhere could identify with that. This exposure prompted Kevin to write a note thanking those who had supported him. In fact, Kevin often said, "Fighting cancer has been the roughest battle of my life. It is a tough battle, but it has made me a better person. I appreciate people, life, and the simple things even more."

June 2001

The Mailbox ... Wilkes-Journal Patriot
"Fear Of Cancer Made Easier By Kindness"
by Kevin Triplett

Cancer is a scary word. It is even scarier when it attacks you. I have battled bone cancer for over a year and hopefully am on the road to recovery. I would like to thank the many people who have stood by me and given me support. I received many cards, balloons, words of encouragement, and visits from friends and even from people who I did not know, but who cared. The *Wilkes-Journal Patriot* allowed me to tell my story and did several articles about cancer awareness. I feel that the many prayers on my behalf made a big difference in my recovery.

I want to especially thank the Gene Allen Lovette Memorial Fund members from Tyson Foods for their generous financial gift recently and last fall. These people took time off from their jobs to ride by motorcycle to Virginia to raise money for cancer patients like me. I especially enjoyed the motorcycle ride around the parking lot.

The Relay for Life will take place in early August. This is another way you can help by making a donation to the American Cancer Society. They are making progress, but there is still much research to be done before cures can be found.

Thank you, Millers Creek Baptist Church, Millers Creek Intermediate School staff and students, my family, close friends, and all Wilkes Countians who found time to keep me in their thoughts. I will always be grateful. Cancer, as bad as it is, does not always mean your life is over. Sure, you do make adjustments, but with the help of caring people like you, the road to recovery is a lot smoother.

Kevin enjoyed worshipping at his local church, but he also enjoyed listening to television evangelists whose messages spoke to his heart. Kevin's excitement grew as our trip to hear Pastor John Hagee from Cornerstone Church in San Antonio, Texas, was rapidly approaching. He would be delivering a message in neighboring Winston-Salem. Kevin had listened intently to his television sermons, and his tape series on healing scriptures had lifted Kevin's spirit. Kevin decided to send him an e-mail in preparation for his visit.

June 16, 2001

Kevin's E-mail to Pastor John Hagee

Dear Pastor Hagee,

My name is Kevin Triplett and I live in Millers Creek, NC. I hope to attend the June 21 service in Winston-Salem, NC. In April of 2000, I was diagnosed with bone cancer (osteogenic sarcoma) of the right tibia below the knee. I had eleven months of chemotherapy, lost all my hair, and almost lost my leg. I finished chemo in February this year. I often listened to your program, prayed constantly, and listened to your Power to Heal cassettes. They helped give me strength. I was in the hospital 110 days, had 21 chemo treatments, and my dad gave me over 140 shots. I praise God that He brought me through this.

I would really like to meet you, shake your hand, and personally share with you my thanks for all the encouragement you gave me. Although this may not be possible, I will be looking forward to hearing you.

I will be the one on crutches. I have been on them over a year and am on my second pair. I became a Christian in 1999, and some of my friends have come to the Lord recently. I try to be a good witness and invite them to church.

You have been a wonderful inspiration to me. Thank you for all that you do.

Love ... Kevin Triplett

Kevin met Pastor Hagee that evening and they had a time of fellowship together.

Kevin had been asked by Relay for Life organizers if he would agree to be the keynote speaker at the 2001 event. Kevin said yes, and again he delivered. With notes on what he planned on saying in his hand, he approached the microphone on crutches, his mother by his side. Kevin's comments from his heart were sincere and moving. People currently involved in the relay still comment on the impact Kevin's speech had on them. This was one of the most moving speeches ever given at the Relay for Life. Kevin often paused to compose himself and hold back the tears. Everyone on the grounds seemingly paused and listened intently to the message in Kevin's words.

Kevin was introduced by his former principal, Dr. Michael Matheny. He stated, "It's been my privilege to know this young man that I'm going to introduce to you for a couple of years. He has displayed one of the greatest efforts of courage because of his heart and who he is, as we've watched him battle through the difficulties that he's had. The strength that he has shown to us at his age is much stronger than many people my age, and adults that I know. He's a model for us and for the students. He helps our students understand at Millers Creek Intermediate that cancer can affect everyone. I had the privilege to see a whole student body and whole community come together in honor of two gentlemen, and one of them was Kevin Triplett. Stand beside me please, if you can, and your mom. What a blessing he has been to us in our school to see, and he brings home all the things that we know about love and courage. Ladies and gentlemen, I give you Mr. Kevin Triplett."

August 8, 2001

Kevin's Relay for Life Speech
Wilkes Community College

Thank you, Dr. Matheny. Good evening and welcome to the 2001 Wilkes County Relay for Life. My name is Kevin Triplett. I'm fourteen years old and in the ninth grade at West Wilkes High School. I am a cancer survivor.

I'd like to tell you about my cancer story. Back in April of 2000, I'd been having some leg pain and never could find out what the problem was. I had some physical therapy at the Wellness Center. I went to the orthopedist in town and had some x-rays and an MRI done. When the results came back, it showed that I had a tumor below my knee in the tibia bone in my right leg. They didn't know right then if it was cancer, so they sent us down to Baptist Hospital in Winston-Salem. I saw a bone tumor specialist. He did a needle biopsy on my right leg, and when the results came back, it showed that it was cancerous. I was in shock. That's how scared I was. I didn't know if I was going to die, lose my leg, or what was going to happen. I figured that if I ever got cancer, it would be like when I was seventy years old or something. I was just thirteen.

All in all, I stayed close to 115 days in the hospital. I lost all my hair and lost a bunch of weight. I got down to about 108 pounds. I was sick sometimes with the chemo treatments. I had twenty-one of them in all. I had problems with mouth sores and just the side effects. I met some nice people down there. The nurses are great. They have the best doctors. I met some other teenagers that were dealing with the same type stuff as me. I made some real good friends. So, I had some good times.

Probably the main thing in the whole ordeal was my cancer surgery. There was a chance going into the surgery that I could lose my leg. I was scared and worried about that, but the doctor felt like he could save it. I kept on praying and hoping. I felt pretty good going in that I would have my leg. They took out the part of the bone in my right leg with the cancerous tumor on it, put in a dead person's bone, and drove a long, steel rod through the middle of it. After twelve hours of surgery, I woke up, and I had my leg. I'm just real thankful for it.

After surgery and a few days in the hospital, I started my rehabilitation. I wore a long leg cast for about two weeks. I went back to the surgeon and got it taken off, and got my staples took out. I had another long leg cast and wore it about seven or eight weeks. In September of last year, I graduated to this knee immobilizer. My leg is doing real good. I just can't walk on it, yet. I can put some weight on it. I go back to the leg doctor the twenty-second of this month. I'm just hoping and praying that I can start putting some more weight on my leg and doing some walking.

Now, I'd like to share with you about how I dealt with cancer. I really couldn't do much, because of the shape my leg was in, but I loved to play the guitar, and I'd come home and just play my guitar for hours. That helped pass the time. I watched TV and played video games.

The thing that helped me the most was my relationship with the Lord Jesus Christ. I read my Bible every once in a while, read some healing scriptures, always said my prayers, and prayed for healing and strength to get through it. I always had a comfort in knowing that beyond all the doctors and everybody on this earth, there was a greater power that was helping me and taking care of me.

Right now, I'm doing great. I finished up with all my chemo treatments in early February this year. I got to go back to school and finish the eighth grade. I graduated with honors, and I just had a great summer. I went to Myrtle Beach, and I'm about to go into high school now, and really enjoying that. I'd just like to thank God because without Him, I couldn't have pulled through this, and just for helping me through it and for all His many blessings. Thanks to all the contributors for the Relay for Life. It is a worthy cause, and one day we will find a cure.

I'd like to close with a verse of scripture. It comes out of Mark 10:27. "With men it is impossible, but not with God. For with God, all things are possible." That verse gives me hope. It's just a great verse. How many survivors do I have out there? Praise the Lord! I guess that's about it. Thank you for your time.

Kevin's speech had struck a familiar chord of faith and hope for those like him, battling the devastating disease of cancer. His heartfelt comments were shared in the following article.

August 14, 2001

Excerpts from the *Wilkes Journal-Patriot* Article
"Sixth Relay for Life Raises Over $90,000"
by Karin M. Clack

Nearly $90,000 has been raised for the American Cancer Society as 70 cancer survivors walked during the sixth annual Relay for Life at the Wilkes Community College MerleFest area. Forty-one teams assisted in raising funds.

An Emotional Testimony

Millers Creek Intermediate School principal Dr. Mike Matheny introduced the guest speaker, cancer survivor Kevin Triplett, 14, of Millers Creek. He is the son of Wayne and Kathy Triplett.

"Kevin has displayed one of the greatest efforts of courage because of his heart and who he is as we've watched him battle through difficulties that he's had. The strength that he has shown us at his age," said Matheny, "is much stronger than many people my age and the adults that I know. He is a role model for us and for the students."

Triplett gave an emotional testimony about his fight against cancer, often pausing to regain his composure. Triplett's mother, Kathy, assisted him on stage, as he walked to the microphone on crutches.

"In April 2000, I had been having some leg pain and never could find out what the problem was, even though I had had some physical therapy at the Wellness Center," said Triplett. "I went to an orthopedist in town and had some x-rays and an MRI done. When the results came back, it showed I had a tumor below my knee in the tibia bone in my right leg. They didn't know right then if it was cancerous, so they sent us down to Baptist Hospital in Winston-Salem. I saw a bone tumor specialist and he did a needle biopsy on my leg. When the results came back, it showed it was cancerous. I was in shock. I was scared because I didn't know if I was going to die, or lose my leg or what was going to happen," said Triplett. Catching his breath, Triplett said, "I figured if I ever got cancer it would be when I was 70 years old or something. I was just 13. All in all, I stayed about 115 days in the hospital. I lost all my hair and I lost a bunch of weight. I got down to about 108 pounds. I was sick sometimes with the chemo treatments. I had 21 of them in all," said Triplett. "I had problems with mouth sores and other side effects. I met some nice people down there. The nurses were great and they had the best doctors. I met some teenagers who were dealing with the same type of stuff as me. I made some real good friends."

"The main thing of my cancer ordeal," said Triplett, "was my cancer surgery. There was a chance going into the surgery that I would lose my leg. I was scared and worried about that. The doctor said he felt like he could save it, and I just kept praying and hoping. I felt pretty good going in to surgery that I would have my leg." The doctors took out the part of the bone in Triplett's right leg that had the cancerous tumor on it. "They put in a dead person's bone and drove a long steel rod in the middle of it. After 12 hours of surgery, I woke up and I had my leg. I'm just real thankful for that," said Triplett with much emotion in his voice.

A few days after the surgery, Triplett began rehabilitation. "I wore a long leg cast for about two weeks. I went back to the surgeon and got it taken out. I had another long cast and wore it about seven or eight weeks," said Triplett. "In September of last year, I graduated to this knee immobilizer and have had it ever since. My leg is doing real good, I just can't walk on it yet, but I can put some weight on it. I go back to the leg doctor the 22nd of this month."

Triplett then gave a very moving testimony of how he dealt with his cancer, from an emotional perspective. To help pass the time, Triplett would play the guitar for hours, watch television, and play video games.

With his voice breaking with emotion, Triplett said, "The thing that helped me the most was my relationship with the Lord Jesus

Christ." The crowd showed its approval with clapping. "I read my Bible every once in awhile, read some healing scriptures, and always said my prayers. I prayed for healing and strength to get through it. I always had that comfort knowing that beyond all the doctors and everybody on this earth, there was a greater power helping me and taking care of me," said Triplett.

Triplett finished all the chemo treatments in early February and was able to go back to Millers Creek Intermediate School to finish the eighth grade, graduating with honors. He is currently in the ninth grade at West Wilkes High School. "I would just like to thank God, because without Him, I couldn't have pulled through this," Triplett said. Closing with a verse of scripture, Triplett read Mark 10:27, "With men it is impossible, but not with God. For with God, all things are possible."

"That verse just gives me hope and it's just a great verse," said Triplett. He then asked for a show of hands for the number of survivors present. Many raised their hands and Triplett said, "Praise the Lord." With that, the crowd gave Triplett a standing ovation.

Kevin loved many forms of gospel music from Christian rock to Southern gospel. He especially enjoyed the singing of the Inspirations, a male quartet and nationally known Southern gospel artists, based in Bryson City, North Carolina. Ron Hutchins, a friend and group member, kept in touch with Kevin's struggles. When he was able, Kevin loved attending their concerts and sharing with them.

October 17, 2001

Hi Ron,

Kevin, his friend Gwyn, and I are looking forward to 10/13. Now that Kevin is in high school, I try to schedule his oncology checkups around teacher workdays. We have one of those this Friday 10/12.

Kevin will be having outpatient surgery early Friday morning (10/12) to remove the portable catheter which was implanted in his chest in April 2000. Hopefully, there will be no complications. If his doctor will allow it (and I think he will), he should be able to attend the Inspirations reunion concert. We're looking forward to seeing you on the 13th. Wayne

Kevin did attend the concert in Bryson City, North Carolina, and he had a wonderful time.

Follow-up bone, CT, and chest scans were performed routinely on Kevin to look for any telltale signs of the cancer's recurrence. Each time, we held our breaths as our hearts pounded in our chests, waiting for the doctor in the examination room. We had been receiving good news until December 2001. A chest scan revealed another tumor in the upper right lobe of his right lung. Our fears had come true. The ominous words spoken by Dr. Chauvenet months earlier came back to me, "With his low tumor kill, it is possible the cancer may return." Surgery was scheduled for December thirty-first, and a thorocotomy (a wedge resection removing the tumor) was performed by Dr. Tom Pranikoff. A large C-shaped incision was made from Kevin's right shoulder blade area down toward the base of his rib cage. With several weeks of recuperation, excruciating chest pain, and a tender rib cage, Kevin began a new three-month chemotherapy protocol using the chemotherapy drugs topotecan, cytoxan, and methotrexate. Again, he faced the hair loss, nausea, and mouth sores, but this time as a seasoned veteran.

My medical updates on Kevin were being sent with greater frequency with the cancer's recurrence. They became more than just the facts to his growing number of friends. They provided a glimpse into the nature of Kevin, and how he managed to cope. They were constant reminders of his strong faith in God and reflected his inner resilience and strength.

December 10, 2001

Kevin's Medical Update

Kevin was released to begin walking after 18 months on crutches on Wednesday before Thanksgiving. The allograft surgical site had completely healed. With a slight limp, he walked Thanksgiving day. His ankle became sore and slightly swollen as a result. X-rays looked ok at that time.

A bone scan last Friday (12/7) revealed a hot spot or area of concern in his right ankle. Needless to say we were on pins and needles all day. Indications are that his walking created a stress fracture to the ankle area which should heal with continued use of the crutches.

As you can see, it is something you have to always keep tabs on. We are thankful that the report looks encouraging. He is taking drivers ed. and has gained significant weight (196 lbs.). He will repeat the bone scan in six weeks and has a CT chest scan scheduled just before Christmas. Just wanted to keep you updated. Thanks for your continued thoughts and prayers. Wayne

I am glad you are getting good holiday news. My best to you and Kevin as you celebrate the blessings of the year during the coming days and every day. Larry

CHAPTER 4

MAKE-A-WISH ...
2002

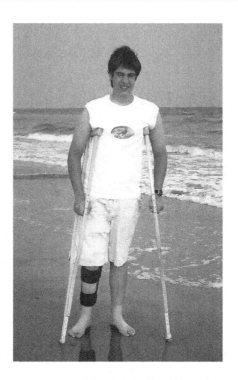

Kevin loved the ocean.
Myrtle Beach, South Carolina, was a great getaway destination for him.
Even crutches and a leg brace could not keep him from enjoying what the beach had
to offer.

Kevin's trip to Paul Newman's Hole in the Wall Gang Camp in Connecticut took him
to new heights!
Horseback riding, rappelling, fishing, and even a
bunkhouse were great therapies for him.

Kevin "gets a lift" from my longtime friend, Ron Hutchins, of the Inspirations.
Summer was welcomed with an opportunity to visit with Ron.
Kevin and his friend, Gwyn McGlamery, bring him up-to-date on Kevin's condition.
Kevin became an "inspiration" to group members Archie Watkins and Jack Laws.

One of Kevin's first stops on his Make-A-Wish cruise was the tremendous Mendenhall Glacier in Alaska. Kevin marveled many times at the beauty of God's creation.

Our merry band of travelers paused for a moment in Ketchikan, Alaska, as a local photographer captured this wonderful Kodak moment.
Kevin, Gwyn with an unidentified birdlike creature clutching him, Kathy, and I had the time of our lives!

What? Know ye not that your body is the temple of the Holy Ghost
which is in you,
which ye have of God, and ye are not your own?
For ye are bought with a price: therefore glorify God in your body,
and in your spirit, which are God's.
1 Corinthians 6:19–20

Kevin began 2002 recovering from pulmonary tumor surgery. The doctor brought in a new device called a spirometer, which Kevin would fit into his mouth and then inhale deeply. I would count down the seconds each time Kevin would inhale, in his attempt to raise the meter to its highest point. Although breathing was painful from the recent surgery, the devise would help reinflate his lung. We often remarked that almost every year around the holidays, he had some type of surgery. He began six courses of chemotherapy alternating cytoxan, topotecan, and methotrexate, which were completed by the end of February.

Again, Kevin's friends came through with numerous encouraging expressions of support. Often, I would sit at the computer and read them aloud to him. Other times, I would print them, hand them to Kevin, and he would read them later.

January 2, 2002

Kevin's Surgical Update

Hi everyone.

On Monday (12/31), Kevin underwent a four hour surgery at Baptist and a small osteogenic (cancerous) tumor was removed from his right lung. If all goes well, he should be coming home Friday (1/4). After a short period of recuperation, he will begin a six month chemotherapy regimen.

We remain optimistic that he will ultimately triumph over this disease. Thanks for keeping him in your prayers. Wayne

That is good news, and I am so glad to hear it. I will continue keeping you and yours in my thoughts and prayers. Garland

It is hard for me to find words. I will pray for Kevin and your family, and ask all the praying people around me to do the same. Thank you for keeping me updated. Please know that you can call on me at anytime for any reason that you would need help. A verse that I am particularly fond of is found in Deuteronomy 33:27 which states, "The Eternal God is my Refuge, and underneath are the everlasting arms; and He shall thrust out the enemy from before thee; and they shall say, destroy them." Keep the faith. You and your family are dear to God. Charles

I felt much remorse that Kevin was missing out on the sports he played at one time. His leg surgery meant the removal of a growth plate, causing his right leg to ultimately be almost an inch shorter than his left. Every right shoe he wore had to be built up in the soles to correct this height differential. Kevin took great care in selecting just the right type of shoe to be altered. I had his Sunday dress shoes adjusted, and he chose New Balance and Vans sneakers. "Dad," he said, "I want the shoes to be cool looking, and I hope the bottoms match, too. I'm gonna wear them when I perform."

If Kevin could get some degree of joy out of something physical, I was determined to make it happen. He became interested in ATVs, or four-wheelers. Dr. Ward had advised against any strenuous activity which could injure his right leg, but Kevin and I had a plan. We visited a number of local bike shops and checked out the four-wheelers. When he climbed on one behind me, and we sped through the parking lot, the only decision left was, which one should we get? I loaded the new four-wheeler onto my trailer and pulling it behind my Toyota Rav4, we headed home. Kevin loved the Arctic Cat 250 and to be careful, we signed up for a safety course. With sand flying on the corners and low-lying tree limbs smacking him in the face, Kevin traversed the safety course in Statesville with ease and left feeling very comfortable with the machine. He spent many joyous hours riding with his friends on trails and in the snow. To his credit, he never had an accident, and we kept it until his interest turned to cars.

January 5, 2002

Hi Fran,

Kevin was a little tired after going all day Friday. Today (Sat.) he had a really good time riding two four-wheelers. He tried out a Honda Recon and an Arctic Cat 250. We were going to get the Arctic Cat today, but the shop has already closed Sat. afternoon. I plan on getting it Monday if possible. He seems to really enjoy riding, very carefully of course. His surgeon doesn't want him to have one, but his minister and several nurses feel that he has been through so much and he really deserves to have a little fun. Wayne ☺

February 9, 2002

Dear Fran,

Kevin's five days of chemo went well and he did not get sick. Dr. Ward saw him Friday and his leg/foot x-rays looked fine. He did have a nose bleed this morning at 5:00 AM (Sat.). He thought about going to school last Friday, but he was tired. He spent today at his grandmother's and at home riding his four-wheeler. What fun! His hair is still there. We will probably see a drop in his counts early next week. I have given him five shots thus far and will do at least five more. He will get chemo #2 beginning 2/8 for three days. He says hi. Gwyn McGlamery, his friend, is staying overnight tonight. He hopes to go to church tomorrow. Happy Nurses Day! Talk to you soon. Wayne

A medicine recall is a rarity in cancer treatment, but this happened on one occasion with Kevin. I had given him a number of Neupogen injections from my latest batch. I received a call from the supplier, repackaged the remaining vials, and sent them back to the pharmacy. They promptly shipped updated vials. This was only a precaution on their part, but it did cause some uneasiness. I watched Kevin closely for any signs of a reaction. Thankfully, he was fine.

April 7, 2002

Fran,

Kevin completed a 5 day treatment last week. We drove back and forth daily. He will go April 18–21 for his last scheduled in hospital treatment. He has been taking drivers ed. and drove last Saturday from West. He drives three days next week. We had a medicine recall Sat. afternoon for the medicine I give him as an injection. I do not know what was wrong with it, but I now have some more. He will probably be okay, even though I gave him four shots.

He is going to fly to Connecticut in June for a seven day camp. This is sponsored by Paul Newman. No adults will be going, and he has never flown. There will be three other chemo patients going.

Also, we think the Alaska cruise for July is a go. Kevin, Gwyn McGlamery, Kevin's mom, and I will be flying to Vancouver and then take an eight day cruise up the Alaska coast with Dr. Charles Stanley. He will see Dr. Ward on the 17th for a leg scan to check for height differential. Hopefully, he will have a CT scan soon and get a clean checkup in order to stop the chemo. We have not done anything for the Relay for Life, yet. I hope someone from West is heavily involved, since the May meeting will be the last before school is out. Kevin may return to West as soon as April 22! Hope you guys are doing well. Keep in touch. Wayne

With surgery behind him, he could then concentrate on two major trips which would bring him much joy. His Hole in the Wall Gang trip in June and his Make-A-Wish trip in July were definitely bright spots and offered solace from the grinding routine of fighting cancer. This was his year to see parts of America he had only dreamed about. An even greater opportunity was the chance to make many new friends.

Kevin had never been away from home before for any length of time alone. To complicate things more, this would be his first time flying. Terri Scott and family brought their son, Aaron, to the airport and we brought Kevin. They would be together for this wonderful outing. Kevin and I did manage to stay in touch.

June 12, 2002

Hi Dad,

I hope you are doing great! I am having a pretty good time at camp. I have done a lot of cool stuff. We went camping one night and had a cookout. It was a lot of fun. I've been fishing a couple of times, since I've been here. Today, I caught a big mouth bass. I have a picture to show you. The plane ride was fun. I think you will like it. I don't know about Gwyn, though! I'll have a lot to tell you, when I get back home! Tell everyone I said hello, and I'm doing good. Love, Kevin

June 13, 2002

Hi Kevin,

I'm glad you are having a great time. It has been lonesome without you here. I talked to the counselors several times and received two post cards from them today. I hope I can find you at the airport in Greensboro, Saturday afternoon. No problem, maybe Gwyn can come along, sweet. It is Thursday night here as I am writing this. Take some pictures with your camera(s) if you want to. I heard the Wall was awesome and that you were a leader, playing the guitar, etc. You might want to apply for the leadership camp next summer. I will go get busy with Taco. You have a fun day tomorrow and enjoy your flights Saturday. See you then. Lots of love … Dad

The camp was just the beginning of some fun and relaxation for a change. Kevin gave tremendous thought to selecting his Make-A-Wish trip. He loved playing guitar and initially felt that he would enjoy a trip to San Francisco to personally meet the heavy metal band Metallica. Perhaps he could get an autographed guitar from them. After giving this possibility a lot of thought and after sharing his feelings with Pastor Jim, he decided this would not be the best choice. Kevin loved the guitar riffs of Metallica, but as a Christian, their lifestyle was not his. He even considered going just to witness to them.

Another option he considered was a possible trip to New York City (at that time it would have been in September 2001). After praying about his decision, he ultimately chose a Christian cruise to Alaska with Dr. Charles Stanley and a number of Christian artists. Kevin admired Dr. Stanley and gained spiritual strength from listening to his weekly sermons on television from Atlanta, Georgia. This eight-day excursion would be his trip of a lifetime!

Mike Greene and the Make-A-Wish Foundation made arrangements with Templeton Tours from Boone, North Carolina, and soon we had our trip brochures. Since Kevin was an only child, he was allowed to take a friend along. Gwyn McGlamery, Kevin's best friend, got the call. Kevin, his mom, Gwyn, and I reveled in all the pampering we received. A highlight was meeting and talking with Dr. Charles Stanley as Kevin shared his personal experiences with cancer with him.

Kevin's tremendous admiration of Pastor Jim prompted him to share his thoughts on his Make-A-Wish trip options with him. Kevin wanted his trip to be special. A Christian cruise would be his ultimate choice, but not before he did some soul-searching.

June 21, 2002

Dear Pastor Jim,

I don't know if I told you about my Make-A-Wish trip or not. As a cancer patient, I have been given a wish. Most kids choose a trip somewhere. It could be a trip to meet someone or some type of gift.

Since I love to play the guitar and I am in a band, I thought about meeting a rock group. I really do like the group Metallica and have almost made up my mind to go meet them. You may or may not have heard of them. I am a little bit hesitant about going to meet them because of the life style that they live. I have seen videos of them and heard how they talk offstage and it is pretty bad. Their music has hardly no bad words in it. My meeting them might be a positive thing for them. I could possibly get a new guitar from them, too. Going to Disney World or Hawaii don't interest me that much. People tell me to do something that I really want to do. By sending you this letter, I am not trying to get you to make up my mind for me, but I really do respect your opinion on things. Please e-mail me your thoughts and any suggestions. Love … Kevin Triplett

The Make-A-Wish Alaskan cruise was waiting. His cruise adventure became the subject of a human interest article by our local newspaper. God's grace had allowed Kevin this trip of a lifetime. Kevin often stated that he would like to return to Alaska one day. He felt the pristine beauty there was a testament to the handiwork of God.

August 7, 2002

Excerpts from the *Wilkes Journal-Patriot* Article
"Triplett Granted Wish While Battling Cancer"
by Karin M. Clack

Kevin Triplett of Millers Creek, a two-year cancer survivor, recently returned from a seven-day cruise in Alaska having been granted a wish by the Make-A-Wish Foundation of Charlotte.

Kevin, fifteen, has been battling bone cancer since being diagnosed in April 2000. It was during that this time he found out about the Make-A-Wish Foundation. After about 15–16 chemotherapy treatments and two surgeries, Kevin was finally physically able to pursue his wish, a Christian-oriented Alaskan cruise.

While at Wake Forest University Baptist Medical Center, a social worker spoke with Kevin and his parents, Wayne and Kathy Triplett, about granting him a wish. People who have had six months or more of chemotherapy, or have a life-threatening illness, and are between the ages of 10–18 are eligible for a wish through the Make-A-Wish Foundation.

The social worker at Baptist, along with Mike Greene, teacher at North Wilkes High School and Northwest North Carolina representative for Make-A-Wish Foundation, helped organize the trip for Kevin. Initially, he considered going to California, Hawaii, or New York.

"Some children choose to go to Disney World in Florida, to meet a celebrity, or go on a shopping spree," said Kevin's Dad, Wayne Triplett. "He wanted to go see the beauty of Alaska. In addition, he wanted a Christian-oriented way of getting there."

Kevin was interested in taking a cruise with Dr. Charles Stanley, pastor of the First Baptist Church in Atlanta, Georgia and speaker on the In Touch Ministries radio and television broadcasts.

With this in mind, Green and the Make-A-Wish Foundation coordinated the cruise through Templeton Tours of Boone, NC which chartered the ms Volendam of Holland America Line for friends of In Touch Ministries. The bars, casinos, and slot machines aboard the ship were closed, and the ship's entertainers were replaced by Christian speakers and entertainers.

The Make-A-Wish Foundation pays for any part of the wish that isn't contributed through private donations of corporate sponsors. Templeton Tours made a cabin available for Kevin, his parents, and one of his friends.

"Usually, the wish is only granted to the child and their immediate family, to include parents and siblings," said Triplett. "However, in the case of an only child, like Kevin, the wish is extended to one friend as well. Kevin chose Gwyn McGlamery of Purlear, North Carolina."

A limousine donated by Mike Fox of Charlotte picked up the Tripletts and McGlamery to and from the airport in Charlotte. The Make-A-Wish Foundation picked up the tab on the airfare from Charlotte to Vancouver, British Columbia in Canada. The foundation also provided a $900 check for spending. Part of the money from this check paid for taxes and airport fees. The Tripletts paid for their own extra excursions not included in the cruise.

The Itinerary

The Tripletts and McGlamery flew out of Charlotte on July 14, flying into Dallas then on to Vancouver. They boarded the ship and departed Vancouver on Monday night, July 15.

On board were 1,410 people and 650 crew members. In addition to Dr. Stanley, the cruise included a lineup of Christian musicians, entertainers, and preachers. These were: The Mike Speck Trio, Alicia Williamson, soloist; Gary Smalley, author and speaker on family relationships; Legacy Five, Gospel quartet; Dr. Jerry Vines, pastor of First Baptist Church, Jacksonville, Fla.; Andy Stanley, pastor of North Point Community Church in Alpharetta, Ga. and son of Dr. Charles Stanley; Ken Davis, inspirational speaker and comedian; Greater Vision, Gospel trio, Stan Whitmire, Gospel pianist; John Starnes, soloist, and Geraldine and Ricky, ventriloquist.

Tuesday was spent cruising the Inside Passage of Alaska. By around noon on Wednesday, the ship docked in Alaska's state capital, Juneau. It was here they were given an opportunity to visit the Mendenhall Glacier.

The cruise then continued in the Inside Passage, docking at Skagway. Much of Thursday was spent touring Skagway, which included a scenic train trip outside of the town. On Friday, the ship cruised through Glacier Bay National Park where the captain strategically positioned the ship near the face of a glacier. While viewing the ominous ice formation, Dr. Stanley read a passage of scripture from the book of Genesis, detailing God's creation. Afterwards, John Starnes sang, "How Great Thou Art."

While in Glacier National Bay, the Tripletts and McGlamery took a whale watching excursion in which they saw humpback whales. "Many of the whales even came right up to the ship," said Triplett. While on the cruise, several bald eagles and sea lions were also spotted.

The ship then docked at Ketchikan early Saturday morning, allowing passengers an opportunity to tour the town known for its great selection of totem poles. An old salmon cannery was also seen in town.

Dr. Stanley preached during the morning worship service on Sunday as the ship toured the Inside Passage again on its way back to Vancouver. The weather on the seven-day cruise was wonderful. In fact, after talking with organizers of the cruise, Triplett learned, "It was one of the best cruises they had ever had." There was low to no humidity with temperatures in the 50–60s. It sprinkled only one day. There were about three or four cruise ships in every port.

On Monday, July 22, the Tripletts and McGlamery returned to Vancouver where they flew out to Chicago and experienced a one day layover due to storms in Charlotte. Triplett said, "We owe a debt of gratitude for all who made this wish possible."

On the Road to Recovery

In April 2000, at age 13, Kevin was diagnosed with osteosarcoma (bone cancer). Following surgery in June 2000, Kevin endured 11½ months of chemotherapy. For the next eleven months there were virtually no problems, other than Kevin being on crutches. "We thought we were home free," said Triplett.

Every six months Kevin visited Dr. Bill Ward for a CT scan of the leg and every three months he had a chest scan. Every month he visited his doctor at Brenner's to have his chest catheter flushed and checked to make sure it was operating properly.

It was on a routine visit for a chest scan in December 2001 that the doctor notified Kevin that a tumor was found in his lung. "It was the size of a pea," said Kevin.

Doctors performed a four-hour surgery on December 31, 2001, and removed the tumor and did a biopsy on three sections of his right lung. The lung had to be collapsed and Kevin had to use an inflation aspirator for a week to strengthen the lung. He was in the hospital five days.

Now, said Triplett, "We just hold our breath every time we go for a check up." Shortly after being released from the hospital in January, Kevin began another regimen of chemotherapy which lasted until mid-April.

Through this ordeal, Kevin missed about two months of school in seventh grade, seven months in eighth grade, and half the school year in ninth grade. Nonetheless, he has managed to maintain good grades. The last chest scan looked okay, and Kevin is scheduled for another chest scan in September 2002.

As for Kevin's right leg, it has healed very well. He cannot run, bike or play basketball, but he is able to walk on it without crutches. His right leg is now shorter than his left. To compensate, he has added a cushion support in his right shoe. If Kevin takes care of his right leg and doesn't overly abuse it by doing anything stressful, he will be okay.

Kevin now wears a specially made titanium brace which supports his knee. "He will probably be in the leg brace forever," said Triplett. He is able to take the brace off at night, though. "We just feel fortunate that they saved his leg," said Triplett.

With bone cancer, during the first five years there is a high rate of reoccurrence, then it levels off to about 20 percent. "You never get to zero," Triplett said.

Later on down the road, Kevin may require surgery again, and there is always a chance the tumor will develop again. Usually, this form of bone cancer appears in one limb only, the long bones of the leg or upper arm. It usually affects at most about 200 children out of a million and primarily boys. This form of bone cancer will affect children during their growth spurt in their teenage years. "Most often, children don't think it's cancer. They just think it is growing pains," said Triplett.

Kevin said he has managed to get through this ordeal by praying and trusting God and through the support of others. He said he has faith that he will possibly be healed completely one of these days.

Upon graduation from high school, Kevin said he hopes to attend college. Right now, though, he is focusing on driving. He recently got his driver's permit.

In his free time, Kevin plays the guitar, rides a four-wheeler, and studies his Bible. He also plays in the band, The Edge, and is in the process of forming a praise band at church.

We met many wonderful people on the Alaskan cruise. One lady from Washington state, Ida Grace, shared with us her tremendous faith and we kept in touch with her via e-mails. Kevin even struck up a close friendship which endured with Maurice Templeton, owner of Templeton Tours. They had a lot in common. They were both cancer survivors.

July 28, 2002

Hi Ida,

I hope you had a safe trip home from the Alaska cruise. We got brave and thought we could get home earlier through a Chicago to Charlotte route. When we got to the Windy City, we discovered that thunderstorms had closed the Charlotte airport. We had to stay in Chicago overnight and fly out on Tuesday morning.

Maurice Templeton and his granddaughter were also stranded on that same flight. Gwyn, Kevin's friend, talked Maurice to death. It was great meeting you and Nancy. I will get some photos to you later this week. Take care and happy trails to you. Wayne

Kevin's Thank-You Letter to Templeton Tours

Mr. Maurice Templeton
Templeton Tours Inc.
PO Box 2630
Boone, NC 28607

Dear Maurice,

Cancer is a scary word. It is even scarier when it attacks you. I have battled bone cancer for over two years (since the age of twelve). During that time, I have had two major surgeries and two courses of chemotherapy lasting almost sixteen months. While on crutches for eighteen months, I had plenty of time to think about my Make-A-Wish, and I wanted it to be very special.

I have always admired Dr. Charles Stanley and it was a wish come true when you made it possible for my family and me to go on the Alaska cruise this month. The preaching was inspiring, the music ministered to my spirit, and the Alaska scenery was awesome!

Thank you for working with the Make-A-Wish chapter of central and western North Carolina. Everyone has been so good to me. It was wonderful meeting you and realizing that your genuine Christian concern for others made my trip possible. I will always cherish the great times we experienced on the cruise and especially meeting other wonderful Christians. The memories will last a life time! May God bless you in all that you do for Him and for others. Your friend, Kevin

Kevin continued his support of the Relay for Life and was honored to carry the banner for the opening Survivors' Lap in 2002, 2004, 2005, and 2006. As a survivor myself, I carried it with him in 2005 and 2006.

August 12, 2002

Excerpts from the *Wilkes-Journal Patriot*
Article by Frances Hayes

Relay for Life fighting against cancer brought out the largest crowd ever to the two-day annual fundraising event. It also brought out the largest number of cancer survivors, 118, to participate in the survivor's walk at 6:00 PM Friday and the largest number of luminaries, 2,600, in the seven year history of the Wilkes Relay for Life. Approximately $110,042 was raised by the 40 Relay for Life teams, but more is expected.

Kevin Triplett and Marsha Sidden, cancer survivors, led the cancer survivor's walk that opened up the seventh annual event. The two were holding a large Wilkes Relay for Life banner.

In October, Kevin's allograft (donor bone) failed (fractured) causing his lower right leg to become unstable. Again, Kevin was faced with making a difficult decision.

Dr. Ward stated, "Kevin, I can implant another allograft, which possibly could fail like this one. You would be on crutches and healing for another eighteen months. I could also amputate the leg above the knee, and you could be fitted with a prosthetic lower leg. Finally, I could replace your knee and tibia with a prosthetic knee and appliance."

"Which would you do?" Kevin asked him.

"That's your decision, Kevin, but patients who opt for the prosthetic knee are usually up and about very soon after surgery. I have had a very good success rate with them."

Kevin chose the total right knee and tibia replacement. "It took so long for my leg to heal this time, and there is no guarantee the allograft would hold up. I want to be able to walk and soon. I want the prosthetic knee," Kevin exclaimed. There were no problems with the surgery and the device served him well. Soon, he was walking.

October 2, 2002

Kevin's Medical Update

Hi everyone.

Kevin had a wonderful summer and a great Make-A-Wish cruise to Alaska. Recently, he has been experiencing problems walking.

Yesterday, his surgeon at Baptist discovered the allograft (donor bone implant) had fractured near the knee. This happens in about fifteen percent of donor bone patients. Three options were available: amputation of the leg, a new allograft implant which would take another eighteen months of rehabilitation, or a total right knee replacement including removing the allograft (bone and rod), and installing an artificial tibia. He is scheduled for the third option (knee replacement) on Oct. 21. He should be in the hospital only five days if there are no complications.

The good news is that with a little post-op therapy, he should be walking very soon without a brace or crutches. His knee area should be stronger and this is unrelated to cancer. Down the road, he may require an additional knee replacement and/or amputation. We are very optimistic that the procedure will be successful. As always, thanks for your prayers and support. Wayne

October 3, 2002

Kevin and Wayne,

I will be praying for you from now until I hear you are up and running again. May our glorious, healing, reconstructing Savior be with you every minute of every day to give you the strength and power to overcome all attacks of the enemy.

Wayne, you are covered as well, for the caregivers need to be held up to God for the strength to endure the fatigues and stress of being on the waiting and assisting line-up. I have been in that position many times in life and sometimes I think that is as hard as being in the hospital bed but not as painful.

Hope you are both keeping strong in your walk and personal relationship with our Lord, for in Him alone will you find all your needs to be met. Sorry this is so late in getting back to you; I don't find much time to get on the internet, volunteering, child-care, and now chiropractor appt. three times a week keep me exhausted. Thanks for keeping in touch. Blessings of peace, hope, love, and joy to you. Ida Grace

October 25, 2002

You have both been on my mind so much lately that I was sure something was happening. I keep your picture on my dresser to remind me to pray often, and lately it has drawn my attention even more than usual.

So happy to hear Kevin's spirits are staying up. May the Holy Spirit continually keep you all spiritually, mentally, and physically strong. I feel very blessed to have met you both and am happy we exchanged e-mail addresses to continue our friendship via cyberspace. May our Lord and King continually send you all of his blessings of peace, hope, love, and joy. Ida Grace

November 2, 2002

Thanks for the update. I am sure Kevin will do well. He is a young man of great faith. May Jesus be real close to him during his recovery. Bro. Gearl

Kevin's trips were tenuously planned, knowing that cancer surgery or chemotherapy side effects could change our plans at a moment's notice. Yet another tumor was apparently growing in Kevin's right lung. A follow-up chest CT revealed another pulmonary tumor. It was time to collect data again and fashion a plan of attack. His surgery was scheduled for January 2003.

November 22, 2002

Kevin's Medical Update

Hi everyone.

Kevin's CT (chest scan) at Baptist Hospital yesterday revealed another tumor located in the same general area as the one removed last December (right lung where lobes meet in the central cavity). This was a suspicious area when viewed this past August. We plan to meet with the oncology team at the Brenner Children's Hospital Wednesday (11/27) to discuss treatment options (more surgery, further chemo, different drug regimen, etc.).

Kevin remains in good spirits and, like before, will face whatever he must with courage to overcome yet another hurdle. Thanks again for your continued prayers and support. I will update you again in early December. Wayne

December 2, 2002

Kevin's Medical Update

Hi everyone.

We are still waiting for some definitive information on Kevin's next treatment. The Baptist tumor committee will meet tomorrow (Thursday) and discuss his situation. Options will probably include surgery to remove the lung tumor within the next two weeks, continued treatment at Baptist or perhaps NIT (Bethesda) or Johns Hopkins. Kevin recorded (last week) a brief radio spot for the Make-A-Wish radiothon which will be held on Oldies 93.1 tomorrow (Thursday, 12/5) from 7:00 AM to 4:00 PM. The station is raising money for kids' upcoming wishes. If you get a chance, tune in during the day for his airtime. He is looking forward to his 16th birthday this Saturday (12/7) and continues to have a very positive attitude! Keep the faith, more later. Wayne

The cancer was back, if it had even left. Often, cancer cells are deposited early on throughout various areas of the body only to begin forming tumors later. We knew Kevin was up against some pretty stiff odds. Unlike when he was first diagnosed in 2000, and we were dumbfounded, it seemed almost surreal and just another bend in the road. We had heard this bad news before. As Kevin said many times, "I just keep going." Still, our loyal friends stood by us.

December 4, 2002

Thank you so much for keeping us updated as to Kevin's progress. I have already lifted Kevin's name up to the Lord several times this morning and will continue to pray for him in the days ahead. His name is on our prayer list at Goshen and his name is mentioned each week. Also, we remember him in our prayers at CYO meetings each morning here at NWHS. Wayne, I'm also praying for you. Several times it has seeped deep into my spirit as to what it would be like if I was in the same situation that you are, and it has brought me down low. I know that we can find hope, comfort, and strength in the Word of God (all things work together for good to those who love the Lord, if God be for us who can be against us, He will not allow us to be tried above what we are able, My grace is sufficient for every need, etc.), and that is my prayer for you and Kevin. I pray that God's perfect, wondrous Will be done in your life. Thanks again for keeping me updated. You and yours are (and will continue to be) in our prayers. May God bless and keep. Charles

Thanks for being so faithful on Kevin's update. I can't imagine what you and Kathy are going through. I am keeping all of you in my prayers, because I am sure you need them as well as Kevin. When your kids suffer, you suffer, also. Please let us know if there is anything you need. Keep in touch. Cheryl

December 6, 2002

As always, thanks for keeping us updated as to Kevin's condition. I'm printing your e-mail as we speak and plan to share it with my brothers and sisters at Goshen as well as the CYO group. It's so easy for me to sit back and say things from my position, having no idea what it is like from your or Kevin's position, but I truly am praying for you and truly do want God's very best for both of you. I also know that if you took all the love, concern, and care of everyone involved in your situation, it cannot compare to the great love and concern that our Almighty God has for you. He never makes a mistake. He knows exactly what He is doing. Jeremiah 29:11 comes to my spirit when I think of you and Kevin. "For I know the thoughts that I think toward you, saith the Lord, thoughts of good, and not of evil, to give you an expected end." I'm praying that God will continue to give you faith and that you will tenaciously hold onto Jesus and look to Him completely. May God bless you, Wayne. Charlie

Conventional cancer therapies showed minimal improvements in Kevin's condition. At best, the cancer was held at bay for a few months each time before progressing. Dr. McLean, Kevin, and I were ready to try a new approach. Kevin would be the first osteosarcoma patient to try this new treatment at Baptist. When the day to begin came, a number of doctors and assistants looked on as the medication was carefully drawn from the vial and deposited into the nebulizer. After mixing in inhalation water, Kevin began inhaling it through his mouth for what seemed a long time (fifteen minutes). It was manageable. We had a new weapon in our arsenal.

December 19, 2002

Kevin's Medical Update

Hi everyone.

After looking at numerous treatment protocols and consulting with national experts, we have begun a clinical phase 2 trial of a drug which is typically used to treat breast cancer patients (GM-CSF). Preliminary studies indicate that it is also effective in patients like Kevin who have developed metastatic tumors in the lung from bone cancer. This is an at home treatment (thank goodness). He breathes a nebulized mist for about 10 to 15 minutes twice daily which I prepare for him. This will continue for 3 weeks.

He will then have thoracic (lung)surgery on Jan. 7 to remove one-third (upper lobe) of his right lung along with the tumor discovered last month. He should be out of school from one to two weeks with this procedure (teacher alert). The in home treatment of GM-CSF will then continue on alternating weeks indefinitely (up to several months).

This is cutting edge stuff which has never been done before at Baptist Hospital. We will basically do like most cancer patients, wait and see what happens. With the research I have been doing with the doctors, in my next life I may go into oncology/hematology (holiday humor).

Kevin's friend of three years whom he shared a lot of chemo-therapy sessions with, Aaron Scott, passed away suddenly last week after a long battle with cancer. He had gone through several years of chemo as well as an arm amputation and later developed leukemia. We went to the viewing and visited with the family this past week-end in Beckley, WV. Aaron's mother is a teacher and his dad is a coal miner. Both Kevin and Aaron had a wonderful week retreat this past summer at Paul Newman's Hole in the Wall Camp in Connecticut.

Kevin is in good spirits and seemingly doesn't let the situation and the sometimes grim statistical stuff phase him very much. He is look-ing forward to the holidays and is mentally preparing for the upcom-ing surgery.

Thanks for your continued support and enjoy the fellowship of family and friends (we certainly will) which this season offers. I will update you periodically (post surgery) with any new developments. Have a great holiday! Wayne

Thank you so much for the update on Kevin. I appreciate it so much. I pray for Kevin everyday. I mention him in prayer requests each morning in CYO and also at Goshen Baptist. I guess it is all in the hands of the Lord at this point.

I'm so sorry to hear about Kevin losing his friend to cancer. That must have been difficult for him. Wayne, you and Kevin are an encouragement to me. I ask myself often, What would I do if it were me or my child? Just that thought (let alone the reality) is hard to swallow. And yet, you both remain upbeat and steadfast. I will continue to pray for you and ask that you keep us abreast of things if you can. I pray a very blessed Christmas for you and yours. Charles

CHAPTER 5

ONE STEP FORWARD ... TWO STEPS BACK ... 2003

Kevin experimented with a variety of musical riffs on his ESP guitar
and enjoyed learning new songs and writing lyrics.

Ruby Triplett, Kevin's grandmother and my mom, loved to visit Kevin.
She always prayed for his healing and embroidered pillowcases and special items for him.

Kevin's first car was this blue 1998 Pontiac Grand Am.
Once he backed it out of the garage, catching the right side mirror on the garage
facing, and the mirror went flying.

"I know that God is in control.
It just gives me comfort, because I know that when I die, I'm going to be with Him,"
said Kevin.
Kevin's testimony was the amazing life he lived.

And Jesus looking upon them saith,
With men it is impossible, but not with God:
for with God all things are possible.
Mark 10:27

True to form, Kevin found himself recovering from another surgery as the year began. The upper lobe of his right lung was removed which contained a golf ball-sized tumor. The cancer was clearly advancing. Our optimism still flourished, since he had been down the surgical route before. The pain from this surgery proved to be his most excruciating. We also discovered that an earlier chemotherapy agent, adriamycin, had damaged his heart valves. Soon he would be taking heart medication for the remainder of his life. He became the first osteosarcoma patient at Baptist to begin a new form of therapy, inhaled GM-CSF, which I administered fifteen minutes, two times a day, for over a year. The vial of medication was mixed with inhalation water and poured into a nebulizer. He also began a new drug, Gleevec, in October after disease progression was noted. Another drug, Avastin, which inhibited tumor blood vessel growth was started as well. There were bright spots with the additional new, cutting-edge therapies which lay ahead, that Kevin pioneered. He realized a dream, too, as his 2000 Mustang was just a few months away.

January 2, 2003

Kevin's Surgery Update

Kevin underwent surgery Tuesday to remove the upper lobe of his right lung, which contained the tumor. Although the procedure was successful, there are some complications. The surgery lasted longer (8 hours) than anticipated due to earlier surgical scar tissue and the tumor location. Late Tuesday, he developed swelling in his left (good) leg. After a series of tests and ruling out a fracture and possible blood clot, specialists feel that he may have sustained an internal bruise (subhematoma) due to his prolonged surgery and positioning on the operating table. He will be in intensive care at least through Thursday.

I have been with him since Tuesday but hope to be at school Friday. I am in contact with the Career Center staff and things are going well.

As before, it will take him time to recuperate and get back on his feet. I will get a Special Friends and e-mail update out hopefully on Friday. Thanks ... Wayne

This subhematoma was unexpected. Kevin's leg looked very swollen and was as hard as a rock to the touch. The doctors were perplexed and considered performing a fasciotomy, cutting the outer layer of skin to relieve underlying pressure. I kept busy in his hospital room, feeling for a pulse on his ankle. Finally, there it was, a slight pulse was felt in his left foot and the crisis passed. Weeks of therapy were needed to get the leg back into operation.

January 10, 2003

Kevin's Medical Update

Kevin is out of intensive care and is now in intermediate care. His leg and kidney functions are returning to normal. As he puts it, "I don't want anymore surgeries anytime soon." I concur. He should be going home early next week if everything goes well. I hope to begin the inhaled GM-CSF treatments again early next week. He may be returning to school by Jan. 21.

I think this crisis is almost over and he is on the way to another recovery. I'll keep you updated. Thanks ... Wayne.

January 31, 2003

Kevin's Medical Update

Hi everyone.

The upper lobe of Kevin's right lung containing a sizable tumor was removed earlier this month. Yesterday's CT chest scan looked good with no indication of additional lung tumors at this time! We were really holding our breath all day yesterday waiting for the results. In keeping with standard practice, a repeat CT scan will be given at three months (late April) to monitor his progress.

We will be continuing the twice daily GM-CSF nebulizer treatments at home indefinitely, while hoping that this immune system stimulant (experimental) will help keep him cancer free.

Last weekend with his leg brace just removed, he suffered a fall with minimal bruising. He will be back on crutches for about a month giving his leg time to strengthen. Currently, he is getting the lung treatments, left leg therapy for stiffness and tutoring to get him back up to speed. With a number of setbacks recently, it is great getting a three-month reprieve! He is in good spirits and manages to keep a very positive outlook. I have learned many lessons from him, not the least being, that every day is a gift to cherish. Thanks for your continued support and I will keep you updated. Wayne

I have always been the sentimental type and delighted in doing little things for others. Our dear friends in West Virginia, the Scott family, were very close to our hearts. Their son, Aaron, had recently lost his battle with cancer. I assembled several photos of Kevin and Aaron, had them framed, and made a copy for each of us. It depicted an earlier, happier time, even though cancer loomed over both of them. My copy hangs near Kevin's room. It reminds me of the bonds which are much stronger than cancer.

February 3, 2003

Hi Terri,

I put a package in the mail today for you and Steve (priority mail). It should arrive within the next few days, so be watching for it.

Kevin is still recuperating from what he calls his worst surgery. He can hardly walk. We see Dr. Ward and Dr. Pranikoff tomorrow afternoon. I suppose it will take some time for the leg/hip bruise to heal.

The tumor removed along with his upper right lung lobe was of substantial size. I don't see how they missed it on the August exam (a gray area ... suspicious). I have started up the inhaled GM-CSF again. He has another CT scan on Jan. 23. Keep in touch and let me know if the package doesn't arrive soon. Take care ... Wayne

April 24, 2003

Wayne, thank you for the photographs and the copy of Model Railroader. They both brought a smile. I hope all is well for you personally and professionally. Since I'm not hearing anything, I have to guess no news is good news. I'm glad things seem better for Kevin. You guys keep hanging in there. Joe

Kevin wanted to earn a little extra money, but there were not many job opportunities out there for someone with weight-bearing issues and a prosthetic knee. Finally, he struck gold at Wendy's in Wilkesboro. Roy, a huge Carolina Panthers fan, hired him, and he worked there for two years, mainly after school and on weekends, until his disease progressed too far. He spent most of his time there working on the grill, cooking hamburgers and chicken patties. Occasionally, he would work up front and assist in the serving area. At first, he was concerned about being able to cook the burgers quickly enough.

"Dad, I'm not going to serve burgers that are not done. I've got to learn to speed up!"

"Kevin," I reassured him, "you have a great work ethic. Give it a little time. You just started! Soon, you will be flipping burgers like crazy!"

True to my prediction, Kevin became one of the main cooks. He was very meticulous about having his cap and uniform just right, clean, and neat. He would have me inspect his hands before work, looking for any minute cut which might need a Band-Aid or could contaminate the meat.

"Dad, does this look like a cut? Should I wear rubber gloves?" he would ask.

He truly cared about doing the best job possible, and now he was part of a great team. I usually stayed up waiting to hear the rumble of his Mustang's engine, as he pulled into the garage after work.

August 13, 2003

Kevin's Medical Update

Hi everyone.

Kevin has been doing well since my last update in January 2003. He has been receiving chest CT scans and x-rays at three month intervals, and as of July 2003, no tumors have been spotted. I am continuing the experimental immune system treatments (GM-CSF) at home twice daily (30 minutes) every other week. We have followed this routine since December 2002. There is evidence of calcification in his lung which is due to the two major lung surgeries. His prosthetic knee is functioning well, but his orthopedist will not allow any physical activity other than walking and upper body strengthening. He is not to lift weight in excess of twenty pounds.

Last month, after several heart tests, it was discovered that he has diminished cardiac activity. This is most likely due to the drug adriamycin which he received in 2000–2001 (18 treatments). Some patients exhibit this problem months or years later. His cardiac function is down from 34% to 25%. In layman's terms, he is not in the danger zone (no swelling or shortness of breath), but he is being closely monitored and is taking two types of medication to strengthen his heart. The condition can stabilize, improve or deteriorate.

He is looking great and has been working part-time at Wendy's in Wilkesboro. He maintains a very positive attitude and just completed the local Relay for Life celebration (his church group played).

We feel very fortunate that he has remained cancer free these past eight months. Your positive support and prayers mean so much. Thanks ... Wayne.

August 14, 2003

Thank you for updating me on Kevin's progress. There truly is power in prayer. I am glad that the cancer has not returned and concerned that his heart appears to have suffered damage from the treatment. However, the treatments did not touch his insurmountable love and compassion that lives in his heart. You and Kevin are my inspiration. May God be close to you! Donna

I am so very glad to hear this wonderful news! We will pray that the heart condition improves! I'll copy this e-mail and read it in church tonight so the people of Goshen can join in our prayer support. Thanks, Wayne, for keeping us updated. You and Kevin have been an inspiration to so many. May God bless you is my prayer. Charlie

Given the history of Kevin's cancer recurring, I continued my research and sent Dr. McLean the results. I had found a drug, which in preclinical trials appeared to be very effective against Kevin's form of cancer. Panzem, a new antiangiogenic drug, topped my list. Acquiring that drug for Kevin would take me another year and a half.

September 27, 2003

Hi Tom,

After continuing my internet search, Kevin, his mom, and I feel that one of the below drugs should be our next line of therapy.

... Panzem (2ME2) ... Take 800mg dose twice daily (capsule) or perhaps a more potent liquid oral version. This is in trial at Dana-Farber with Dr. Paul Richardson.

... Vatalanib ... Available in caplet form. This will work well with Gleevec since they are in similar trial (mentioned in my last email).

... Neovastat ... Available in caplet form. This is another antiangiogenesis drug with few side effects.

... Avastin ... The premiere drug to use, but it must be administered thru IV twice monthly.

... Erbitux ... Not interested (chemo derivative).

I think the Panzem is more osteosarcoma specific. A website to consult is www.entremed.com. We want to continue with Gleevec, since it is producing positive results in his lung. I don't see any drug interaction complications with either of the three choices. We want to move with this right away. If you have a better plan, let me know. I feel good about this form of treatment. The sooner, the better.

Thanks, Wayne

The cancer became more aggressive and frequent. Cancer was found in several new pulmonary areas. Kevin never gave up or even complained. He knew he had to go on. He would not relinquish his life to this foe. This constant battle was now almost routine, a way of life for him and for me. We had been there before, and we could rise above it again.

October 14, 2003

Kevin's Medical Update

Hi everyone.

Kevin's regular (3 month) chest CT revealed two new nodules (one in each lung). They appear to be cancerous. This is the first occurrence of the disease in the left lung. He will be seeing the pediatric surgeon this Thursday morning, possibly go through pre-op that day and have the surgery to remove the nodules early next week (tentative plan). This will be his seventh surgery.

He had remained cancer free for the past ten months. We plan to continue the experimental GM-CSF treatments while looking at other protocols. The nodules are small and removing them ASAP is important. He will probably miss two weeks of school.

In the meantime, he continues "business as usual" with his schooling, church involvement, and after school part-time job. We remain upbeat and optimistic that things will go well and he remains in very good spirits. More later as things develop. Thanks ... Wayne

The church youth group periodically carried out the Sunday evening worship services in the church gym. Skits were performed, the praise team ministered with music, Pastor Craig delivered the message, and Kevin shared his testimony on this special evening.

October 2003

Kevin's Praise Team Testimony
Millers Creek Baptist Church Gym

Hello. My name is Kevin Triplett, and I'd just like to take a few minutes to share a word of testimony with you about my salvation experience, and how God has just blessed my life and just is my strength. Back in 1999, I was twelve years old, and I'd been going to church here for a little while. I knew I was a sinner, and the conviction of the Holy Spirit was on me to get saved. I wanted to get saved, but I was afraid to go up to the altar because of all the people in the congregation just kind of scared me. I believed in Jesus, that He was God's Son, that He died for my sins, and that He rose again. I knew I was a sinner, and I wanted to get saved, but I was just afraid to take that step of faith and just commit to it. I was at my grandparents' house one day, and we were all in the living room talking. We were talking about church and God. I told them how God was dealing with me, and I wanted to be saved. My grandpa told me it was between me and the Lord and not to be afraid. They encouraged me and got me "unscared" you might say. After that, I told my dad about it, and he took me to see Pastor Gore. In his office, he presented the Gospel to me. I prayed a prayer of salvation and invited Jesus into my life. That's the greatest thing I have ever done.

Not too long after that in the year 2000 in April, I was diagnosed with cancer. I guess you could say that was a tragedy. God has helped me through it. Even though it's bad to have cancer, it has brought me closer to Him. They told me this week they saw a couple more spots on my lungs. It's not too good, but I'm not really that concerned about it, because I know that God is in control. It just gives me comfort, because I know that when I die, I'm going to be with Him.

God has been real to me this week. I've been trying to seek Him and get hold of Him. He has just given me comfort every time. It's just a joy, when you've got Jesus in your heart. He's with you, and He's not going to leave you. He brought me through this cancer. I praise

Him for that. If anybody is sore with any kind of problem, spiritual or physical or just any kind of problem, just get on your knees and talk to Him about it. Read His Word, and claim His promises, He'll see you through. I just love Him. I just praise Him for what He has done in my life, and what He's doing, and what He ultimately will do. I just keep on going, keep trusting, and keep believing. It's kind of like that song says, it gets sweeter as the days go by. Thank you for your time. Just know that God is in control. If there is anybody out there that doesn't know Him, tonight is the night. It would be a good night to come to Him, if He is drawing you. You know, today is the day of salvation. It's just great living.

The Brenner Children's Hospital oncologists met each week to discuss possible treatment options for their patients. Knowing this, I asked Dr. McLean to take my suggestions before them. Gleevec, a lung cancer inhibitor, would be the drug of choice to use next.

October 15, 2003

Dr. McLean,
After researching the attached protocols, the following avenues look promising. Please let me know what you and the team recommend: imatinib mesylate (Gleevec, STI571, protein inhibitor), Protocols 1, 16, 19, gemcitabine (perhaps with docetaxel) Protocol 20, bortezomib (enzyme inhibitor), Protocol 7. All of these are Phase II trials. Please advise of additional protocols which look promising. If complications would not result, I'd like to continue GM-CSF. Thanks, Wayne

October 17, 2003

Kevin's Medical Update

Hi everyone.
The battle continues. After meeting with Kevin's surgeon yesterday, we have decided to put the lung surgery on hold for at least six weeks. After reviewing over fifty treatment protocols, I found four which looked promising. Since the nodules are small the oncologists agreed with me to try a fairly new drug (imitab myselate or Gleevec)

which has shown positive results in patients with pediatric leukemia and stomach cancer, and is now being used with osteogenic sarcoma patients. Unlike chemotherapy, this is an enzyme/protein inhibitor which thwarts the reproduction of certain rapidly growing cancer cells. Since it is a tablet, it is manageable at home with minimal side effects (nausea, cramps, fluid retention), so, Kevin's teachers be warned (lol). He will have a CBC to keep tabs on his white blood count. Sorry about all the pharmaceutical terminology, but after reading dozens of protocols, I feel that a career in oncology may be feasible (lol … again)! We will repeat the CT at six weeks, evaluate the treatment effectiveness around Thanksgiving, and make additional decisions at that time.

Thank for your e-mails and support. Kevin and I read each of them, and it does lighten the load. You guys are great! Wayne

Even people we did not personally know kept up with Kevin's fight. My e-mails were often passed from computer to computer, with people adding his name to their church's prayer lists. Kevin was inspiring others.

October 22, 2003

Kevin and Family,

I know you don't know who I am, but I wanted to let you know that we will be praying for you and your family. I am updated on your condition through your dad's e-mails to the school principals and staff, and I just wanted you to know that I am very proud of you. You may have a few obstacles trying to get in your way, but you "keep on truckin'" and don't let anything get you down. I wish all the students in our schools had the determination and drive that you have. I am a school social worker and I talk with kids everyday, trying to get them to come to school, and trying to keep them in school. They just don't take their education seriously. When I hear how courageous and strong you have been, and how you are almost always in school, it gives me confidence that maybe you can help me make a difference. Sometimes it is frustrating working with kids and parents who don't value their education, but hearing about you helps me "keep on truckin'," and it helps me realize there are students out there who really and truly care about their education, and who don't take anything for granted. Thank you for being such an inspiration to me. We will be keeping you and your family in our prayers. Angel

Kevin fell in love with the look of the Ford Mustang and talked about owning one someday. Knowing his health was a major factor, I suggested we begin looking right away. His mind was set on a black, hardtop coupe; but when we drove up to Boone Trail Autohaus in Wilkesboro and saw the Atlantic Blue 2000 'Stang sitting there, I knew it might be the one. It was a straight transmission, so I opted to chauffeur Kevin around in it. The white decals really made it look sporty! The dealer gave us several days to think it over. As I dropped Kevin at West High Monday morning, he began having second thoughts about it. We had to decide that day.

That afternoon as I picked him up he asked, "You didn't get it, did you?"

"Of course I did. You know you love it!" I said.

A huge smile broke across his face. He continued to add extras to his Mustang and loved riding with the windows down, with the sound of the Flow Master mufflers rumbling underneath. I owe a special thank-you to Maurice Templeton and Millers Creek Baptist Church. Kevin learned to drive with a straight transmission in your neck of the woods.

October 28, 2003

Wayne and Kevin,

It was so good to hear from you. The Mustang is awesome! Cool car! And I love the name Taco for your pup.

This weekend was our homecoming. It was nice, but it brought back a lot of bittersweet memories for me. Let me know what the doctors tell you. It sounds as if you're doing your research, but I know you have to. I didn't realize that Gleevec was used for tumors like this, either. We knew so much about Ewing's Sarcoma, but when Aaron developed AML, I felt totally lost. We were in the midst of the battle and I didn't get to go online to learn a lot either. Aaron needed me right there, so I couldn't go to the RM Room and research. Dr. Martin from Duke had hoped to use the new drug, Mylotarg, with Aaron when he relapsed in December, but it was just too aggressive. I still can't make sense of it all. I don't think I ever will.

Take care. We think of you as some of our closest friends, too. We've been through more together and have a better understanding of each other than our own families. I feel closer to you, because of what we've been through. Love you both! Terri

December 3, 2003

Dr. McLean,

After reviewing osteosarcoma and non-small cell lung cancer protocols, the following approaches may be viable if Kevin's CT proves discouraging. I am leaning more toward the gemcitabine/docetaxyl protocol at the moment. If you feel a protein/enzyme inhibitor may be better (gefinitib), I would endorse that, too. The meds of choice from my research include: gemcitabine plus docetaxyl, bortezomib, gefitinib and celecoxib, alanosine and vincristine. I have starred and circled possible protocols if you'd like to visit them in depth at www.clinicaltrials.gov. Other issues include whether to operate soon or use the existing tumors as test areas as well as the continuation or cessation of GM-CSF and Gleevec. Kevin's CT is scheduled for 12/11/03. Thanks for your continued support.
Wayne

CHAPTER 6

THE CHRISTMAS GIFT ... 2004

Kevin graduated from crutches to a cane.
Kevin and Gwyn McGlamery were inseparable, and Gwyn was like a brother to him.

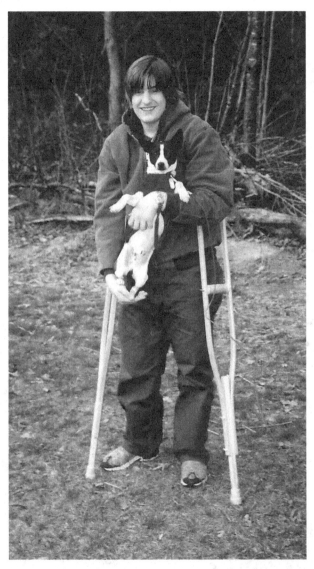

Taco, Kevin's rat terrier, was raised from a pup by Kevin and me.
Taco remains my energetic, little companion.

The 2004 Wilkes Relay for Life event was a celebration honoring cancer survivors and remembering those who had fought the good fight. Kevin and Marsha Sidden carried the banner for the survivors' lap.

Kevin's Pa and Granny, Ralph and Martha Shew, enjoyed many special times with him. They supported Kevin in everything he did and were always there for him. The love they had for each other was immeasurable.

Kevin began a part-time job at Wendy's in July of 2003.
He loved working with others and the extra money came in handy.
He worked there two years mainly on the grill and, ironically, was the Employee of the
Month in July of 2005, his last month of work due to his illness.

Kevin's blue 2000 Ford Mustang was his pride and joy.
He added bullitt wheels, a new exhaust system, and other amenities
and had hoped one day to trade up to a Mustang GT.
I remember its deep, rumbling purr as Kevin pulled into the garage after work.
He loved riding with the windows down, the wind swirling around inside.
Kevin and his "Pony" were quite a pair.

The Scott family met us for dinner in Winston-Salem.
Lindsay, Steve, Terri, Kathy (Kevin's mom), Kevin, and Andrew renewed old acquaintances.
We reflected on Aaron, on how much we missed him, and on how much we loved each other.

Barry and Gary Shew, Kevin's cousins, celebrated Christmas with Kevin each year at Pa and Granny Shew's house. They loved Kevin dearly.

Delta Miller, assistant manager at Wendy's, presented Kevin with this beautiful, handmade quilt complete with the Wendy's logo and individual patchwork by employees. Kevin is all bundled up in Christmas joy.

The Christmas surprise was about to become a reality, as Gwyn has just awakened Kevin from a nap and presents him with a card. Kevin eyes the beautifully wrapped package.

Kevin proudly displays his beautiful Schecter C-1 Classic sunburst guitar as friends Zeb Wright, Brandon Conley, and Gwyn McGlamery savor the moment.
Kevin's hundreds of friends and staff members at West Wilkes High School had succeeded in surprising him with this wonderful Christmas gift and giant get-well card!

The beautiful guitar begged to be played, and Kevin readily obliged.
Kevin proceeded to jam with his friends and christen the new guitar.
Their jam sessions were legendary!

For by grace are ye saved through faith; and that not of yourselves:
it is the gift of God: Not of works, lest any man should boast.
Ephesians 2:8–9

Kevin began the new drug, Gleevec, during the summer of 2003, and results looked promising with little growth noted in the pulmonary tumors. He continued getting monthly checkups at Brenner's, along with regular blood counts and port flushes. I had concerns about Kevin's weight loss, since it was the precursor to his original cancer diagnosis in 2000.

July 21, 2004

Hi Terri,

I opened Aaron's website at work. I couldn't hold back the tears. What an awesome site! As I read so many memories flooded back into my mind. It is a labor of love, and you did a magnificent job. It's true, we will always love you guys, even across the miles. I think of you and your family often. The framed picture is upstairs, and I pass it each day.

Kevin has had several good scans with the small 3 mm tumor still contained and stable in his left lung. The experimental pill, Gleevec, is still what he is taking daily. Kevin has lost about 25 pounds this past year (still 196). I alerted the doctors of my concern, but they don't seem alarmed and say this is probably a normal loss. As you know, every two or three months we hold our breath at the scans. Kevin has been experiencing a lot of anxiety and tension this week. It may be a medication thing (zoloft). I'm trying to hook him up again with a therapist. We're seeing Jeff Ungetheim tomorrow. Other than that, he is fine.

My mom had a stroke in February, and my older sister had a heart attack two days later. They are doing well now, and I've been trying to get my mom on Medicaid.

Kevin is working about five evenings a week at Wendy's cooking burgers! I'm too old to handle all these changes (lol). Stay safe. You did and are doing a marvelous job with the web site. Aaron would be so proud of you. All our love, Wayne and Kevin.

September 14, 2004

Possible Treatment Options I Researched

Inhibitor Options: ***2ME2 (methoxyestradiol, angiogenesis inhibitor), ***bortezemib (velcade), ***avastin (bevacizumab), ***gefitinib (iressa), erlotinib (tarceva), PKC-412, PS-341 (proteasome inhibitor), MTP-PE, PTK-787 (oral angiogenesis), CDKN2A (gene targeting)

Chemotherapy Options: gemcitabine and docetaxel, ABT-751 (binds with tubulin), BMS-247550 (epothilones)

*** = suggested treatments if Gleevec becomes obsolete

Kevin's weight loss was a harbinger of things to come. The cancer, although stable in his lungs, had migrated to lymph nodes in his mid-chest cavity.

September 25, 2004

Kevin's Medical Update

Hi everyone,
   As you know, Kevin has been battling osteosarcoma (bone cancer) since being diagnosed in April 2000. After chemotherapy and a number of surgeries (leg and lung), he began experimental therapies in December 2002. The drug GM-CSF (leukine) helped keep him cancer free for eleven months. When a new lung tumor developed, he began taking a new drug in October 2003 called Gleevec (imatinib mesylate). While on this medication the tumor has been stable in his lung for an additional eleven months.
   Last week's CT chest scan revealed additional calcification in a mid-chest lymph node (paratracheal node). After closer examination the oncologists believe that the cancer has migrated to that site (extremely rare for this to happen). With Kevin's weight loss this year, I was increasingly concerned. The options include removing the lymph node (3 to 4 weeks to recover), monitor his condition with follow up CT/PET scans, or begin additional therapies. The oncologists and I are currently researching several new targeted therapies that have shown promise in slowing or stopping tumor growth. While not

a cure, this approach could buy us some valuable time as research continues.

In the meantime, it is business as usual with Kevin. He is a senior at West Wilkes and continues his part-time job at Wendy's. We prefer to keep a normal routine and take one day at a time focusing on once again possibly finding a magic bullet that will stop the cancer's advance.

My e-mail list is extensive including Kevin's former and current teachers, and friends we have made in many places. It is difficult talking openly about his ups and downs. E-mail seems the best way to keep you updated (and I will), and we know you are very supportive. Keep Kevin in your prayers. Wayne

I appreciate your honesty. I continue to want to know of his progression and, of course, all of you are in my prayers. Joe

Dear Wayne,

I'm so glad you e-mailed with Kevin's update. I have had Kevin on my mind for the past few weeks and called Kathy at work yesterday. She told me about the CT scan, and gave me much of the information. I'm so sorry that this is happening. Words can't begin to tell you how I feel. I hope you know that you are all in my prayers constantly.

Please let us know what the docs decide. I'm sure you are doing all the research via the net that you can do. This all just makes me so mad, though. It just seems so unfair and wrong that such wonderful kids with such promise have to face such a disease. Of all the people we've met during these years, Kevin has meant more to us than anyone. Give Kevin a big WV hug from us all. We love you all, Terri

Sometimes venting is therapeutic. The Scott family and our family had shared so many ups and downs trying to beat cancer. My e-mail to Terri was especially poignant. We were mutual caregivers, and we spoke a language all our own.

September 26, 2004

Hi Terri,

Kevin is at Wendy's working and you're right, I have been online researching. I talked with Tom McLean last week and gave him several drug protocols for him to consider. Right now, I'm looking at angiogenesis inhibitors, which stop some cancerous tumors from forming blood vessels. I'm still looking for that magic bullet. I don't think Tom wants to operate. His posture indicates that he thinks it could reappear somewhere else anyway. Kevin has lost about 30 pounds this year. I mentioned it to them several times, but that wasn't a major concern for them. He has been taking Wellbutrin for a periodic depressive state of mind tendency. He is usually upbeat and emotionally he is doing well. Some "novices" have no idea that you and I measure and treasure the gift of just an extra month or two, if we are lucky enough to get a good scan with our kids. You just have to live through it like us to know the impact these horrible diseases have on all of us.

About a year and a half ago, I felt compelled to put together some video footage from Kevin's life, a tribute. Occasionally, I look at parts of it. It is to be his story, a gift from me, a labor of love. I think of you and the wonderful web page you created for Aaron, your tribute to him. We have to do something to add meaning to what we are going through. In some ways it is therapeutic. We still fight the fight daily, and hope that something will stop it. The lung tumor is stable, so the Gleevec must be impacting it. I hope Tom will go with the pill form of vatalanib.

I just e-mailed Tom some drug recommendations tonight. As you know, we just carry on, not oblivious to what lies ahead but trying to savor the gift of the moment. I'm not saying anything you don't know. Somehow, you go on, one day at a time. I admire you, Steve, and especially Andrew for his perseverance without Aaron there beside him. I know it is difficult for all of you. As you know, we find a way to manage. I will give Kevin a big hug for you guys. He is thinking about getting another guitar. I hope he can maintain that positive focus.

You keep the faith and know that you guys are never far from our thoughts. Even with so much calamity in our lives, the friendships we have made give us much comfort. As long as we have that, our kids will be with us. We shared so much, and as I said before, special is too less a word to describe your family, and Aaron. God bless, Wayne

We finally received news that the Walk for Friends plaque was becoming a reality at Baptist Hospital. Kevin and Justin's schools and the Millers Creek community had made a difference in helping less fortunate children through their donations.

Dear Wayne and Kevin,

I have some news for you to think about. I got a call from NCBH that they were putting up a display in the new Cancer Center that was recognizing contributors of $10,000 and more. I asked if they could put Millers Creek Schools for Kevin and Justin. They said they were just putting the names of the contributors. It reads, Millers Creek School—Primary and Intermediate. I really think someone at our newspaper should know about this. I am very proud, for you and Justin's family. I have not talked to Justin's mom, yet. Take care, and I will talk to you real soon. Fran

The following e-mails confirm again the tremendous support Kevin and I had from our growing network of friends. Even more, our correspondence became a sounding board. We did not have answers to all the questions of why cancer had to strike our Kevin, but we had strong shoulders to help bear our burdens and to occasionally cry on.

September 27, 2004

I cannot imagine what this is like for you and your family. For what it is worth, you and Kevin continue to be an incredible witness for Jesus Christ. I truly wish there was something I could do to help. You are in our prayers. Thank you for keeping us updated on the situation. I pray God's very best for you as you continue walking through this valley. Charles

Morning Wayne,

I thought about Kevin last week when I was driving somewhere to do something, that part I do not remember, but I do remember wondering how he is and how you are as well. You both have courage beyond what I can comprehend. A very close friend of mine has a thirty-one year old daughter who was diagnosed with a massive brain tumor the day after her birthday. It had grown for years and years but because it was so slow, it was only detected after she had a seizure. She has three small children and has just now started chemo. She did seven weeks with radiation. Another friend found out last week she had breast cancer. Why and what is causing so much? After my John went through a Microsoft systems engineering program in Charlotte a couple of years ago, he came home one night and told me he thinks computers contribute to cancer. He did not go into detail when I asked him but still believes electronics have something to do with mutation of the cells. Please keep me updated on what is happening. May God continue to be with you both. Pat

I will definitely remember you and Kevin in my prayers. I enjoy seeing him so much as he passes in the hall. Sometimes our eyes meet and we speak, other times he doesn't see me. I admire him so much. He's one of my heroes. Take care. Becky

I absolutely want to continue receiving updates. With all of our lives being so busy, it is the only way we seem to keep in touch. We enjoyed visiting with Kevin on several late night trips to Wendy's after ballgames this past summer, and he is the same ole Kevin, happy and smiling. That's a strong tribute to his faith and his family support. You will continue to be in our prayers always. Keep believing and keep fighting, because you never know what's right across the horizon in terms of new treatments! Ricki

Miracles happen every day. Here's praying for another for Kevin and you. Your strength and optimism amaze me! Steve

Thank you so much for keeping me up to date. I think of Kevin a lot and of you. I have admired your faithfulness to stay positive and upbeat in all this. I want you to know that I will pray for Kevin and for God's grace to be richly poured out on this situation. You tell Kevin I was asking about him. He is a great young man just like his father. Garland

I am so sorry that you and Kevin have yet another down time going on. I certainly want to be on the list to stay informed. You are such a positive person, and Kevin is so lucky to have you. Together, you guys are an inspiration of hope to many others. I will continue to keep you both in my prayers and thoughts daily. Thanks for sharing. Sharon

I really mean to call, but I'm still more than a little emotional now and don't want to put you through that :). Your letter brought back so many memories. Ever so often, I'll still find myself on the computer looking for clinical trials, or some new drug for Ewing's and AML. Then it hits me, and I think, "What are you doing?" I understand completely about looking for that elusive magic bullet. I had to smile at your reference to the "novice" not understanding. I'm on an internet support group, Day By Day for parents who lost children to cancer. We refer to them as "the clueless."

I have a friend who is thinking about retirement, and I'm encouraging her even though I'll miss working with her. Her son is twenty, has Spina Bifida, and his health is not good. He wants his mom home with him. Every second of every day is so precious with our kids, and the clueless just don't get it.

I'm not surprised that Dr. McLean does not want to operate. He always explained to us that they wanted to use the tumor to gauge if the meds are working or not. As parents, we just want our kids free of it. I do understand his reasoning, it just went against my thinking as a mother.

As for Kevin's weight loss, thirty pounds is quite a bit. Do you think the loss could be from using Wellbutrin? There's only so much our kids can deal with.

I am sure the video footage is wonderful. I know how therapeutic it is when I work on Aaron's web site. I want the world to know what a great kid he was. I haven't been able to look at videos yet, but I will eventually.

I'm so glad Kevin is keeping up with his job; it must help to be with friends and staying busy. I hope he gets the guitar. I know he always loved to play.

As I said before, I find myself being so angry now. I think I'm only now facing that emotion. We had a young boy, only 9, die in August from a very rare sarcoma, epitheloid. I made friends with his family, and the loss is just so senseless. I just want Kevin to be well, and whole, and to live a long, healthy life with children, grandchildren, keeping all of you busy! That's my prayer for your family. Know that you're always in our prayers. Love, Terri and family

October 1, 2004

I appreciated your e-mail the other day. I think about and pray for you and Kevin everyday. He is truly an amazing young man. I can not image the agony that you are facing in your decision making process. The Lord has been there with you through many valleys, I know he will walk with you again. Thank you for keeping me and the Career

Center posted on Kevin's progress, we love and miss you!!! I wanted to share this poem with you, it is one of my favorites.

> The tree that never had to fight
> For sun and sky and air and light,
> But stood out in the open plain
> And always got its share of rain,
> Never became a forest king
> But lived and died a scrubby thing ...
> Good timber does not grow with ease,
> The stronger wind, the stronger trees.

May God be Close to You, Donna

Thank you so much for everything you've done for me over the past four years. You have been a great mentor, and I will look to your example to follow as I move into the administrative field. Kevin is always in my prayers. Take care, John

October 2, 2004

Hi Tom,
Thanks for getting back to me. I feel that with Kevin's weight loss over the past year "something" is remiss somewhere. I didn't think osteo was susceptible to any form of radiation treatment. When you mentioned "radiation oncologists" I felt that might be in the offing. I feel that Panzem (2ME2) could be very effective. I don't see a risk factor in him taking it, since clinical trials point to its efficacy in completed trials. We were at this point last year when we you introduced gleevec, and we witnessed the positive results. I'm not opposed to looking at some new intervention, but since something is obviously at work and Panzem (or vatalanib) are possibly available, I'd like you to consider that option as well. I'll wait to hear from you soon. Thanks for keeping me posted. Wayne

October 4, 2004

Hi Tom,
Thanks for your call. The manufacturer of avastin can be reached at www.gene.com (Genentech). The above website suggests a dos-

age (twice monthly, day 1 and 14) of 5mg/kg as an IV in solution. Using metric conversions with Kevin weighing 184 lbs. or (83kg) a 16 mL vial (400 mg) would just about cover his body weight for one administration. Using the suggested price list at www.drugstore.com, a 100mL vial costs roughly $653 (4 vials approx. $2612). Given twice monthly costs would appear to be approx. $5300. I could be wrong of course.

Please continue to pursue the gamma knife approach if it seems feasible. I think we need to eliminate the suspicious lymph node by some means. As always, thanks for your help. Hope to hear from you in a few days. Wayne

Avastin, a relatively new antiangiogenic drug, was on the market for specific cancers and in additional clinical trials for others. Tom and I joined forces to procure this drug for Kevin, using this approach to hopefully starve developing tumors from their blood supply. Ultimately, we were able to secure the use of the drug for him.

October 12, 2004

From Dr. Keith Flaherty, Philadelphia

Dr. McLean,
The Avastin-Gleevec trial was initially a phase I trial open to all tumor types. However we completed accrual to that portion of that study. At this point, it becomes a phase II trial in melanoma. Unfortunately, I don't think that we will be able to help out. I apologize. Keith Flaherty

October 18, 2004

Hi Tom,
Our visit Friday to Dr. McMullen went well. Today I talked with Dr. Pranikoff. Tom feels that he and his associate can effectively remove the lymph node. He suggests doing this surgery in January, since the CT scan showed a slow progression. He feels that the photon radiation could pose the possibility of damaging surrounding esophageal, etc. tissue.

Kevin wants to go the surgery route with Dr. Pranikoff. I suggest doing a CT scan perhaps in November to monitor the nodes enlargement. Also, Tom along with Kevin and I, feel that starting avastin immediately is what we should do. Please facilitate this and let me know when you would like him to come down for his first iv dose.

I have also talked with EntreMed about the new Panzem NCD oral formula which should go into clinical trials in early 2005. I really want to pursue this new antiangiogenesis drug and hopefully get in on a trial (Dana Farber, etc.). As usual, we will look to you for assistance here. Eagerly awaiting your call. Wayne.

I will work on the avastin. Regarding a clinical trail, most would require some measurable disease, in which case you would not want to operate first (because he wouldn't be eligible if the disease is "gone"). Rather, he could be enrolled and treated, and the node size could be followed on CT scan. Of course, the best plans for initiating clinical trials are often delayed. It could be mid or even late 2005 before that trial opens, so I don't think I'd wait for that. Overall, I think surgery in Jan. is a reasonable option. We should probably get a CT scan immediately prior to starting avastin, and then another after three months or so to see if it's doing anything. I'll be in touch. Tom

Nothing would stop me from pursuing what I thought was a possible magic bullet to stop Kevin's cancer. Panzem, an experimental drug, seemed out of reach. Newer therapies are largely just being tested, and companies had their own stringent guidelines before a cancer patient could participate in the trial. I e-mailed the manufacturer a number of times, enlisted the help of the FDA, and even considered the *Oprah Winfrey Show* or the *O'Reilly Factor*. If I could convince our elected officials to intercede for me, I might have a chance. The tumultuous back-and-forth of e-mails which follow chronicle my passion for saving Kevin's life. It was a no-brainer. Short of a miracle, if we did not stop the cancer, it would ultimately claim his life. I knew that, and he did, too. The roller-coaster ride was beginning again.

November 12, 2004

Hi Ginny (Entremed spokesperson),

I spoke with you a month or so ago regarding my son's battle with osteosarcoma. After four and a half years, a number of leg and lung surgeries and several rounds of chemotherapy, his metastatic cancer continues to advance. A cancerous paratracheal lymph node continues to enlarge and a small outbreak may be in a shoulder blade.

In short, chemo and inhaled GM-CSF have been only partially successful in slowing its advance and have been discontinued. Currently he is taking Gleevec (a multiple myeloma drug) which seems to have stabilized his lung metastases for almost a year. We have just started avastin (antiangiogenesis drug). It is my mission to overlook no possible intervention which might slow or even stop the cancer's advance. Panzem, from my research, has made dramatic improvements in many osteo patients. It has shown impressive results in vitro and with mice in increasing osteosarcoma tumor cell apothesis. Time is critical, and I'm relying on you as my conduit to forward this e-mail to someone who might assist me in getting Panzem for my son. I would gladly abandon avastin for a regimen of Panzem (tablet or new oral suspension formula).

Our medical facility (Wake Forest Univ. Bpt. Med. Center) in Winston-Salem, NC has an excellent team of oncologists who have partnered with several clinical trial groups on a consultative basis. Surely, there must be some way to either enroll him in or be a partner to an ongoing study in the interest of saving a young man's life. Please let me know what channels I need to pursue. Thanks for listening and I'm hopeful you can intervene in a positive manner. Wayne Triplett

November 13, 2004

Virginia Foxx, U.S. Congress
Richard Burr, U.S. Senate
John Garwood, N.C. Senate
David Banks, FDA

I am a principal in the Wilkes County Schools' system (Mt. Pleasant Elementary) and a former high school principal here. My teenage son, Kevin, was diagnosed over four years ago with bone cancer (osteosarcoma). It has been an uphill battle ever since. He has had two leg surgeries (prosthetic knee) and two lung surgeries when the cancer spread. It is now in a lymph node and in his shoulder.

We have done the usual chemotherapy and several new drugs (GM-CSF, gleevec and now avastin). Each slowed the cancer's advance somewhat. There is a relatively new drug in clinical trial (not FDA approved yet) called Panzem (2ME2). I have been unable to get him enrolled in a trial, since no one is offering it just for bone cancer. Research clearly shows that it has been very successful in killing ostersarcoma cells in vitro and in other area tests.

The pharmaceutical company says maybe in late 2005. It may be too late then, since his cancer is spreading. The doctors at Brenner's (Baptist Hospital in Winston-Salem) have worked with me well but do not have that drug. If you can help by contacting the below company which makes Panzem and can sway them, I would be eternally grateful. Usually Kevin's doctors get what we need, run it through our two major medical policies and there are no problems. I am even willing to pay. If we could try it a few months to see if it is helping. It is available as two pills a day or a new liquid version. I certainly would not hold the company responsible, and it would be monitored by Baptist Hospital doctors. This is the information you might need: Drug Name: Panzem (2ME2), Company: EntreMed, Contact Person: Ginny Dunn ginnyd@entremed.com.

I hope you will get back to me with some information or refer me to someone who might help. I have seen you at several political rallies locally. As a parent, I will leave no stone unturned to try and save my son's life. Thanks for your help. Wayne Triplett

November 16, 2004

Hi Tom,

I talked with Dr. Pranikoff this afternoon and he feels removing Kevin's lymph node should be our next step (shortly after Thanksgiving). He advises not to continue avastin at this time with surgery being imminent. I did not get a response yet from Dr. Ward. Kevin and I will be in clinic tomorrow around 11:00 AM (after my prostate biopsy) to pick up his statement of excessive absences form and share some clinical info with you. Congressman Richard Burr's medical issues' secretary, Jenny Hansen, called me this afternoon. She advises that if you will contact EntreMed (the company that makes Panzem) and state that our need for the drug is for "compassionate use," they might comply. You may site his critical situation. If they agree the drug (tablets or preferably the new oral suspension) would be free to you to dispense to Kevin. Then you would contact the FDA for some paperwork both you and I would submit for final clearance. I will list the numbers below and share this hard copy with you tomorrow. EntreMed (maker of Panzem ... 2ME2), Contact Person: Ginny, ginnyd@entremed.com, FDA Approval Number (after EntreMed agrees to dispense medication), Congressman Richard Burr's contact (if all else fails), Jenny Hansen.

I am determined to get this drug, even if I have to camp out on their doorstep. It is in the same category as avastin and is in clinical trial. The research backs up its viable use with osteosarcoma patients. It may be a long shot, but then we are used to taking the path less traveled. If I can help in any way let me know. Thanks for all you do. Wayne.

November 18, 2004

Hi Terri,

Kevin's tumorous lymph node (paratracheal) has grown to golf ball size. Dr. Pranikoff thinks he should remove it shortly after Thanksgiving. That is the plan. It is somewhat like open heart surgery involving the upper sternum. The CT also revealed a worrisome area in his left scapula (shoulder blade). I spoke with Dr. Ward and he thinks he can remove it if necessary.

Basically, I am suggesting what I think he should have. I found a drug called Panzem (2ME2) which has shown promise with osteo patients. It is in clinical trial, but not for osteo. The company told me, maybe next year. We may not have next year, so I have called three congressmen's offices and heard from two of them. They gave me some info, which I passed on to Dr. McLean. He has called the company and is asking for the drug's use based on "compassionate use." If I have to guess I'll go up to Maryland and camp out on their doorstep.

It seems the cancer is taking bits and pieces of Kevin, but he remains upbeat and really enjoys his Wendy's work. Who knows? He'll probably be in the hospital on his 18th birthday, Dec. 7, for surgery. The bone scan should tell us if it is progressing or not. It's a roller coaster as you well know. I often wonder why it had to strike our boys who had so much to give and didn't deserve the lousy hand they were dealt. It is very easy to be cynical. Sometimes, I get so angry and at other times am resolved to just keep on keeping on one day at a time. My mission, to keep Kevin alive, for as long as possible and support him, like I have done for almost seven years.

Thanks for listening. As we both know, you have to go through these valleys to really empathize with someone. You've been there and sharing with you is a positive thing for me. We love you guys. Say hello to everyone. Keep in touch. Love, Wayne and Kevin.

November 19, 2004

[Thank-You Note to U. S. Congresswoman Virginia Foxx]

Virginia,
Thanks so much for your call this afternoon. If you can help get this company to release the drug after reading this e-mail, I will be forever grateful. Thanks ... Wayne

November 21, 2004

Thanks for the info. It has not shown up in my Charter account as far as I know, so I'm glad you sent it here. I will make a call on Monday. Virginia

November 22, 2004

[E-mails to David Banks, FDA]

Hi David,
This e-mail to my son's oncologist chronicles my current frustration with not being able to get the drug Panzem. Next stop, Oprah or Bill O'Reilly. Hope to hear from you soon. Wayne

Ginny [EntreMed spokesperson],
    As you may have gathered I have tried through my oncologists at WFUBMC to communicate to you the urgency for my son to get a trial sampling of Panzem. I have talked with three congressmen all of whom have done their part to convince you of his "compassionate use" need for this medication. Needless to say, I am disappointed with our negotiations thus far.
    You may have children. If you do you must know that if there is a possible drug which could save that child's life, it would be inhumane to deny that child the possible benefit of its use. I have contacted the FDA for further assistance. I plan on continuing my efforts through contacting larger media markets. I do not want to point the finger of disdain at Entremed, but in the interest of fairness and the preserva-

tion of life, I think you are denying my son a possible major cancer intervention. If this drug works, think of the boost it would give your company in this area of cancer research. Perhaps someone can see the humanitarian nature of my plight and can convince your CEO of this great need. If need be, I will schedule an appointment to talk with Entremed officials in Maryland. Keeping my son alive is my mission. I will leave no possible route to getting this drug unsolicited. What good is developing a medication if it is withheld from someone in great need of it? Research backs this up that Panzem possibly could be very effective against his cancer. I would appreciate a call so we might discuss this further. Wayne Triplett

Wayne,
I heard back from Ginny at EntreMed. She said they will not release it on a compassionate basis and that Kevin is not eligible for any current trial with Panzem, so I think this will not be an option. Let's proceed with the bone scan and surgery as planned, and keep thinking of other options. Tom

November 25, 2004

Wayne,
I did speak to Ginny, but she explained what you have. She was very pleasant and said she hoped to be of more help after the first of the year, but I stressed to her that time is of the essence. She said she understands your advocacy. Please keep in touch and let me know if there is anything else you need me to do. Virginia

Kevin's Medical Update

Hi everyone.
I last e-mailed you in September and there are some new developments with Kevin. The tumor in Kevin's paratracheal lymph node (chest cavity) has grown considerably (golf ball size) since his last CT scan six weeks ago. This rapid growth has possibly been the main reason he has lost some fifty pounds this year. He is scheduled for pre-op on December 7 (his 18th birthday) with surgery to remove it scheduled for the next day (Dec. 8). He will be in the hospital around five days, and then spend some additional time recuperating at home. This seventh surgery (fifth major one) should be well tolerated by

him. It is similar to open heart surgery just below the sternum. He may not be back to school before Christmas. Current teachers: please touch base with me on a plan for his exams.

He does have a worrisome area in his left shoulder blade which appears on CT to be osteosarcoma. This area was not clearly visible on last week's bone scan which may indicate it is manageable.

I have been very busy researching possible treatment options. He began the drug avastin (approved by the FDA in Feb.) which in some patients has shown promise in delaying tumor development. We are off the drug temporarily in preparation for surgery. I have been actively pursuing a new non-approved drug called Panzem (2ME2) which is in the same antiangiogenesis family. The drug company did not have a clinical trial open for him. I contacted Congressman Richard Burr's office, spoke personally with Congresswoman Virginia Foxx and Senator John Garwood as well as with a member of the FDA and Kevin's chief oncologist Dr. Tom McLean. I thank each of them for going to bat for me in negotiating with the drug manufacturer, but the company located in Maryland still will not cooperate. I actually considered going the "mass media" route (Oprah, O'Reilly, regional television news outlets) for more exposure on the "compassionate use" of the drug for Kevin. In order to keep the possibility open with EntreMed and perhaps get in on an early 2005 trial, I have decided to take the route of diplomacy and wait. After he recovers from surgery, we plan to begin the twice monthly treatments of avastin again and see what happens.

It has been a whirlwind of activity. Kevin is enjoying guitar jamming with his friend (Gwyn) and working part time at Wendy's after school. We are meeting this holiday with some friends from West Virginia who lost their son to cancer whom we have not seen in several years.

Kevin has purchased a number of the Lance Armstrong and Carolina Panthers cancer awareness bracelets and has been handing them out to his friends. His resilience is remarkable, and as you can imagine is on a first name basis with several of his surgeons.

Thank you for your continued support and prayers for him. This Thanksgiving, I continue to be thankful that Kevin will continue touching lives in a positive way through his struggles. As the bracelets he hands out proclaim, "Keep Pounding" and "Livestrong," those are the phrases he would have each of us live by. I would expect nothing less from Kevin. I'll keep you updated and Happy Thanksgiving! Love, Wayne and Kevin

Kevin was facing surgery, again. Wonderful words of encouragement and support began flowing into my e-mail inbox as friends read Kevin's latest update. Kevin and I were overwhelmed with the compassion our extended family had shown us. Those messages warmed our hearts, and we knew that whatever happened, we felt their love and caring.

November 28, 2004

Your message really puts the meaning of Thanksgiving in perspective for us all. I will continue to remember Kevin and you in my prayers. Thanks for keeping me posted. Mike

I am sorry about Kevin. Tell him I am praying for him. Take care of yourself. Hope you had a good Thanksgiving. I really missed my son. He is not able to call or e-mail us much. He is going out in the field in Iraq now and that worries me a lot. I will be praying for you, too. Love, Kathryn

Knowing how busy you must be, I'll keep this brief. We will all be praying that all possible avenues will be cleared and that Kevin will be healed soon. My (and our) prayers are with you both. Ron

Wayne and Kevin, What can I say? I admire you two so much. You know you are in mine and my families thoughts and prayers. Linda

Thanks for the inspirational e-mail. I really needed it today. You are the most deserving person I know to receive your e-mail. You are always thinking of others and strive to make life easier for your employees and those close to you. I hope you take some time for yourself and relax this weekend. I think of you and Kevin often and remember you in my prayers. Take care ... Donna

November 29, 2004

Well, I certainly will continue to pray for Kevin. He has touched my soul, and I am pulling for him. As far as an exam in anatomy, I think that Kevin probably knows more anatomy and physiology than a young man his age should. But, many things in life are simply not our choice, and we take what comes along, don't we? His exam in this class is to have this surgery and spend his time in restful recovery, so he can enjoy Christmas. I have not asked anyone's permission, but surely as a classroom teacher, I do still have the option of making that decision myself. At least, I am exercising that option anyway. If this is not agreeable with you, just let me know and we will work out something else. If he feels like it after he returns home, maybe he could e-mail me and let us know about his progress. Again, I will do the one thing I know I can, pray for him and for you. Thank you for letting me know what is going on. Paula

Morning Wayne,
What an inspiration you two are. You both have my utmost respect and are continued in my thoughts and prayers. You know, we always really know God knows what He is doing, but we do wonder sometimes which only makes us human. But one thing is for certain, He blessed Kevin with the right father. I'll especially remember to say a prayer those mornings. Pat

I'm so sorry to hear that Kevin is going to have to undergo yet another surgery. You don't know how much I admire him. Just seeing him in the hall adds sunshine to my day. Just wanted you to know that if there is anything that I can do to help in anyway, please don't hesitate to call me. Kevin is special, and I will certainly keep him in my daily prayers and will ask my church family to pray also. Take care, Becky

I just read your e-mail and I want to give you words of encouragement, but I don't know if I have the strength to say something in person, and I don't know if you prefer for us to talk to you or not. So I will e-mail for now, and please let me know if you would prefer to talk. I lost a brother to cancer last Christmas, and my mother has cancer, so I can empathize a little. I say "a little" because I cannot imagine the suffering of having a child with cancer. Kevin is blessed to have a wonderful father like you. May God grant you both the spiritual, physical, and emotional strength you need, and I pray He heals you both in every way. You remain always in our prayers. Carol

Very touching report. While prayers are still and will always be a part of Kevin's treatment, I just have to say if there is an award out there someplace for Dad of the year, you need to receive it. Such love for one's son. Kevin is a lucky child even though his life is tough. Keep strong as always. If I can do anything to help let me know. Al

I have known Wayne and his son, Kevin for many years. Wayne is the principal at Mt. Pleasant school. His son, Kevin, has been a warrior against cancer for a large part of his life. I asked Wayne to keep me posted, so that I will continue my prayers for Kevin. As you will notice in the most recent e-mail from Wayne, Kevin continues to work at Wendy's and does the things a typical teenager would do. He is one tough young man. Please keep him in your thoughts and prayers. I am sure the Great Physician will attend to his health needs. Take care, C

When I asked how to get in touch with you at work, Steve forwarded your e-mail. I hesitated to ask about Kevin when you called me the other night, but I wanted to find out what was in store for him, especially since I was a little worried that he wasn't in class today. I really appreciated being able to read the update, although the news was what it was.

However, after reading Kevin's autobiography, I too am optimistic about Kevin! What an attitude. And, I might add, what a dad!

Please don't worry about Kevin's work after December 7. If Kevin had not had to have medical absences, he would not have to take an exam. So, tell him from me that if he simply does his class work and maintains his "B," we'll call it even for the semester with a Merry Christmas and no exam. Best, Jenny

You are such a wonderful Dad with all the ways you have tried to get what Kevin needs. He sounds like a very special kid, and he is blessed to have such a caring father. I just wanted to remind you of that. You're in my prayers. Tammy

November 30, 2004

Kevin's Medical Update

Hi everyone.

As you know, Kevin has been battling osteosarcoma (bone cancer) since being diagnosed in April 2000. After chemotherapy and a number of surgeries (leg and lung), he began experimental therapies in December 2002. The drug GM-CSF (leukine) helped keep him cancer free for eleven months. When a new lung tumor developed, he began taking a new drug in October 2003 called Gleevec (imatinib mesylate). While on this medication the tumor has been stable in his lung for an additional eleven months.

Last week's CT chest scan revealed additional calcification in a mid-chest lymph node (paratracheal node). After closer examination, the oncologists believe that the cancer has migrated to that site (extremely rare for this to happen). With Kevin's weight loss this year, I was increasingly concerned. The options include removing the lymph node (3 to 4 weeks to recover), monitor his condition with follow-up CT/PET scans or begin additional therapies. The oncologists and I are currently researching several new targeted therapies that have shown promise in slowing or stopping tumor growth. While not a cure, this approach could buy us some valuable time as research continues.

In the meantime, it is business as usual with Kevin. He is a senior at West Wilkes and continues his part-time job at Wendy's. We prefer to keep a normal routine and take one day at a time focusing on once again possibly finding a magic bullet that will stop the cancer's advance.

My e-mail list is extensive including Kevin's former and current teachers, and friends we have made in many places. It is difficult talking openly about his ups and downs. E-mail seems the best way to keep you updated (and I will) and we know you are very supportive. Keep Kevin in your prayers. Wayne

December 1, 2004

What a letter! My heart really goes out to you. I know you have faith, but you and Kevin have been through so much. I hope only the best for him. I will put him on our prayer list at church. Please keep us informed. Is there anything we can do for you at North? We still think so much of you and wish you were back. Are you taking a leave? You know how rumors are and I have heard that you were. If you need any leave, let us know! Cheryl

You tell Kevin I think he is a very special guy, and I admire him. Garland

Even though the tumors were advancing in his mid-chest area, Kevin's determination and zeal to live thrived. He had surgical removal of the paratracheal mass in early December 2004. Although the scar ran down Kevin's sternum and was wired together, his accompanying pain was minimal. He was pleasantly surprised by this. In fact, he said, "I think this is the easiest surgery I've had." Sensing that the conventional and even newer therapies were only yielding mediocre reduction in his tumor growth, I again launched a major effort to secure the new drug, Panzem (2ME2), which was in phase one clinical trial in Indianapolis. Dr. McLean and I still clung to the belief that it might be the drug which could turn the tide in our favor.

December 9, 2004

Kevin's Medical Update

Hi everyone.
Kevin came through surgery yesterday (Wed.) well. The cancerous tumor was removed, and he was in ICU until mid-morning today (Thurs.). I stayed with him until midday today and wanted to update you prior to my attending PTO tonight. He will be taking it easy for about a month (no driving, working at Wendy's, etc. for several weeks). He is now in the Brenner's suite on the 9th floor. He may go home or to his Granny's tomorrow or possibly on Saturday. If you have time, he would love to hear from any of you. Thanks for the wonderful banner from West. I sneaked a quick peak, but I will not read it until Kevin has seen it. You guys are wonderful, more later. Wayne

I am so glad to hear about Kevin, and you are terrific to update us. Our classes are doing a card today, and I believe Cathy Sebastian is headed to Winston, so she will deliver it. Please tell Kevin I really miss him, and think about him every day. Take care of yourself. Get good food and rest. Very best wishes. Jenny

December 12, 2004

Becky,

Thank you so much for the wonderful banner! Kevin enjoyed reading it, and we are going to find a huge wall in his music room and post it. You are so faithful, and your words always touch my heart. I am including a photo of Kevin with the banner. Use it as you see fit. I'll keep you posted, and your caring makes you very special to both of us. Wayne

Kevin's Medical Update

Hi everyone.

Kevin's surgery on Wed. (12/8) went very well. The cancerous lymph node in his mid-chest area was successfully removed, and there seem to be no complications. The tumor had compressed his trachea somewhat, but the resulting soft area of the trachea should heal. He spent several days in ICU but returned home late Friday. He goes for a recheck on Friday (12/17). He is restricted from activity (no driving, no opening car doors, no lifting, etc.) for a week and his chest will be sensitive for about six weeks. It will take several months to get to business as usual. He now has another mid-chest scar to add to his collection. This surgery, in his words, was not too bad. He should be able to return to school after Christmas.

In early January, we plan to begin the drug avastin again and take a closer look at the potential developing tumor in his shoulder blade. For now, we give thanks for the successful surgery, for your well wishes, and for your generous support.

We especially say "thank you" to the students and staff at West Wilkes High School for the wonderful banner and written words of encouragement. It really meant a lot to know that so many of you are pulling for him. He has a special spot for it on the wall of his music room.

Kevin's five year struggle with cancer has reaffirmed in our hearts a central theme of this season, the greatest gifts come adorned with no ribbons and bows but instead are words of encouragement and prayers of hope offered from caring hearts. Thank you for your many gifts. We hope each of you have a wonderful holiday season. Wayne and Kevin

Thanks so much for the update on Kevin. I am so glad that things have gone well and will certainly continue to keep you all in my thoughts and prayers. It was good to hear he had gotten to go home. Cathy Sebastian had gone by the hospital Friday night, and said he had already been discharged. I have a little gift for Kevin and wondered the best way to get it to him. I can send it to Mt. Pleasant, but I wasn't sure if you would be working this week. I can always just drop it in the mail. Just let me know. Please give Kevin my good wishes. Jim

Wayne, thanks for the update. What a courageous young man Kevin is. He's an inspiration to countless folks who are following his care and treatment. He's setting an example for others to follow. And what a fine father you are! Both of you are handling this with amazing strength and upbeat outlook. Kevin's going to triumph in the end. No doubt!

Pauletta told me she saw you recently. I hope you're taking care of yourself. I know the stress of Kevin's illness plus work are taking their toll on you. Take time to get your rest. Kevin needs you to remain strong. You are all in our thoughts and prayers. God's Peace, Chuck

Praising God for all the success! Jim

December 13, 2004

Yes, Kevin is a gift. It's wonderful to think of Kevin in the midst of the tragedy we are experiencing at West. As a matter of fact, the seniors in Kevin's English class really are holding onto Kevin's successful surgery and progress while thinking of what happened to Aaron. Thanks so much for the updates. You can imagine what that means to all of us. Very best wishes to you both, Jenny

I'm so glad that Kevin is doing well, and I am thrilled to get the picture. He looks so good that it's hard to believe that he just had surgery. Everyone at West loves Kevin, and the banner was just one way for us to express our care and concern for him. I pray that he will get stronger every day, and I can't wait to see him in the halls again. Like I said before, he's my hero. I hope that you both have a Merry Christmas and that 2005 will be the best year yet for Kevin. God Bless Always, Becky

Thanks for the update. You and Kevin are in my thoughts and prayers. Kevin is fortunate to have a dad like you. Both you and Kevin over these last few years have impressed me with your faith, hope and positive outlook. Hope you both have a joyful Christmas, Randy

What wonderful news! Please tell Kevin that I am so impressed with his spirit. He truly is a special young man. I will continue to pray for his full recovery and for your continued strength. God Bless you both and Happy Holidays, Kaye

Everyone loved Kevin. Never was this expressed more by the staff and students of West Wilkes High School, than the welcoming of their Christmas gift to him, a brand-new Schecter C-1 Classic guitar and case. The guitar and the many hours he spent playing it opened up a new world for him, and one which ultimately would culminate in his forming the Christian rock band Taking Up Arms.

The Christmas surprise, the beautiful guitar and case, epitomized how special Kevin was to the staff and students. He absolutely loved it and was totally surprised when he received it. It brought him many hours of pleasure. May God richly bless all of those who contributed for that magnificent gift. The story of how it all came about was beautifully captured in the following article.

December 31, 2004

Article from the *Wilkes-Journal Patriot*
"Role Model: Kevin Triplett Battles Cancer With A Smile"
by Frances Hayes

The students and staff at West Wilkes High School have grown almost accustomed to the heroism exemplified by Kevin Triplett, a senior who was diagnosed with osteosarcoma (bone cancer) in the spring of 2000.

For almost five years, the approximately 700 student body at West, the staff and Triplett's teachers have seen him beat the odds, successfully coming out of seven surgeries with no complaints. He has attended school and kept a part-time job at Wendy's despite surgeries and caner treatment.

Cathy Sebastian, one of Triplett's teachers at West, says she realized two years ago that "nothing was going to stop Kevin from surviving."

The lessons learned from Triplett's amazingly resilient and strong nature are many. "We have all been inspired by Kevin's optimistic attitude in meeting all obstacles," said Ms. Sebastian. "Kevin has been a role model for the students, going good even in the hard times."

Triplett, his family, and friends have been actively involved in the Wilkes Relay for Life after he was diagnosed with cancer. Following his example, students at West have been involved with the fund-raiser to find a cure for cancer since 2001.

Recently, Triplett bought a large number of Lance Armstrong and Carolina Panther cancer awareness bracelets. He handed them out to his friends with the implicit message to "Keep Pounding" and "Livestrong," the words printed on the bracelets. These are also words that Triplett lives by.

"You can see Kevin's goodness in his desire to go through experimental drug therapy, because it helps people find a cure for cancer," said Ms. Sebastian. For over four years, Wayne Triplett, Kevin's father, has searched tirelessly for experimental therapies that will cure his son's cancer when more traditional methods have not worked. He undertook that search again when a CT chest scan taken in early September 2004 showed the cancer had migrated to a mid-chest lymph node. Doctors decided surgery would be the best course of action, as well as taking the drug avastin, approved by the FDA in February 2004.

In this situation, as in every other one, the Triplett family has been an example of strength and courage. It can be seen in the e-mail, on September 25, Wayne sent to the extensive list of people who love his son.

"The oncologists and I are currently researching several new targeted therapies that have shown promise in slowing or stopping tumor growth. While not a cure, this approach could buy us some valuable time as research continues. In the meantime, it is business as usual with Kevin. He is a senior at West Wilkes and continues his part-time job at Wendy's. We prefer to keep a normal routine and take one day at a time, focusing on once again possibly finding a magic bullet that will stop the cancer's advance."

With Triplett's imminent surgery, the students at West decided it was time to do something major to show Triplett how much they loved him this Christmas, said Ms. Sebastian. "Kevin's friends have done things for him all along, but this year we wanted to do something that included the entire school," said Ms. Sebastian. "Kevin is really loved. The love students feel for Kevin is obvious. He is so sweet and loving no matter what."

Motivating them was the news that doctors had found a tumor in Triplett's chest cavity that was growing rapidly. That meant he would be undergoing his fifth major surgery and his seventh surgery since 2000. This fifth major one, similar to open-heart surgery, was scheduled for December 8, a day after Triplett's 18th birthday. Ms. Sebastian says news of Triplett's surgeries comes through Kevin's father. "Kevin never talks about it," said Ms. Sebastian. His father told teachers he would return to school in January.

Gwyn McGlamery and Aaron Nersthimer, two of Kevin's closest friends, decided the perfect gift would be a Schecter C-1 Classic guitar and case. Triplett has been an avid guitar player for many years and enjoys playing with his friends, McGlamery, Nersthimer, Zeb Wright, and Brandon Conley. Students placed $1 buckets all over the school and more money was collected during lunch. Within three days the $813 needed to buy the guitar was raised through contributions from students and staff at West, as well as parents of West students.

"We raised the money quickly even though seniors were really only there for one of those two days, since the last two were for exams," said Ms. Sebastian. Leading the fund-raising for the guitar was Laura Staley, student body president. A large, original get-well card with a guitar printed on the front was signed by most of the students. The card project was led by Brittney Witscher.

Surprising Triplett with the large card and guitar required planning. There were a few mishaps before that goal was achieved, says McGlamery. Initially, it appeared the guitar would not be in stock till mid-January. Ms. Sebastian and several other students spent several hours on the computer, searching for a site that had a Schecter C-1 Classic guitar available immediately.

Finally, on December 23, his friends told Triplett they would be coming by his house to play guitars with him. "Kevin enjoys his jam sessions with friends," says his father, Wayne Triplett.

This time Triplett's friends were late and he fell asleep, only to wake up with his friends clustered around his bed. They achieved their goal, surprising him with the guitar and life-size card.

Earlier in the week, Triplett had received a large get-well banner from the West Wilkes students and staff after he returned from cancer surgery. The Wendy's of Wilkesboro employees also presented him a quilt complete with employee signatures woven into the fabric. Delta Miller, the assistant manager at Wendy's, presented the quilt to Triplett.

The outpouring of love and support for Triplett has shown his family how loving teenagers can be. "Sometimes stereotypes of teens can be misleading in its negativity. If they find a cause, they are adamant to get it done," said Triplett.

For the Tripletts, the support from the community has been a continuous source of strength, says Triplett. In an e-mail from December 12, Wayne Triplett wrote, "Kevin's five year struggle with cancer has reaffirmed in our hearts a central theme of this season, the greatest gifts come adorned with no ribbons and bows, but instead are words of encouragement and prayers of hope offered from caring hearts."

CHAPTER 7

KEVIN'S AUTOBIOGRAPHY

For God so loved the world, that he gave his only begotten Son,
that whosoever believeth in him should not perish, but have everlasting life.
John 3:16

Kevin's English IV class had a major project to complete to fulfill their course requirements. Each student had to write an autobiography. Kevin approached this task seriously and spent many hours writing it. His handwritten, original version, contained in a binder, is a prized possession of mine. Kevin's goodness, strong moral character, and faith in Jesus Christ shines through. I think one comes to know him much better after reading it. It offers a unique glimpse into the young man he was becoming.

Kevin Triplett
An Autobiography

for
English IV—Third Period
Ms. Nelson

November 22, 2004

Section One:
My Early Life and Family

Favorite Holiday

My favorite holiday is Christmas. I like it because it is a time when all my family gets together. We always have a good time together. On Christmas Eve, I go to my grandma's house. This is an annual tradition. We gather around the Christmas tree, pass out gifts, and take turns opening them. On Christmas day, I go to my other grandma's house. Everyone gathers in for a big meal with turkey, ham, and all of the trimmings. After that, we usually pass out gifts and open them.

Church is a big part of my Christmas, too. The Christmas play and the musical cantata bring out the true meaning of Christmas. Our youth group has a Christmas party that is a good time of fellowship.

It is always nice to have two weeks out of school. I enjoy taking it easy around the house and enjoying the Christmas break. It is always nice if it snows for Christmas. One of my favorite snows was when I rode my four-wheeler around. It was fun sliding on the ice and snow. The free time on Christmas break is a good opportunity to get with friends and make music. We gather at my house and play guitars. If we're lucky, we have new sheet music and learn new songs.

A few times the power has gone off during the break. We managed to drive to Bojangles for food, even though the snow was kind of deep. You can see that Christmas has many meanings for me and a lot of memories.

Favorite Vacation

My favorite vacation ever was when I went to Alaska. This was a very special trip for me. It was what I chose for my Make-A-Wish.

My dad, mom, one of my best friends, and I went on an Alaskan cruise. It was an eight day cruise through the inside passage of Alaska. We went in July and the weather was great for the whole trip. Surprisingly, it wasn't too cold.

We visited Juneau which is the capital of Alaska. Also, we visited Skagway, Ketchikan, and cruised through Glacier Bay. We had a lot of fun at each of these places. One of the best things was when we went whale watching. We were fortunate enough to actually see some humpback whales. In Skagway, we took a train ride and saw all kinds of breathtaking scenery. We toured an old salmon cannery in Ketchikan. That was rather interesting.

The cruise ship was also very nice. The food was excellent all through the cruise. You could eat like a king. The ship also had plenty of recreation areas. I had fun in the arcade and playing ping-pong. I also went swimming.

Every part of this vacation was awesome. I will never forget my Alaskan cruise. Maybe someday, I can go back.

Early School Memories

I really can't seem to remember my first day at school, but I do have bits and pieces of memories from those days.

I remember going to preschool at Mt. Pleasant. One of the funniest things I remember doing was riding big wheels in the gym. I don't know how fast we got on them, but it seemed like we were race car drivers. There was an old red tricycle that you had to ride sometimes if you couldn't get a big wheel. It was no fun.

Not long after that, kindergarten began. Our kindergarten room was neat. It had an actual upstairs in it. I remember learning my ABC's. We made a kind of book, I think. We would take yarn and glue it to the paper in the shape of the letter, lower case and upper case. We also made a book in kindergarten. Most of the boys did their books about bugs. One boy mentioned bugs, and it seemed like we all wanted to do bugs. That is what I did. I can't remember what the girls did.

I also recall times when I didn't want to go to school. I remember times when I would cry. I didn't want my mom to leave me. I guess it was all a part of adjusting to the routine. Eventually, I believe I began to enjoy school. When I really think about it, I remember more from my early school days than I thought I did.

Favorite Relative

I love all of my relatives. I spend more time with some, though. My grandpa is one of my favorite relatives. We have spent a lot of time together. His name is Ralph Shew. He is my mother's father. Unless the circumstances are very unusual, he is always there if I ever need to talk. My grandpa is always encouraging me and asking about me. He is a simple man. He tries to live one day at a time and just enjoy life. I believe his heart is full of love for his family, friends, and others.

My grandpa has taught me a lot through the years. He taught and showed me the importance of coming to God and being saved. He tries to lead me and my family in the right direction. He has also taught me and probably others perseverance. He had a stroke and even though he is not back like he used to be, he has worked hard and came a long way. He did not give up during this setback.

During times in my life when I have been sick, he has helped me. He was always there with my grandma doing all he could do. When I have had surgeries, he has always come down and seen me in the hospital. Anything I wanted to eat, he was usually more than willing to go and get.

My grandpa has always shown me love, and I am blessed to have a special grandpa like him. I hope that one day I can be a good grandpa like him.

Immediate Family

My immediate family is small. I have no other siblings. So really, my immediate family is just my father and my mother. They are very special to me.

My father's name is Wayne Triplett. He was born on May 29, 1952. He has a good work ethic, and I respect him for this. He finished high school and went to college afterwards. He has four college degrees. My dad works in the school system. He was a teacher for eighteen years. Then, he moved up to assistant principal for awhile. He is currently the principal at a local elementary school. My dad and I have a very close relationship. My parents are divorced, and I live mainly with him. He is very smart and always tries to help me when I need help.

My mother's name is Kathy Triplett. She was born on March 12, 1958. She is originally from Baltimore, Maryland. She works at Tyson Foods in the transportation department. I enjoy spending time with her. We have a lot of fun doing things like going out to eat. She is always nice to my friends and lets them come over. My mom supports me in all that I do. She loves to travel. She has been to Hawaii, Aruba, and some of the Caribbean Islands. She also likes to read, watch television, and spend time with her friends. That is my immediate family. I love them.

Favorite Family Tradition

Thanksgiving is a wonderful holiday. Actually, everyday should be a day of Thanksgiving. My family loves to celebrate this holiday.

It is a yearly tradition for our family to gather at my grandma's house for Thanksgiving. I always look forward to this event. My cousins and other family members that I do not get to see often are there. My grandma and other family members prepare a big meal. There is always plenty for everyone. The main thing is of course the turkey. I like turkey, especially the legs. My uncle never eats turkey. He says it is an ugly bird, and he doesn't want to eat it. When I was younger, I would always want to get the wishbone and break it. We also have sides to go along with the turkey. Everyone loves my grandma's mashed potatoes. We also have rolls, dressing, cranberry sauce, and yams. Then, for dessert we have fresh pumpkin pie with whipped cream. Before we eat everyone always gathers around the table and someone says the blessing.

Thanksgiving is always a good time of fellowship and bonding for my family. We usually watch some of the parade on television or a football game. Sometimes after everyone is done eating, we play card games like Rook. You can see why this is a favorite tradition for my family. I wish we could do it more often.

A Biography of Kevin Triplett

It isn't often that a child can be someone's greatest teacher, but for me Kevin is that person. Kevin was born on December 7, 1986, which is also known as Pearl Harbor Day. As his father, his birth was the most significant event of my life. I remember being in the delivery room and catching a quick smile from him as he was born. My life has been so enriched from knowing him.

As a child and toddler, we were inseparable. Our lives revolved around playing with blocks, riding in the stroller, making baby formula, and looking for Ninja Turtle characters all over town. We took our nature walks, played in the newly fallen leaves, and made great snowmen. I loved seeing him play with his next door friends (rollerblading, biking, sword fighting). What fun we had! Those were great days!

In elementary school, he truly enjoyed tee-ball, baseball, and YMCA basketball as well as being on the school basketball team (undefeated). I have precious videos of many of these activities.

When bone cancer (osteosarcoma) struck him in his seventh grade year, we were devastated. For nearly five years, he has fought this deadly disease valiantly (chemotherapy, two leg surgeries, three lung surgeries, on crutches eighteen months). As a surgeon said, "He went in a child but came out a man." This is true of Kevin. He never complains and sees his predicament as God's will for him that the new cutting edge cancer therapies, many of which pioneered by him, will ultimately benefit many other people.

I have known many people in my life and have even talked with presidents, but Kevin is the greatest person I have ever known. He has touched so many lives in a positive way and has been an inspiration to hundreds of others by his perseverance even in the face of overwhelming odds. Now, as he faces more surgery, his determination and mine are even stronger to somehow slow or stop this disease.

He has been an inspiration spiritually to his peers by his active involvement in his church youth programs and praise band. He has even been the keynote speaker for the local Relay for Life cancer fundraiser. Numerous articles and interviews detailing his battle with cancer have been chronicled in the local newspaper. He takes all this in stride and is very modest about it.

To have a normal life again may not be in the offing for Kevin, but as long as he has his music, great sense of humor, support of his doctors, and most of all his dad, he will be fine. He is my inspiration and has taken what might be a death sentence for many people and made it a beginning. This beginning carries with it the hope for a cure, and the promise that whatever happens he will be fine, because he is in God's hands. This acceptance gives him an inner peace.

Yes, Kevin is a model for us all. His life and struggles continue to be life's lesson for me. Kevin, my mentor, teacher, little buddy, my son, of whom I could not be more proud.

Submitted by Wayne Triplett

Section Two:
The Times of My Life

Most Embarrassing Moment

An embarrassing moment for me happened not too long ago. It was last August at the Relay for Life.

The Relay for Life is always a very fun, inspirational, and touching event for me. This one was no exception, but there was a slight technical problem that happened.

There is always entertainment on the Watson Stage at the Relay for Life. Our church Praise Band had a spot on the bill this year. Last year, we played at this event, and we had a good show. The show was still good this year. I just had a slight problem. Anyway, we began playing. Everything was going good. Then, one of my guitar strings broke. It was not a good feeling. There I was on the Merle Watson Stage in the middle of a song standing there with a broken string. This is the same stage that country greats like Willie Nelson and Vince Gill had performed on.

Even though this was an embarrassing moment, everything still turned out good. There are two guitarists in our Praise Band, and we pretty much play the same thing, so I was covered. Although there was a sweet solo I was going to play but couldn't because of the broken string. I stayed on stage and tried to play what I could. Basically, I just stood there and acted like I was playing.

I learned a valuable lesson through this experience. If it is possible, you should always have a backup guitar on stage.

Most Frightening Moment

Myrtle Beach has always been a favorite vacationing spot for my family and me. I always look forward to going. It is a lot of fun. One time things got a little scary.

I don't remember exactly how old I was, but I was a little fella. My parents and I were out on the beach. It was a nice sunny day. The beach was crowded. My dad and I were out playing in the ocean. We had our rafts, and we were getting knocked down by the waves. We were just having a good ol' time.

Suddenly, I lost sight of my parents. It wasn't too long before I realized I was lost at Myrtle Beach. The ocean and beach and everything kind of seem to look the same, so I guess I just got mixed up and wandered too far off. I had gotten lost before in stores or places like that, but this was Myrtle Beach, South Carolina, and I had no idea where my parents were. I was frightened. I kept walking around searching, hoping I would find them. I thought about talking to a lifeguard and probably eventually would have. Then I saw my dad walking towards me. I was so glad and relieved to see him. At the age I was, this was definitely a frightening moment.

A Sad Day

I believe one of the saddest events in my life was the day I found out that I might have cancer. My life has never been the same since that day.

It was in the spring of my seventh grade year at school. My right knee had been bothering me for quite sometime. It was also swollen, and my range of motion was limited. My doctor ordered some x-rays and an MRI to be done. Not long after that, my dad and I went to his office to hear how they turned out. I had no idea about the news we were getting ready to hear, and how forever it would alter our lives. The doctor came in the room. I was sitting on the examination table and my dad was sitting nearby in a chair. The doctor put his hand on my knee and said something like, "I need to get serious for a while." I don't remember all that he said, but when I heard cancer it got me. I was shocked. My dad said I turned white. I was only thirteen years old. I thought cancer was what you got when you were old.

When my dad and I left the doctor's office, we both were saddened. I was scared. I did not know what was going to happen next. We shed our tears and just hoped for the best. There was still a chance that it wasn't cancer, and we held on to that hope. The next day, a needle biopsy revealed that it was cancer.

An Influential Person

Many people in life have had an influence on me. One person who has really influenced me in a positive way was my guitar teacher Tony Mancusi.

I guess when I was in the fifth grade I decided I was going to play the guitar. One of my friends and I wanted to start a band. He and I both started taking lessons from Tony around the same time. My friend was not as devoted as I was, and he eventually dropped out of the lessons. I kept playing and taking lessons, and it paid off.

Tony is a real nice, easy going guy. I always enjoyed my lessons with him. He made sense to me, and I understood him. I liked the way he taught. I had a lesson book, and we would play in it for awhile. Then he would try and teach me any songs I wanted to learn. Songs that I heard on the radio I liked, he would teach me. He figured a lot of them out himself. He is also a thoughtful guy. While I was taking lessons, he would send his students a birthday and Christmas card. The Christmas card had a little gift in it.

I give Tony credit. He has had an influence on me learning and playing the guitar. He is a good friend. I tell people if I never took guitar lessons, I probably never would have stuck with it.

Leisure Time

It is always nice to have some leisure time. A time when you can clear your mind and just have fun is always refreshing. There are so many activities you can do.

One of my favorite leisure activities is playing music. I love to play guitar as often and as much as I can. When time allows, I like to work on songs from my favorite bands or just try to write some of my own. Sometimes, I get the opportunity to play with my friends. This is very rare because of our different schedules, but when we do play, it's awesome.

Another thing I like to do is visit with my family. My family means a lot to me and is always there for me. I especially like to visit with my grandparents and spend time with them. Family time is special because you never know how much longer they will be with you.

I also enjoy being with my friends when I have leisure time. Sometimes we go out to eat. We also enjoy playing video games together. Talking on the phone is another thing my friends and I like to do when we can't hang out together.

As you can see, leisure time is very valuable and important to me. We should always enjoy and cherish our leisure time.

Just Laugh

Ha, ha, ha, ha, ha, ha, that was so funny! I believe everyone loves to laugh. Laugher is good for a person. It relieves tension and stress. It makes you feel good.

I love to laugh. There are many things that make me laugh. My dad can really make me laugh. He is so funny. We used to play this laughing game. Most of the time, we would play it in the car. I would look at him, and he would do something funny to try and make me laugh. If I showed my teeth or anything like that, he would win. As you might expect, of course he won almost all the time.

Something really simple that makes me laugh and laugh hard is the fact that I am ticklish. I am ticklish under my arms and on the bottoms of my feet. If you grab my knee and start squeezing it suddenly, that also can make me laugh.

My friends also make me laugh. I can be out with them sometimes and one of them will just really do something goofy. Sometimes, one of them will just have a really funny joke to tell that cracks us all up.

Movies, music, plays, and literature make me laugh, too. Movies that have Jim Carrey in them, I think are some of the funniest movies I have ever seen. Laughter is good and healthy. Remember to take the time and laugh.

My Faults

As human beings, we all have our faults. Nobody is perfect. We will mess up. There is no way around it. Each individual has different faults, but we probably share some, also. I know my faults. I may have some that I have not yet realized.

One of my biggest faults is laziness. I have a job, and I'm usually not lazy on the job. School is kind of different, though. I try to do a decent job with keeping up on my work, but sometimes I get lazy and turn in incomplete assignments or sometimes not turn them in at all. Another fault I have that goes along with being lazy is not studying enough. I make fairly good grades, but I know if I applied myself better and studied more, I could be much more successful. Math is a weak subject for me. One of the reasons is probably because I don't study enough.

Another one of my faults is procrastination. I have a bad habit at school of putting work off to the last minute. Sometimes, I can handle it and get it done. Then there are other times that I don't get the work done. If I would not procrastinate, I would probably make better grades.

These are a few of my faults. They hinder me and hold me back in some ways, and I don't do my best. I need to try and work on these faults and not let them get to me so much in life.

Favorite Music

I love music. I listen to it, sing, and play it. My favorite style of music is rock, although I also like a lot of other styles. The guitar is probably the main reason why I enjoy rock music so much. I love to hear a good rock song with crunchy, distorted guitars and a nice wailing guitar solo.

Rock music may be my favorite style of music, but contemporary Christian music is one of my favorite genres. Since I am a Christian, I like listening to music that is uplifting, hopeful, and encourages spiritual growth. A lot of secular music is so corrupted by profanity and drug references. In Christian music, there is a positive message about life and encouraging lyrics to help you out in your everyday life.

Some of my favorite bands are Kutless, Audio Adrenaline, Switchfoot, Falling Up, and Disciple. Even though I really don't listen to Metallica that much anymore, they are kind of an influence on my playing style. I have seen some of these bands live, and they really put on a good show. They have a lot of energy and get the audience pumped up. I got to meet Kutless after a performance, and that was a lot of fun. They are really a great group of guys.

Music has always helped me through life. No matter what I'm going through, all I have to do is listen to some music and I feel better.

Section Three:
My Philosophy

Life's Most Important Things

Everyone has got their view on what they think is most important in life. It's sad that some people get so caught up in drugs and alcohol that they miss what is most important in life.

The most important thing in life is your relationship with God. God has a special plan for everyone. The greatest decision anyone can make is deciding to trust God's son, Jesus Christ, as personal Lord and Savior and repent of their sins.

Another important thing in life is your relationships with others. We should love others, even our enemies. We should treat others the way that we want to be treated. When someone does us wrong, we should not hold grudges. We should forgive them and love them. It is better to encourage others rather than bring them down.

An education is very important to have in life. Times have radically changed and without a good education, it is hard for some people to find a good paying job. I don't always like going to school. I am a senior in high school, and I realize and appreciate more how blessed I am to have had a good education all my life with teachers that care.

Those are three things that I believe are most important in life. They really impacted my life and always will. It's great to be alive. Enjoy life!

America

I am proud to be an American. We are blessed as Americans to have so many freedoms. As great as our country is, there needs to be a lot of changes made.

The values of America are on a decline. Some people believe homosexuals should have the right to get married. I think this is horrible. Marriage should be between a man and a woman. Drugs are out of control in a lot of places. You hear on the news about meth labs and stuff like that. Also, a lot of kids are on drugs. They have become too easy to get. Pornography is widespread throughout the country. The porn industry should be shut down.

It would be nice, though, if citizens were told more about what goes on in the country. I have always wondered about Area fifty-one. That place is so protected, and our leaders don't ever tell us what's going on inside. You hear stories about aliens and spaceships being inside. I wish somebody would just step out and tell us exactly what goes on there.

I think our country has made good steps on keeping us safe from terrorists. We are stricter in our airports and other places. It's wonderful that we have not had another horrible attack like 9/11. Instead of criticizing our president so much, I think people should give more support. These are some of my thoughts and opinions about America for the present.

Optimist or Pessimist

I am definitely an optimist and proud of it. Whether the situation is good or bad, I always try to have a positive outlook. The glass is half full, not half empty.

When I was thirteen years old, I was diagnosed with bone cancer. This was a great shock and tragedy. I believe that because I have had a positive attitude, I have gotten to where I am today. Cancer is very scary, but a positive attitude goes a long way. If I would have just curled up in a ball and cried all the time and worried about dying, I don't believe I would have done as well. With an optimistic outlook, you can take on life's toughest challenges. As long as there is life, there is hope.

I believe that optimistic people are probably much happier than pessimistic people. It must be so depressing to always look at life from a pessimistic point of view. Even in the worst of circumstances, look on the bright side and be optimistic. If people would just change their perspectives on life, they would see that it's not really so bad.

In life you have two choices. Will I be an optimist or pessimist? Will I turn lemons into lemonade? Do I see the glass half empty or half full? I believe being an optimist is the best choice.

Religion

There are many religions in the world. All of them claim to be the right way. There is only one that is the right way. It is Christianity.

I am a Christian. I believe that there is only one true God. Christianity is more of a relationship than it is a religion. It is a personal relationship with God through His Son Jesus Christ. The Bible says in the book of John chapter fourteen verse six (Jesus speaking), "I am the way, the truth, and the life. No one comes to the Father except through me." Jesus clearly says that He is the only way to heaven. He said He is the Way, not a way. The Bible also says that broad is the road that leads to destruction and narrow is the way that leads to life, and few be that find it.

A lot of people rely on their good works to get them into heaven. No matter how good a person is, they are still a sinner. Everyone has sinned. Everyone has done wrong. I believe that everybody who does not trust Jesus Christ as their personal Lord and Savior is going to hell.

As a Christian, I try to point people to Jesus. I don't do as good as I should, but if someone asks me about my religion I will tell them what I believe. God loves us all, and He sent His only Son to die for us, and He arose from the grave on the third day. Eternity is too long to be wrong. Choose Jesus!

Censorship

I think censorship can be a good thing. I don't think cursing, pornography or drugs are right. Some things should be censored. People do have the right to express themselves as long as it does not infringe on the rights of others.

I don't think the American flag should be burned unless it is done in a respectful and reverent way. An author has the right to write about anything in their work. If someone doesn't agree with them, then they don't have to read their work. Sometimes the media censors graphic violence which should be done, because you never know who might be watching.

We need to consider what the media is feeding children. We should be aware that graphic violence can be harmful to them. Pornography can give them the wrong view about sex and love. Some of the stuff in the media can scar children. There has been controversy about some children's programs such as the *Teletubbies*. It might have been something to do with homosexuality. I have even heard about stuff being in Disney movies. There could be subliminal messages or suggestive themes in children's programs. Maybe some people just have too much time on their hands.

Like I stated earlier, people have the right to express themselves as long as they don't infringe on the rights of others.

Abortion

I oppose abortion. This is a very controversial issue concerning a woman's right to have an abortion. In 1973, the Supreme Court ruled in Roe v. Wade that women do have the right to choose an abortion during the first three months of pregnancy. Many people like me who believe it is wrong are labeled pro-life. I believe human life begins at conception, and no woman has the right to end a human life. It is not just a personal health issue. Many women have even died from abortions performed by unskilled people. Each state now can have new restrictions on abortion. If you believe the Bible, it is obvious that an abortion results in the death of an unborn human. Even though it may only be a fetus, it is still a human being. I believe it is against the law of God to kill. One of the Ten Commandments states that thou shalt not kill. Pro-life people must persuade the Supreme Court to reverse this decision. A woman's right to choose should not result in the death of an unborn child. It is not the child's fault that it was conceived. A good option would be having the child and putting it up for adoption. Many couples would love to have these children. Another option would be that family members, like grandparents, could raise the children. I believe that life is sacred and should be protected. This legalized killing of the unborn is a black mark on our society. The lifestyle of many women should be altered. It has become too easy to get an abortion on demand. The morning after pill also fits into this category (RU-486). The right thing to do may not be popular, but in the eyes of God, a life is our most precious gift.

Prayer in Public Schools

I think having prayer in public schools is great. Prayer is very important to me, other students, and teachers. I think that if there was prayer time every morning and some Bible reading, it would help our public schools.

If you really look at the situation, it's kind of like God is being taken out of schools. I have heard that back in the old days, they would pray and maybe read the Bible at school. Now, prayer is being pushed out of schools. Some people think that under God should be taken out of the pledge of allegiance. Our schools are blessed, and we should take time each day at school to thank God.

I am glad that we have clubs like the FCA that promote prayer at school. It's great that we can have prayer on the square and share our prayer requests. Mrs. Williams always reminds everybody. You can hear her yelling in the hall, "Prayer in the courtyard, five minutes."

If we had daily prayer at school, there might be fewer discipline problems. The Holy Spirit might speak to students about their sin and draw them closer to God.

It might not be all that controversial if we had prayer at school in our community. There are churches all over the place. I am not trying to force my beliefs on anyone else. I would just encourage them to check it out and pray.

Smoking in Public Places

I despise smoking. I think smoking is crazy. It has many health risks like cancer and emphysema. Smoking in public places is bad.

As a cancer patient I have no use for smoking. I have enough to deal with the way it is. I think smoking should be banned in public places. Why should non-smokers have to breathe in secondary smoke? They say secondary smoke is worse for a person, anyway. At least most restaurants that allow smoking have a separate section, but the smoke is still getting in the air, and it carries. I have loved ones that smoke, and sometimes it just kills me when I see them smoking, because I know how it is hurting them.

Thankfully though, some public places and restaurants are banning smoking. I work part-time at Wendy's. I am glad that at our Wendy's, it is a non-smoking restaurant. I would hate to have to breathe in a lot of smoke every time I was on break or cleaning the dining room.

Hopefully, as time goes on, people will get wiser and quit smoking. It would be great if the medical world came out with a one-time pill that made you quit smoking and never do it again.

I am just going to keep encouraging people to quit smoking. Also, as often as possible, I will try to sit in the non-smoking section.

Section Four:
My Hopes and Dreams

If I Could Be Anyone

If I could be anyone, I would be a guitar player in a band. I love music, and I love the guitar. It makes me feel so good to play guitar. It is an adrenaline rush. I would love to have a career in the music business.

The guitar has been a labor of love for me for a few years now. The reason I started playing the guitar was to be in a band. I have been in a band before, and it was good while it lasted. I want to be in a band that makes it fairly big and is known by people. It's not that I crave being a rock star. I just want to be in a successful band and a great guitarist that writes encouraging music to help people through their lives. I want to be humble. I don't want the fame to go to my head.

My friends are in a band that in my opinion is doing great. Tethered inspires me that hard work does pay off and to stick with something.

The kind of band I want to be in and the kind of songs I would want us to write, I believe, would help a lot of people. That is the kind of person I want to be, a person that loves and cares for others, a person that inspires people, and helps people out no matter what the situation. I will keep practicing guitar and always keep it fun. That is what it is all about.

Travel Anywhere

If I could travel anywhere I believe I would go to Europe. I think Europe would be an interesting place to visit.

It would be nice to see Buckingham Palace and all of the guards. They say their expression never changes. The clock, Big Ben, in London would be very interesting. I would like to see the Eiffel Tower in France.

Experiencing the different cultures would also be fun. There would be different foods to try, drinks to sample, languages to hear, and different accents to appreciate. It would be fun sight seeing and exploring the cities. The different currencies would probably be hard to adjust to. In Europe, they also drive on the opposite side of the road than what we do. If I drove over there, that would probably be scary at first. Hopefully, I wouldn't wreck. I don't know what the speed limit would be. Maybe it would be similar to ours.

It is important that we try to understand and learn about other cultures. If I went to Europe, it would be a great opportunity to learn about the European culture and how their ways of life are different from ours. Europe is a place I would definitely go to. I would probably have lots of fun.

Plans and Goals for the Next Five, Ten, and Twenty Years

What will I be doing in the next few years? After I finish high school, I plan on going to college for a couple of years and then maybe transfer to Appalachian. I'm not exactly sure what kind of career I want to have. Well, I know what I'd like to be doing. I'd like to be full time in a band. I might go into teaching. I have thought about becoming some kind of history teacher, maybe high school history. I still plan to continue working at Wendy's. I am going to try and play guitar as much as I can and try to become the best player I can be. Basically, I just want to stay in Wilkes County for awhile.

Further on down the road, I plan on getting married sometime, if it is meant to be. There is a season for everything. I want to enjoy my single life for awhile before I commit to marriage. As you can tell from my autobiography, my family and friends mean a lot to me. I hope I will have plenty of good times with them in the future. If I ever get married, I plan on having at least two children. I don't want one to have to grow up alone.

I just want to have a healthy quality of life and enjoy being alive. If I continue to have health problems, it will be okay. I will be optimistic and persevere through them. I want to help others in whatever ways I can and develop close relationships with people. These are some of my plans and goals.

Section Five:
Summing Up

A Poem by Kevin Triplett

Cancer

I found out about you when I was thirteen.
You made your presence known.

Only God knows how long you had been
lurking inside of me.
Only He knows how long you had been
growing
trying to take over my body.
I don't know why you came to me.
I guess that's just what was meant to be.
You shook us up,
but we didn't give up.
Things were dark like the night,
but we chose to fight
battle after battle we began to see the light.
You put us to the test.
We gave you our best.

What I Have Learned

This project has been a journey. It has been a lot of writing and typing. It has required thought. I believe this project has been good for me. It's like a stroll down memory lane. Composing this project has been a reflection of my life thus far. I dreaded doing it, but now that it's over, it really didn't seem all that bad. I have learned from this project. As I wrote about my faults earlier, I mentioned procrastination as one of them. It almost got the best of me. If the due date hadn't been extended, more than likely it would not have been complete. I know now I need to set more of a steady pace for myself.

I would definitely recommend this assignment to future seniors. It's a good way to learn about yourself and examine yourself. While doing this project they may ask themselves, what will I be doing in the future? Why am I living life this way? As I have been working on my autobiography, a song came to mind by a band named Switchfoot. In the chorus of the song the singer says, "This is your life. Are you who you want to be?" It's really a good song. Throughout my four years in high school, this has been the most I have written. I am probably a better writer, since I have written this.

Summing it all up, I feel that this is a positive project. If you look at it with the right attitude, it's not so bad.

Alternative Projects

What the World Needs Most.

```
S  S  E  N  E  V  I  G  R  O  F  G  J  H  N
E  Z  K  H  E  E  M  J  E  J  N  E  R  T  H
M  W  A  Y  T  M  X  C  C  I  S  V  U  I  W
G  W  K  V  D  F  A  V  L  U  M  O  X  A  H
C  I  S  U  M  E  V  A  S  H  O  P  E  F  U
N  F  M  M  P  R  E  I  L  M  Z  E  H  V  G
N  O  U  V  I  H  D  C  S  O  M  Q  Q  P  S
Y  L  I  L  C  Q  G  R  X  I  V  A  W  Z  D
R  T  S  T  H  K  O  Y  T  A  O  E  I  C  Z
K  R  I  D  A  H  V  T  R  H  Y  N  S  Q  K
J  N  C  N  Q  V  K  U  O  Q  G  M  D  H  C
B  M  C  Q  U  X  I  W  F  G  J  J  O  Z  Y
S  I  N  G  I  N  G  T  M  P  M  D  M  C  M
A  Y  N  Z  M  X  B  Q  O  A  Y  B  L  O  A
B  V  J  T  Q  F  H  G  C  M  N  H  V  P  D
```

COMFORT	FAITH	FORGIVENESS
HEALING	HOPE	HUGS
JESUS	LOVE	MOTIVATION
MUSIC	PEACE	SINGING
UNITY	VISION	WISDOM

What the World Needs Most. Solution

```
S  S  E  N  E  V  I  G  R  O  F  G  J  H  +
+  +  +  +  +  +  +  +  E  +  N  E  +  T  +
+  +  +  +  +  +  +  C  +  I  S  +  +  I  +
+  +  +  +  +  +  A  +  L  U  +  +  +  A  H
C  I  S  U  M  E  V  A  S  H  O  P  E  F  U
N  +  +  +  P  +  E  I  L  +  +  +  +  +  G
+  O  +  +  +  H  +  +  S  O  +  +  +  +  S
Y  +  I  +  +  +  +  +  +  I  V  +  W  +  +
+  T  +  T  +  +  +  +  T  +  O  E  I  +  +
+  +  I  +  A  +  +  +  R  +  +  N  S  +  +
+  +  +  N  +  V  +  +  O  +  +  +  D  +  +
+  +  +  +  U  +  I  +  F  +  +  +  O  +  +
S  I  N  G  I  N  G  T  M  +  +  +  M  +  +
+  +  +  +  +  +  +  +  O  +  +  +  +  +  +
+  +  +  +  +  +  +  +  C  M  +  +  +  +  +
```

(Over, Down, Direction)
COMFORT(9,15,N)
FAITH(14,5,N)
FORGIVENESS(11,1,W)
HEALING(6,7,NE)
HOPE(10,5,E)
HUGS(15,4,S)
JESUS(13,1,SW)
LOVE(9,6,SE)
MOTIVATION(10,15,NW)
MUSIC(5,5,W)
PEACE(5,6,NE)
SINGING(1,13,E)
UNITY(5,12,NW)
VISION(7,5,SE)
WISDOM(13,8,S)

THE END
30 COMPONENTS

CHAPTER 8

THE END
AND A NEW
BEGINNING ... 2005

A highlight of Kevin's Junior-Senior Prom was his being named Prom King!
Kevin and Prom Queen Lauren Privette (top left) reigned as coroyalty.
Larisa Kilby (top right) was Kevin's prom date for the evening.
Graduation from high school was a dream come true for Kevin.
Steve Moree, the West Wilkes High School principal, congratulates him and presents
his diploma.

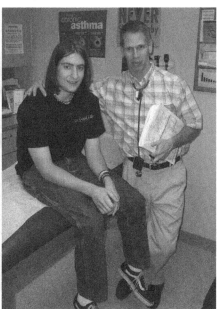

Rev. Jim Gore and Rev. Shannon Critcher provided meaningful, spiritual guidance and counsel for Kevin throughout his life.

Dr. John Pontzer, pediatrician, offered valuable assistance with Kevin's medical issues through the years and became a good friend.

Kevin's character in his early, formative years was molded by the nurturing, Christian atmosphere provided by his babysitter, Miss Martha (Martha McGee) and her husband, Mr. David.

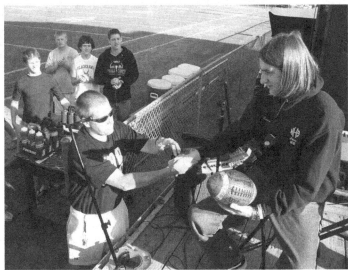

Kevin played his ESP guitar at West Wilkes High's Fifth Quarter event.

Tim Pruitt, Blackhawk head football coach, presented Kevin with the game ball in appreciation of his courage and being a role model to the team.

The first edition of Taking Up Arms included Adam Minton, Grant Miller, and Kevin. Their first major performance, a local talent show, gave them great exposure.

A great friend to Kevin, Crista Baker, attended most of his shows and visited him often.

Cancer therapy really makes a guy sleepy. Sometimes Kevin had to catch a few zzzz's. The teddy was a gift from Crista.

One meaningful way Kevin served his Lord was by playing guitar for the church's youth praise team.
Kevin and his friend, David Dyer, often ministered to the congregation through music and song.

Two of my favorite photos of us. Even while on oxygen, Kevin's attitude remained positive. We made a great team and shared all of his concerts together.

Taking Up Arms in one of their first publicity photos (top).
Kevin (guitar), Charlie Coleman (drums), Adam Minton (bass and vocals), and
Jim Coleman (guitar and vocals) were ready to tour.

Joe Hutchinson's (center) amazing vocals and guitar expertise gave Taking Up Arms
the finishing touch it needed. Each member was accomplished with their instruments,
while Adam and Joe wrote most of the song lyrics. Their performances consisted of all
original material.

Kevin's always upbeat attitude was a great inspiration for the group.

Taking Up Arms performed often at the Bassment in North Wilkesboro, North Carolina.
(l–r) Jim, Kevin, Adam, Charlie, Joe
Kevin loved being on stage and always got into the spirit of his music.

Kevin's favorite guitar was his Schecter C-1 Classic (the Christmas gift).
He played many shows with it and bought a Schecter Blackjack as a backup.
He used Peavey amps and had a well-endowed pedal board.

Trust in the Lord with all thine heart; and lean not unto thine own understanding.
In all thy ways acknowledge him, and he shall direct thy paths.
Proverbs 3:5–6

The year 2005 was a year like no other. It was the single most pivotal year of Kevin's therapy. It was a trip to death's door and back. This chapter in Kevin's life was filled with highs and lows. His senior year was a time of joy with the prom, him being named Prom King, and graduation in late May. My own diagnosis of prostate cancer and surgery in June would not stop my continuing quest for the drug Panzem.

This year would also see Kevin form his beloved Christian rock band Taking Up Arms. He had played several years with friends and Adam Minton, a good Christian friend and fellow guitarist, teamed up with him, and began searching for additional band members. The search was short-lived. Kevin's friend and co-worker at Wendy's, Charlie Coleman, was an excellent drummer and his brother, Jim, a budding guitarist. A few months later, the tremendous vocals of Joe Hutchinson were added to round out the group. The band played multiple gigs for almost two years. Early on, Kevin was a mainstay when the band performed and practiced regularly with them. Kevin was receiving therapy in Houston in 2006, but he encouraged the band to continue without him, and they did. The bandmates were budding songwriters, always playing original material, and had quite a following. One song in particular was inspired by Kevin's battle with cancer. Joe and Adam teamed up to write it, and I recall that Kevin titled it "Chemical Warfare." A CD with original songs was cut and they prospered. Kevin played with passion in his last performance with the band at the Bassment, afterward becoming nauseated. He returned several times to witness the band's success and was called on stage as a tribute to him. Kevin could not play their final engagements due to his illness; nonetheless, the band won Best Amateur Band at the regional 2006 Battle of the Bands, and they presented Kevin with the first place trophy. "I can't believe it," he said. "This is great! I'm happy for you guys. We can trade the trophy around if you like." Today, it sits in a place of honor in my home.

Kevin enjoyed surfing the Internet and designed his personal Web page on MySpace.com. This way he kept up with the music scene, bands of interest, and his growing number of friends. Later, I purchased a laptop computer for him which he took on his last trip to Houston.

"Chemical Warfare"
Lyrics by Joe Hutchinson and Adam Minton
Title by Kevin Triplett
Music by Taking Up Arms

You're running out of time. Fighting to stay alive. You've never felt
this way before.
You pretend that you don't care. There's a silence in the air. You've
never felt this way …

You feel so far away (it's killing me). It's killing me.
But I find my faith in you. I find my cure in you.

Now you're running for you life. Fighting for more time. You've
never felt so insecure.
So take one last breath. Before your final rest. You've never felt so …

You feel so far away (it's killing me).
It's killing me.

But I find my faith in you. I find my cure in you.
It's killing me …

You feel so far away (it's killing me). It's killing me.
But I find my faith in you. I find my cure in you.

You feel so far away (it's killing me). It's killing me.
But I find my faith in you. I find my cure in you.

It's killing me.

Kevin's MySpace.com Web page
(in his own words)

Kevin's Interests

General: Growing closer to God, Music, Guitars, Cars, ATV's, video
games, Internet, being with family and friends, nature, sitting on
the porch, Carolina Panthers Football, Nascar racing

Music: I listen to mainly rock, metal, and Christian rock. I also like
some country and bluegrass. Some of my favorite bands right
now are ... The Showdown, Kutless, 12 Stones, Demon Hunter,
Taking Up Arms, Chevelle

Movies: *A Walk to Remember*, *Godzilla* movies, Horror and Sci-Fi
movies (not the really gory ones), *Gods and Generals*, *Gettysburg*,
Glory, *The Lord of the Rings* Trilogy, all of the *Star Wars* movies

Television: ATV Television and anything about ATV's, Music channels, Carolina Panthers Football, Nascar racing, Speed channel,
Spike TV's *Powerblock*, sometimes *Monsters HD*, Sci-Fi channel

Books: The Holy Bible, Christian devotionals, *All Quiet on the Western
Front*, *At Risk*

Heroes: Jesus Christ, my dad, my grandpa, our military service men
and women

Groups: Guitar Geeks, The Chosen Many, o so hardcore, Taking Up
Arms owns your face, Tethered (just Tethered), As I Lay Dying

About Me

I am an easy going guy most of the time. I was diagnosed with bone
cancer when I was thirteen years old. Fighting cancer has been the
roughest battle of my life, but I believe it has brought me closer to
God and made me a better person. I love music, and I love to play the
guitar. I helped start a band called Taking Up Arms. If you want to
know more about me, you can send me a message.

I began the new year wasting no time and resumed my quest to enroll Kevin
in a Panzem drug trial. I pulled out all the stops and e-mailed some of the coun-
tries leading doctors, hoping to persuade them to include him in an upcoming
trial.

Perhaps, I was a thorn in the researchers' sides, but Kevin's life hung in the
balance. I had to keep up my efforts to enroll him in a Panzem protocol. The
premier doctors with familiarity with this drug would soon be getting my
e-mail.

January 1, 2005

Letter to Dr. Charles Erlichman, the Mayo Clinic
Dr. Paul Richardson, Harvard Medical School
Dr. William Dahut, National Institute of Health

Dr. Chris Sweeney, University of Indiana, and
Dr. George Wilding, University of Wisconsin

My son Kevin Triplett (age 18) has been battling osteosarcoma
since June 2000. He had a right tibia allograft implanted (tumor site)
which ultimately failed followed by a knee replacement. He has had
three recurrences of tumors in his lung followed by resections and
a lobectomy (upper right lobe). He currently has a small tumor in
one lung which appears to be stable (assumption that Gleevec may
be working) and has just had a paratracheal lymph node removed
(osteorsarcoma). His meds have included the standard chemos and
several cutting edge drugs (inhaled GM-CSF, currently Gleevec).
Each of these protein/enzyme inhibitors have bought him additional
time. I have done extensive research and am intrigued with the possible efficacy of Panzem (2ME2) in either the capsule or new NCD
suspension formulation. The antiangiogenesis drugs seem to hold
much promise. He has had one course of avastin since it is in the
same family.

I have consulted with Entremed and I'm currently looking for a
trial that he might fit into. If you may have a spot for him Dr. Tom
McLean (Wake Forest University Baptist Medical Center) can provide
you with additional patient specific information. His email address is
tmclean@wfubmc.edu.

Kevin keeps an optimistic attitude even with options being few
and far between. At this point, he has beaten the odds. I hope you
can share with me briefly any information which might be helpful.
Thank you … Wayne Triplett

Memo from Dr. William Dahut

Unfortunately our trial is not open @ this time. Check back in about
6 weeks because we may have new information @ that time. Good
luck!! Dr. William Dahut (NIH/NCI)

Dr. Sweeney,

Kevin keeps an optimistic attitude even with options being few
and far between. At this point, he has beaten the odds. I hope you
can share with me briefly any information which might be helpful.
We would greatly appreciate his induction into the Panzem trial and

would gladly schedule a visit there if you feel optimistic. Dr. McLean would and could handle the drugs dispensation (in home use) if that would be possible. I look forward to your response. Please let me know via phone or e-mail what you find out. I'm counting on you! Thanks, Wayne Triplett

I had for some time been included on EntreMed's recipient list for drug trial updates. One evening, I saw that the Panzem trial was again open, which gave me renewed hope that Kevin might get in.

January 5, 2005

Hi Tom,

Entremed, the maker of Panzem, notified me that new trials are now open for the drug. Areas include advanced cancer and multiple myeloma. I have contacted current trial physicians but have had no success in enrollment to date. These new trials may be what we need. Please go to entremed.com and click on clinical trials. The two new areas will pop up along with phone numbers. I am sending Entremed an e-mail, too. There are doctor phone numbers, etc. on that page. If you have any luck, please let me know. Thanks ... Wayne

January 6, 2005

The 2ME2 trial will be opening soon. It is not clear how the new formulation will work, and we could not give it in combo with Gleevec, although that is a good idea, something to consider as a subsequent trial after the single agent phase I. He would need to travel to Wisconsin or Indiana on a frequent basis if he was on the 2ME2 trials. As he seems not to be growing on the Gleevec, I would be hesitant to stop it. There are other oral antiangio agents that are further along, especially the tyrosine kinase inhibitors from Pfizer (sugen and agouron agents) and Bayer. Astrazeneca and Bristol Myers Squib also have agents in trials. Most recently, the NCI was seeking combo trials with the Bayer agent. I think a Gleevec combo was in there. Best of Luck

George Wilding, M.D.
Director, UWCCC
Assistant Dean for Oncology
Anderson Professor of Medicine
Madison, WI 53792

January 10, 2005

Dear Mr Triplett:
Thank you for your e-mail. As you have detailed, this Panzem study is about to be activated at IU. It is very intense and patients will have to be seen at IU weekly for the first six weeks. It is a novel drug, but as with all new drugs, there is a lot to be done. As with all phase I trials, the chance of benefit is less than 5 percent. The protocol requires patients be off all other treatments. I think the Avastin at home is as good an option and because it is closer to you, better. Good Luck. Dr. Chris Sweeney

Kevin's stamina was still strong, and I relished taking him to concerts with his friends. We had already seen the Christian Cornerstone event with a host of groups including Kutless and Disciple. The Alter Bridge concert was awesome. Now, it was time to see the up and coming group Chevelle.

March 20, 2005

Hi Debbie,
I took Kevin and two friends to a rock concert in W-S Friday night at the Millennium Center and it was really wild, so much moshing and body surfing that the band had to call a halt to it. We stood up almost six hours and outside for over an hour. It took me all day Saturday to recover, since we were almost at stage level. Of course, Kevin loved it! Keep in touch … great hearing from you. Wayne

April 8, 2005

Kevin's Medical Update

Hi everyone.
Kevin and I hope you are well. He had a wonderful. Junior/Senior Prom this weekend and was even named the Prom King!
As I shared with you in December, Kevin's mid-chest lymph node removal went well. His January 2005 CT scan looked fine, but this week's CT revealed two to four paratracheal lymph nodes which have grown and now have the resemblance of calcified osteosarcoma (bone cancer). He has essentially had four months without evidence of cancer, until now.

We plan to continue the chemo drug avastin twice monthly (it seems to have slowed the progression) along with the protein inhibitor gleevec. Our oncologists will continue to monitor the lymph nodes for possible removal later. That will be Kevin's decision. A person reaches a point when the quality of life (and his has been very good) must be weighed against the possibility of another surgery. Given the choice, I think he would go under the knife again.

Now it's my turn. After monitoring my escalating PSA level since October 2004 and with the second biopsy just in, my urologist has confirmed that I have prostate cancer. It is somewhat aggressive with a gleason score of seven, but it is confined just to the gland in two small areas. I have opted to go with a relatively new surgical procedure ... the da Vinci robotic laparoscopic radical prostatectomy. The spelling is correct and it is state-of-the-art. Essentially the surgeon will make four or five small abdominal incisions and operate robotically, talk about cutting edge. This will be done in mid-June and the recuperation time is half that of the usual open surgical method (2 days in hospital, 3 weeks then back to normal, 6 weeks no lifting). A word of advice, you GUYS, upper 40's and beyond, get your PSA level checked (this cancer strikes 1 in 6 men, not usually this early though).

I suppose it is Kevin's turn to look after dear old dad! Some people ask how we manage to go on with all that has happened and with what may lie ahead. As I have shared these past five years with you, our life's journey has been a highway. Some parts of the trip have been "happy motoring," but we have encountered more than our share of speed bumps, too. We will continue to maneuver our way around hoping to find the right combination of turns with hopefully occasional rest stops as needed. We learned a long time ago that you get into a routine, and you just keep on going. It's our way of life. It's business as usual with Kevin and me. No time to feel sorry for oneself. Many of you who have loved ones in similar situations know exactly where I'm coming from. As always, I will continue to update you, now, on BOTH of us! We remain grateful for your prayers and support. Wayne and Kevin

The news was out. I had cancer, too. Strangely, it did not seem to phase me that much. Perhaps, it was because I had been around cancer so long. In fact, with the research I had done on my prostate PSA escalation, I figured it could be cancer. I remember saying to Kevin, "It's probably cancer and not an enlarged prostate."

Kevin would chime back in, "Dad, you probably don't have cancer. Even if you do, you know all about it anyway. Just trust in the Lord."

Our special friends answered the call and bolstered our spirits with their comforting e-mails.

As always, thanks for keeping us updated on things. I feel almost ashamed to even attempt to respond to this e-mail because I just don't have the words. Courage, respect, perseverance, faith are just a few that immediately come to mind. Please know that you guys are an inspiration to so many. If someone was tempted to cry baby or complain about something, all they would need to do is think about your situation and that temptation would quickly leave. May God bless you, Wayne. I know what the Scriptures say about these things and that is my prayer for you. If we could ever help in anyway, please let us know. Honestly. Charles

I am so sorry. I promise that I will dedicate my rosary to you and Kevin every day. I will pray for your recovery. You and Kevin have been a complete inspiration to me and I admire your strength and courage above all else. Keep the faith. Always in my prayers, John

Wayne, thanks for sharing with us again. You and Kevin have my utmost admiration for your spirit and drive. I hope that someday when faced with similar situations, that I can handle the speed bumps with half as much dignity and grace as you guys. You are both in my thoughts and prayers daily. Hang in there. It will get better. I wish you good luck with your surgery. Sharon

Since our conversation last week, I have been praying even more earnestly for you and Kevin. Frankly, beyond prayer, I sometimes feel at a loss of what else to be doing. That being said, please know that I, like all of your peers and co-workers, stand ready to assist in any way. You are a shining example to all of us on perseverance and strength through faith. Please call on me at any time. I, like all of your friends, love and care for you. Steve

Everyone was so pleased Kevin was chosen Prom King. He appeared to have a good time, and I'm sure you are both looking forward to graduation. I'm sorry to hear about your latest medical updates. I admire your strength, and I hope everything goes well for both of you. Remember, everyone here is pulling for you. Take care. Becky

Encouraging comments can seem so repetitive, but you know I care and pray for you guys. Take care and hang in there. God put a lot on Job, but it is difficult to understand his will, but there is a reason. Charles

Thanks so much for keeping us updated. I will continue to keep you and Kevin in my thoughts and prayers. What role models you both have been. It just doesn't seem fair that one family would have to deal with so much. You guys are an inspiration. I was so pleased to see Kevin named Prom King. So many folks were happy about that. Take care, Jim

Hi Wayne ...

I heard last night about Kevin's wonderful prom experience. In my estimation, there is no better person for that honor. I'd love to see prom pictures when you get them!

I hate to hear the latest news about your prostate cancer, but it sounds like you have found a fabulous doctor and treatment alternative. Please keep us posted on your progress. Our thoughts and prayers will continue to be with you both.

Wayne, if it's any consolation at all, it's people like you and Kevin and the things you've dealt with over the past five years that make my faith stronger. I can't imagine how you guys do it with such strength and conviction, but you have been such an inspiration to me and so, so many people. God has two wonderful messengers on this Earth, and they are named Wayne and Kevin. Becky

I was glad to hear about Kevin's prom and his reign as West High's King. He is certainly a King in my book. I am constantly amazed by his ability to persevere and to make a difficult and challenging situation seem somehow bearable. You and Kevin both have inspiring faith and strength. I will continue to pray for you and Kevin. Please know that I am close by and will help in any way. Much Love, Donna

April 13, 2005

I am sorry to hear that Kevin continues to have to deal with cancer concerns. And now you have been diagnosed. My heart goes out to both of you. Yours and Kevin's God-centered attitude about all of this is very evident and such a powerful witness to all around you. I just wanted you to know that Linda and I will continue to pray for you and Kevin. I think of you often, and I have very fond memories of the years we worked together. Take care of yourself and Kevin. Just know that we join hands with the rest of your Christian brothers and sisters in surrounding the two of you with our love and prayers. Hope to see you soon. Tony

April 14, 2005

Wayne and Kevin,

My heart dropped when I read this. I want both of you to know how much you mean to me. Kevin, there is not another young man that has had more impact on my life than you. Wayne, one word sums you up, a fighter. I am praying diligently, and I will do anything that I can. Please know how much I love you, and I am here for you both. I don't understand, and I don't claim to understand, but all we can do is trust, and it is so hard. I am reminded of John 16:33 "These things I have spoken unto you, that in me you might have peace. In the world ye shall have tribulation; but be of good cheer; I have overcome the world." If we trust and look to Jesus, we will overcome as well. Please let me know if there is anything I can do. Praying, Craig

Hi Terri,

As you can see, when it rains it sometimes pours. I've been around cancer so long that my diagnosis was less than a revelation. I just don't want to get down and not be able to care for Kevin.

Kevin had a great time at the prom. His Prom King status didn't go to his head. I just e-mailed Tom McLean asking him to try to get Kevin in on a Panzem (2ME2) protocol somewhere up north. I have been trying for months to do this, but he would have to drop gleevec and avastin first. We have decided to do that if he can get in. His lymph node seems to have some osteo in it, and I know Panzem has just been FDA approved as an orphan drug for ovarian cancer treatment.

I had been monitoring my PSA for several months as it began rising last October (3.3, 5.9, 7.9). I knew it was a 50/50 chance of being cancerous. When the second biopsy was positive, it wasn't that much of a shock. I think the robotic surgery will be the best choice.

Kevin graduates May 31 if we don't get any more snow (lol). Not knowing the future (but who does) I booked Kevin, his mother, and me on a bus tour for Washington, DC on July 4–7. My surgeon thinks I should be able to travel by then. If Kevin has surgery, I'll try to work around that (you know how that is). Kevin likes history and I think he would really enjoy seeing that city. Anyway, it will get our minds off this cancer stuff for a few days. I bought some insurance just in case we have to cancel suddenly. I'll probably be laid up a few weeks this summer, so you better call (I'll be bored). If I sound humorous, just ignore me. May as well take it all with a grain of salt.

Thanks for your continued friendship. You know Kevin and I love you guys. The bond we made will never be broken. We went through so much together. I think of your Aaron often. He will never be forgotten, he did so much good and WAS and IS an inspiration to so many. I don't know about you, but I'm getting teary-eyed right now. We love you all. Wayne and Kevin

Finally, the Panzem trial seemed within our reach. All the months of wrangling were finally paying off.

April 20, 2005

Mr. Triplett,

I spoke with Dr. McLean this morning regarding your son and our Panzem trial. We currently have a waiting list for this trial. I will place your son on our waiting list with a projected start time around the end of June or early July. I am going to fax some trial information to Dr. McLean this morning. Thank you for your interest in this program. Jennifer

Hi Jennifer,

Thank you for the good news on including Kevin Triplett in the Panzem study. We will continue to monitor his worrisome lymph nodes by CT scans, and hopefully he can be enrolled before the cancer gets too far advanced.

On another note, I have just been diagnosed with prostate cancer (gleason 3+4=7). The only symptom was an elevated PSA. I am almost 53 and the surgeon is planning on a da Vinci robotic laparoscopic radical prostatectomy in mid-June. I think the cancer is confined to the prostate only.

I know that Panzem was used in a prior prostate study by Dr. Sweeney. If there are any open studies which might be helpful for my enrollment, please let me know (Panzem included). I thought a study might be a better option than surgery at this point for me. If nothing turns up, I will proceed with the surgery.

Again, thanks for your great help. Dr. McLean will fill me in I'm sure on additional information relative to Kevin's inclusion, the sooner the better. Wayne Triplett

April 26, 2005

Hi Jennifer.
I hope this info is helpful. If you require additional specifics please let me or Dr. Tom McLean know, and we will do our best.

Kevin W. Triplett—Cancer Therapy Profile

DOB:
December 7, 1986 (12-07-86) Original diagnosis date: April 7, 2000 … osteogenic sarcoma (right proxima tibia)

Previous treatment protocols and approximate dates:

April 2000-February 2001 (11 months) … ifosfamide, mesna, doxorubicin, methotrexate, adriamycin, cisplatin (23 treatments, 3-5 days duration per session), Children's Cancer Group CCG-7921 POG-9351

January 2002-February 2002 (2 months) … cytoxan/topotecan w/ GCSF, methotrexate (2 courses … alternating 3 weeks and 2 weeks)

December 2002–February 2004 … Inhaled sargramostim (leukine … 250 mcg/mL per session), 7days concurrently then 7 days off (twice daily in a nebulizer w/inhalation water … 15 minutes each session)

March 2004–Present ... Gleevec (imatinib mesylate ... 400 mg tablet daily)

November 2004–Present ... Avastin (IV infusion thru port ... 400 mL over 90 minutes ... twice monthly)

Current Medications and Approximate Start Dates:
Gleevec (400 mg tablet daily) ... since March 2004
Avastin (400 mL twice monthly ... IV infusion) ... since November 2004
Enalapril Tab (10 mg daily) ... since February 2004
Digoxin (.40 mg tablet daily) ... since February 2004
Zoloft (150 mg daily) ... since January 2003
Wellbutrin XL (150 mg tablet daily) ... since May 2004
Genistein (550 mg capsule daily, herbal supplement) ... since December 2004
Megestrol Acetate Oral Suspension (20 mL daily ... appetite stimulant) ... since April 2005

Surgical Overview
Removal of osteosarcoma tumor and insertion of allograf (average 35% tumor apoptosis ... pathology results)
Failure of allograft and insertion of prosthetic right knee and tibia
Lung resection due to metastases
Right upper lobectomy due to metastases
Paratracheal lymph node removal due to metastases
Port-a-catheter insertion (two separate occasions)

Current Symptoms
Interval increase in calcification in a right paratracheal, pre-carinal and right peribronchial location which is worrisome for progression of disease. Stable small area of calcification in right lung. Small area of concern on scapula.

Thanks, Jennifer, for all that you are doing to help! Wayne

Although we were prepping for a possible trip to Indianapolis, Kevin's graduation was almost at hand. He would be receiving several scholarships to further his college education.

May 18, 2005

Hi Terri,

Great hearing from you! Kevin received an American Cancer Society scholarship which he applied for earlier this year. It is for $1,000. I think it maxes out at $2,500 over four years assuming he keeps his GPA up. I contacted a county commissioner, whose wife is a cancer survivor, who will present him with a certificate at the 5/27 awards assembly. The ACS did not have a certificate, so I made my own. He also has received some type of scholarship from our local community college which he hopes to attend. I'm filling out a FAFSA form in order to get him some voc. rehab. money for college. He graduates on 5/31. The principal usually gives out several unsung hero awards during the senior awards assembly. I hope Kevin gets one.

I have finally convinced a doctor in Indianapolis to enroll him in an upcoming Panzem (2ME2) protocol. This is the drug I have been wanting for over a year. He will have to drop gleevec and avastin totally one month prior to that protocol. It will probably be late June or July before he starts. I think I will have to take him (drive or fly) to Indianapolis once a week for at least six weeks initially. I don't see why because it is a liquid and can easily be administered. Maybe I can talk them in to letting Baptist monitor his vitals. He does have two or three small tumors in lymph nodes. I hope we can get up there before they get too large and have to be removed. He has gained a few pounds on the appetite stimulant I'm giving him.

I'm drinking a yucky soy product twice daily and participating in a prostate study at Baptist. June 13 is my big day or morning … so … say a little prayer for me. It's my turn for some TLC.

I found out that Drew Cheatwood had to have a bone marrow transplant. We went to Brenner's to see him, but he was not taking visitors. This suddenly came on him and his uncle said he was really swollen. I think you may have met or heard of him. He had osteo similar to Kevin. I think he's still a patient there.

As you see, the beat goes on and hearing from you is a real pick-me-up. You understand the ways of us cancer folks. Thanks for thinking of us. Hope to hear from you soon. Wayne

Tom and Dr. Chris Sweeney, the coordinator of the Panzem trial in Indianapolis, kept in touch, fine-tuning the particulars regarding Kevin's upcoming trial. Disease progression had to be evident before he could be accepted.

May 24, 2005

Memo from Dr. Chris Sweeney

Dear Dr. McLean,

We will do what we can to accommodate. However, we prefer to see some documentation of progression from prior therapy before putting someone on investigational therapy. It could be that a significant toxicity emerges and the patient could have done better with stable disease for months with the prior therapy and avoided the toxicity of the investigational agent. I recognize there is some degree of urgency on patient and family's behalf.

As such, if his imaging in the week of June 26 shows stable disease or minor response, we would advise we hold off on Panzem (or other investigational therapies). If there is any sign of growth, we would be happy to enroll Kevin. Chris

May 25, 2005

Hi Tom,

Are we to get a CT at Baptist on 6/26 or earlier? I'm a bit confused with what Dr. Sweeney terms "disease progression." Kevin's April CT did yield increased calcification, and I feel that a CT (done with you any time now) would show additional disease progression. I would like you to schedule a CT for Kevin, since it has been almost two months. That should indicate if there is a definite progression. I would hope not, but in light of the April CT, I would think the scan would prove conclusively that Panzem is warranted. Kevin graduates May 31 and I have pre-op in urology on June 2 (that would be a perfect morning for his CT). Give me a call when you have time. Thanks, Wayne

Chris,

Kevin Triplett had a follow up CT scan today (6/2/05) which clearly shows evidence of disease progression (increased calcification and increased size of known lesions), so we would like to get him lined up for the Panzem study as soon as feasible. I believe he has been off all chemo since 5/27/05. (His father Wayne (cc'd on this email) can confirm this.) Thanks very much. Let me know how I can facilitate his enrollment. Tom

Kevin's graduation from high school was a dream come true. No one reveled in it more than Kevin, and rightly so. I never knew, given his many cancer recurrences, that this day would come. Now, it was here and a cause for celebration.

May 31, 2005

Steve,

Kevin's diploma is a miracle in itself. Five years ago, we lived from scan to scan taking each small "you're still clear" as a major victory in his battle with cancer. Frankly, we were afraid to think of high school graduation, since we were not sure that he would ever see that day. Now, it has come and gone and the struggle continues.

The diploma means so much, but your personal note conveys a heartfelt message which is precious to us. Kevin and I hold you in such high regard, and we are so appreciative of the prayers you have sent up for him. I purchased a keepsake box for his graduation mementoes. You can be sure that your note occupies a special place in it. Your caring and compassion speak so much of you. You have taken West very far, and equally so, you have made Kevin's four years there a highlight of his life. I am sending four photos (two per e-mail) in hopes that they will call to mind our special night. You remain a special friend to both of us. That can be summed up in one word, priceless. With deep appreciation, Wayne and Kevin.

From the Desk of Steve Moree
Principal of West Wilkes High School
Special Note to Kevin on His Receiving the Principal's Award

Kevin,

What a wild ride you have had. You have been a rallying point for this class. Throughout your battle, your classmates have had an opportunity to grow and learn caring and compassion. Every single one of your classmates love and support you along with the entire staff here. I have prayed for you many times, and rest assured I will continue to do so. Your strength has been a remarkable thing. Without question, you are the most courageous student I've ever met. May God Bless, Steve Moree

June 5, 2005

Kevin's Medical Update

Hi everyone.

Kevin's high school senior year has just ended with a flurry of celebration and emotion. His graduation from high school was a dream come true, a day which four years ago seemed in terms of his health, a remote possibility. This summer looks unlike any we have seen before.

Kevin's chest CT scan last week revealed a progression of tumor growth in at least four mid-chest lymph node clusters. These nodes have been monitored for several months. With this confirmed, Indiana University oncologists have agreed to admit him into the next Panzem (new drug) treatment protocol. This is the drug I have been trying for almost a year to obtain for him. We plan on flying to Indianapolis within two weeks for a consultation and then begin the drug the last week of June. This is an oral drug which only requires refrigeration and should be taken every six hours. We are planning perhaps weekly trips there (plane or car) for a number of weeks initially. He may be facing additional surgery later to remove the nodes, but I feel that Panzem will make a very positive impact on his cancer.

My prostate surgery will be June 13, and I feel very confident that it will go well. Lifting will be off limits for six weeks, so Kevin will be taking on a new role as caregiver (lol). I'm filling him in on the fine points of yard work and laundry.

If it works out, I plan on taking him on a guided tour of Washington, DC on July 4–7. He loves history and I think it is a great graduation present! His graduation was the best! He received three small scholarships which he will use as he attends Wilkes Community College this fall. Mere words cannot express our heartfelt appreciation for the staff and students of West Wilkes High School. These past four years, West learned a new meaning of courage through Kevin's battles and resilience, while at the same time confirming for him that he was so loved by his extended family there numbering in the hundreds. The diploma and principal's award meant so much to him and your caring over the years, the visits, cards, donations, surprise guitar at

Christmas, and a host of other things have endeared you to us. West High will always be that special school (the best school) that accepted him for who he was and helped make him the fine young man he is today.

Mt. Pleasant Elementary School also has done so much for us. The bake sales and raffles of various items with proceeds going to help us financially are a testament to the giving spirit and caring the students, staff, and school community possesses. We remain grateful for all that you have done and continue to do.

With so much going for us, how can we lose? Through turmoil you discover that each small step you take leads you closer to the goal, winning the battle against cancer. Kevin and I thank each of you for your support over the years and as always, I will keep you updated. We are looking forward to the possibilities which lie ahead.

As Kevin said when I asked him about more surgery, "Whatever happens, it will be all right." It will be all right in great part because your continued prayers and well wishes make all the difference. In a word, priceless. Love, Wayne and Kevin

June 6, 2005

It is so hard for me to even respond to your e-mails. I feel so humbled by the courage and faith of you and your son. Please know that each time you and Kevin are thought of, it evokes tremendous humility and gratitude. You two are continual reminders of faith and hope in God. You've been tremendous role models for both. I admire you so very much. You and Kevin are in our prayers. I pray that the Panzem treatments go well as well as your prostate surgery. Thank you for keeping us updated. You are an inspiration to us all. God bless, Charles

Hey Wayne and Kevin, You are both priceless! Sounds like all is going so wonderful. Wayne, I know how proud you must be of Kevin. Let me know if I can do anything. Frances

June 7, 2005

I'm so sorry to hear about Kevin's latest news. I am glad that he is finally going to be able to get the medication that you think he needs. I hope and pray that it works well for him. I also hope that your surgery goes well and that everything turns out good. If I can do anything for either of you, please let me know. Tell Kevin that I know all about yard work, cleaning house, and laundry, so if he needs some help or a supervisor (ha, ha) to let me know. Seriously, I along with others here at West are willing to do anything to help you out. All you have to do is ask. Thanks for keeping me informed about Kevin. I admire you both for your strength and courage. I don't think I could have handled all of the hurdles life has put before you both. I feel like you both are fine examples of answered prayers and proof that God does carry us through hard times. I know that he will continue to do so for you. You are in my prayers. Please tell Kevin hello for me. I am so proud of him. Take care! Becky

The spring and summer of 2005 had witnessed Kevin's graduation from high school. This was to be his summer to celebrate and enjoy. Things appeared to be going well with the Panzem trial coming up. The trip to Washington DC was my graduation present to him. Kevin, getting into the spirit of things, even briefly considered a body piercing. Like so many other things, his health took priority. Still, in the back of my mind, the question persisted. What if the Panzem did not stop the tumors' growth? All summer in a day may have been a more fitting description.

June 8, 2005

Hi Tom.

I think the July 13 schedule would be a better option given my surgery and no Panzem until July 12 anyway. Also, Kevin wanted me to ask if an eyebrow bar or ring (you've seen some people wearing those body piercings) would be risky for him. I suspect it would with possible infection (port) and tend to discourage it. I hope you concur. Either way, he is fine. I suppose he is developing his own "tastes." Thanks ... Wayne

I don't think Kevin should get any piercings now, because if it got infected that could jeopardize (or delay) him getting on the Panzem trial. I have a CD with his 2 most recent CT scans. I think I will mail it to Jennifer, unless you'd prefer to hand deliver it. Do you have a preference? Any luck with Corporate Angels? Tom

Hi Wayne, Thanks for sharing this! Life is full of challenges and it seems some of us get more than our share. A great teacher of mine once said, "Be thankful for the challenges, God thinks you can handle them!" Anyway, here's some discussion from Andy Weil's site you may be interested in … http://search.drweil.com/search?site. The other book I was talking about was by Dr. Bernard Jenson (who is a Naturopath, I believe). We'll remember you in our thoughts and prayers. Ken

Our church had been very supportive of both Kevin and me. Not only were they prayer warriors, but they had given us several love offerings which really helped with our expenses. We wanted to say thank you.

June 19, 2005

(Note in Millers Creek Baptist Church *Open Door*)
A Note of Thanks

Having a supportive church family is a source of great strength, especially during a time of need. Kevin and I are so grateful for your prayers and support during my recent cancer surgery and over the years. We continue to covet your prayers for him, as Kevin begins a new cancer treatment in Indianapolis in July. Your kindness is truly a reflection of the Christ-centered congregation of which we are blessed to be a part. In Christian Love, Wayne and Kevin Triplett

Kevin's flight to Indianapolis was coming up, but I was still dealing with the after effects of my prostate surgery. It was manageable but very inconvenient, especially when traveling long distances. The return trip through the airport in Indianapolis was especially cumbersome, as I had an insulated bag in each hand filled with five glass bottles of Panzem.

June 22, 2005

Hi Debbie,

I am on day 9 of 10 with the dreaded catheter. I am scheduled to have it removed tomorrow morning at Baptist and get the results of the biopsy. I feel pretty good overall with some abdominal soreness and about four small puncture wounds along with a two inch incision. This catheter is like a ball and chain, and I have been home virtually seven days since getting out of the hospital after three days! I've cultivated more patience anyway. Kevin is poised to begin the new

Panzem treatment in Indianapolis on July 11. I'm trying to hook up with the corporate angels network for free flights up there and back.

The principals took up some money for me last month and Mike and Michele brought it over last Thursday. It was very nice of them. Mt. Pleasant folks took up almost $6K for us thru bake sales and raffles!

Kevin had a great graduation and received three small scholarships which he will use at WCC. His principal's award was very emotional, and Steve Moree mentioned Kevin's courage over the past five years in battling cancer.

Hey, now I officially am a cancer survivor, too! I've had so much going on health wise and still will not be able to lift over a gallon for six weeks. I do want to get out again next week, start driving and even working. Take care ... Wayne

June 24, 2005

Hi Jennifer,

My prostate biopsy indicated the cancer was confined to the prostate only (good news)! I'm now, minus the catheter, dealing with incontinence. Hopefully, that will not last too long. Kevin had a small amount of blood in his spit as he coughed two nights ago. He had been sitting back in his recliner on the phone about an hour and has had some sinus issues (congestion, stuffiness, pediatrician prescribed Sudafed). It may have been just post nasal drip. The blood was bright but of a very small amount. I mentioned this to Dr. McLean's nurse yesterday when we went for his port flush. If it were the cancerous lymph nodes encroaching on his trachea, it could be life threatening. This would indicate an advanced stage of osteosarcoma. I will continue to monitor this closely. Dr. McLean's nurse (in consultation with him by phone) wondered if an earlier start date for Kevin's Panzem would be possible. Let me know what you decide (I left you a voice mail message). Thanks for everything ... Wayne

June 25, 2005

Hi Jennifer,

Glad you monitor your e-mail frequently. Yeah, I went thru a dozen of those, well, (maxi-pads) before bedtime last night. I think it is a little better this morning or it may be the full Depends diaper giving me that added measure of security (lol). I really feel for you ladies. My gleason score was 3 + 4 = 7. Specifics include adeno-carcinoma (conventional), primary pattern: 3. Secondary pattern: 4. Margins clear, high grade prostatic intraepithelial neoplasm (additional findings). 5. right pelvic lymph nodes, 1 left pelvic lymph node and vas deferens were all negative for cancer.

I'll talk with Kevin about his coughing and about monitoring any blood. I have always been straight forward with him. If his status changes or worsens, I'll contact Dr. McLean and e-mail you.

If it is possible to squeeze him in early, I'd gladly forego the DC trip. His life and health are much more important. Let me know if you can put anything together to speed this up. Talk with you later ... Wayne.

June 27, 2005

I was so glad that Kevin is now going to be able to get the new therapy. Our prayers remain with you both. Ron

I scheduled a quick bus tour to Washington DC in July for Kevin, his mom, and me. He loved history and visiting our nation's capital was a must see for him. I thank God that I could get the trip scheduled. It was his last opportunity to have a vacation.

July 8, 2005

Hi Jennifer,

We had a great four days in DC, and this afternoon (Friday) I finalized flight plans to IUCC. We should arrive at the airport there around 9:30 AM on Monday morning (7/11). We will take a cab to your facility shortly thereafter. I'll then check with the Ronald McDonald House on room availability. As of today, there was a waiting list. We may opt for a motel if there is no room in the inn. We're looking forward to meeting Dr. Sweeney and you on Monday. I will bring insurance cards, forms, and copies of Kevin's last two CT scans. If you read this before Monday and need to update me, that will be fine. Otherwise, we'll be in Charlotte, North Carolina, at 5:00 AM on 7/11. Of course, you can reach me by cell phone anytime. Take care, Wayne.

July 18, 2005

(Thank-You in Millers Creek Baptist Church *Open Door*)

Kevin is the first bone cancer patient in the country to receive the new trial drug Panzem. If results are favorable we will be making two trips each month to Indianapolis. As Kevin says, "Whatever the outcome, it will be ok." Your prayers and support continue to lift our spirits as the battle continues, and we greatly appreciate the generous love offering. May God richly bless each of you as He has blessed us with your friendship. In Christian Love, Wayne and Kevin Triplett

July 19, 2005

Hi Tom,

We were in clinic this morning for the Indiana Panzem study blood draws. I hope you received the folder I left for you with an updated IN protocol calendar, overview and IN CT scan on Kevin. I'm hopeful the Panzem will make a positive impact. We plan on continuing the Panzem obviously if progress is made. The CT in IN revealed several areas of concern (the mass effect of the lymph nodes narrowing the arterial and bronchus areas, hypodensity liver bell area, scapula lesion). If advisable, Kevin is up for the paratracheal lymph node removals if the Panzem is ineffective. I ask that you check with Drs. Hines and Pranikoff as to the feasibility of this procedure, if it comes down to it. Kevin has had what I think is a sinus infection (allergies) and has completed a round of amoxicillin followed by augmentin (albuterol inhaler a few days). This has improved. I don't think the nodes are associated with this condition. Jennifer, Dr. Sweeney, and the entire IN team were wonderful and we plan on driving up on Aug. 7 for his re-eval. Kevin is tolerating the Panzem nicely with no obvious side effects. I'd appreciate your checking to be sure Jennifer gets copies of Kevin's blood work along with his vitals from this mornings CBC. I wonder if the blood work indicates the level of Panzem in his blood stream. I'll bring the blood collection vials for his two PKs next Tuesday on our return visit. Always great hearing from you. Wayne

I had focused on the new drug for almost a year and a half, but I knew it might not be the cure-all to end-all. I began making contingency plans with Tom. Something was not quite right. Kevin began to have difficulty breathing.

July 20, 2005

Hi Tom,

Kevin mentioned to me today that he seems to be taking more breaths upon inhalation to get the air he needs. At lunch, he was taking a number of short breaths after walking in from outside. Also, he said he had some pain or soreness in his right chest area (front and rear) when he took deep breaths. I thought he might need to be seen in clinic, perhaps Thursday or Friday even though we are coming down on Tuesday. He has remarked that his breathing seemed a little different. Please let me know what you think we ought to do. I'll call today during the regular call time (2:00–3:00 PM). Thanks, Wayne

July 24, 2005

Dear Wayne,

I'm finally writing, but it's not from lack of thinking of you both. I hope your trip to D.C. was enjoyable. I've only been once, and that was when the boys were a year old. I have a friend who lived in the suburbs of D.C. at that time. She did take us downtown one night, but I didn't get to see much. I am anxious to hear about your trip to Indianapolis. Let me know what you learned there.

Yes, it scared me when I read about Kevin spitting up blood. I pray that the antibiotic took care of it. Your heart just drops to your stomach anytime something like that happens. It's a roller coaster life, isn't it? You have to take the ups and make the most of them while you have them, because you never know when it's going to drop.

I hope you continue to heal and regain your strength. You have to remind yourself that you did have major surgery, and your body needs to recuperate!!

Please let me know what the doctors told you. Even when I don't write, all of you are on my mind. Andrew asks about him very often. You are always in our prayers. Take care, Terri

I always had to sandwich our quick, fun trips between surgeries or chemotherapies. Kevin began wheezing and having some difficulty breathing while in Washington. On the bus trip home, he was very quiet and seemed especially tired.

"Kevin, your breathing sounds different," I said as we came home.

"I know, Dad. Listen."

He exhaled through his mouth and a crackling sound emanated from deep within. I just knew the tumor had become constrictive. He became pale.

"Dad, I can't breathe very well. I think you should take me to Brenner's," he said.

I immediately rushed him there. His oxygen level was very low, and he was almost at the point of passing out. Immediately, they hooked him up to oxygen. Scans revealed that his right lung main bronchus had been blocked by the paratracheal lymph node tumor, rendering his right lung useless. To make matters worse, the tumor was inoperable. I remember the poignant moment when the pulmonologist confirmed that the insertion of a stint in the right bronchus was impossible. I carried the news and a color photo of the blocked airway into the waiting room and told Kevin's mom, grandparents, uncle, and Pastor Craig that it looked like nothing more could be done to save him. His death seemed to be looming.

Days later, our world was turned upside down. "The cancer is advancing and it is inoperable. Kevin probably has days, a few weeks, or a month at most to live," stated a remorseful Dr. McLean in Kevin's hospital room. Kevin ultimately broke the silence with, "Okay, what do we do now?" After having prayer with Kevin, his mom, and me in his hospital room, and with a tearful embrace, Dr. McLean called hospice and ordered oxygen for him at home.

July 28, 2005

Kevin's Medical Update

Hi everyone.

Kevin had a wonderful early July trip to Washington DC. This was followed by our flight to Indianapolis on July 11 to pick up the new drug Panzem. He took the drug orally almost two weeks when he began having some problems breathing (right side pain). After taking him to the ER at Baptist last Wednesday, the chest x-ray and CT revealed additional growth of the mid-chest tumors with one constricting his right bronchus preventing his right lung from functioning. He returned home last Friday. The Indianapolis team called asking us to stop the drug, since it apparently did not impede the tumor growth. He is currently receiving some oxygen assistance and we will return to Baptist tomorrow (Friday) morning, where a pulmonologist will take a look with a possible stint insertion early next week to allow the lung to function again.

With the tumors growing at an accelerated pace, at this point his options according to the oncologists are few. There is the possibility of the right lung removal, but there could be complications. There are a few drugs he has not tried, but the side effects could be more harmful than beneficial. In short, the oncologists suggest making him comfortable and maintaining a good quality of life for a few weeks or months at the most. Hospice has been working with us on a consultative basis.

True to form Kevin is taking all this in stride. He remains in good spirits, although at times he is somewhat short of breath. He is having visits from friends and family and is very much himself. He continues to play guitar with his band and attend church services. It is his decision, and at this point he is very comfortable with his relationship with God and the inevitability of what may happen.

Surgery in April or May may have intervened in this situation short term, but the new drug would not have been available in the absence of tumor growth. As we have seen in other therapies he has tried, hindsight is always 20/20, but his five year battle has resulted in many miracles in maintaining a high quality of life for him. He by no means has given up. We continue to ask God to perform a miracle, and with your prayerful support, anything is possible. His resilience is amazing, and he always has that upward look and fighting spirit which we have all come to appreciate.

Thanks to everyone for your visits and calls. A special thank you is due to Jim McRae, former principal of Mt. Pleasant Elementary School, for stepping in as I take a medical leave to be with and care for Kevin. I will continue to update you. Again, I solicit your continued prayers for Kevin that a mighty work might be done, and that a miracle healing is just around the corner. Love, Wayne and Kevin

I just don't know what to say. You both have been so faithful and courageous and an inspiration to everyone around you. I'm happy to hear that Kevin's spirits are high and his faith is exceptionally strong, I know. Please send him our love and prayers. We would love to stop by one day for a quick visit. We'll call first. Ricki

My thoughts and prayers are with you both. I remember when my little brother was losing his battle and how calm he remained. God gives such strength. It is a miracle in itself. I think of you both every day and wish for you both to hold each other, continue to find laughter and make each day as normal as possible. Wayne, I do so admire and respect the spirit in which you have held it all together. I am confident that Kevin has mirrored what was instilled by his wonderful Dad. I will continue to pray and hope for comfort and miracles. Love to you both, Debbie

You and Kevin are such an inspiration. You both still have such a positive outlook on life. I continue to pray for each of you that God will give you strength and courage to get through this. I am glad that Jim is filling in for you at Mt. Pleasant. That will be one less worry you will have and be able to give Kevin all your attention. Love, Pam

Good Morning Wayne and Kevin,
Both of you have more courage than any people I have ever known. I was thinking of both of you driving to East Middle on Monday and saying a prayer, and it came to me that Kevin is certainly a hero. And what a model he has as a father. The qualities your Kevin possesses as a human being are to be emulated by others. The fight you guys have fought for the last five years is of a quality beyond what is normal. My deepest respect to both of you. With your work through the medical community, you both have touched and changed more lives than you will ever be able to know. Through God, anything is possible. I believe that with all my heart and know that you do too. Know that the entire school community is praying hard, and that you are always on the minds and voices of each of us. Pat

Wayne, we all continue to be with you and with Kevin in our prayers. I have not called, even though I have been getting updates on your fight through Aaron. The reason I have not called is simply that I have recently (within the last three years) gone through this with my mother-in-law, my sister, and both my parents. We are still cancer involved with my father-in-law's fight. From these experiences, I know how difficult it is on family and realize the friendship and love of others while needed can also be burdensome, as you continuously dwell on the same information. I also believe in prayers, and you both certainly have mine as well as those of all at the Career Center (you know how much you are loved here). I know if there is anything that we can do beyond prayers, you will not hesitate to ask. My heart and my tears along with my prayers are with you. Stay strong with your convictions and courage. I have never seen a father who has fought harder for his son. Al

Thanks, Wayne, for the update. Sorry the news wasn't more positive. Healing comes in many forms, not always the outcome we would choose. We will remember you in our prayers and hope for the strength to embrace whatever God has planned for us. Ken and Cindy

Kevin is such an amazing person. I have truly been inspired by him and the way he has handled this situation. Kevin and you are continually in my prayers. Linda

You have my thoughts and many, many prayers, Wayne. Kevin and you are very special, upbeat, positive people who have been thrown many curves over the past few years. Thanks for your updates. Keep them coming, and I will ask everyone I know to continue the prayer chain. Sharon

Dear Wayne and Kevin,
I do hold you in my prayers. I think we all have gained a lot following you through your courageous management of the whole process you both have been through. Maturity is not just an issue of age, is it? Though you have to face discouraging news again, you will never be alone as you make difficult decisions. Thank you for allowing me to keep up with you through these updates. Love, Margi

You have an amazing son, as I know you know. Your medical updates are always both inspirational and hopeful, although Kevin's medical situation is heart wrenching. You both are very strong and upbeat. No doubt, Kevin draws some of that from you as well as from his faith. You both are in my thoughts and prayers, and if I can do anything for you, let me know. Randy

Thank you for the update on Kevin. We are all so interested in how both you and he are doing. I can not imagine the roller coaster of emotions that you must be experiencing right now. I continue to be amazed with your strength as you handle Kevin's illness. He is very fortunate indeed to have you as his father. I will continue to keep both you and Kevin in my prayers. May God surround you both with his love and peace. Kaye

The feeling of helplessness and finality, which crept over us days earlier, did not linger for long. Kevin and I talked, and if the surgeons felt it was feasible, perhaps surgery could again be an option. After much consultation, they felt the risk outweighed the benefit. There were too many probable complications with the tumors' locations.

July 29, 2005

Hi Tom,

With less than desirable news from Dr. Conforti of his inability to find a sizeable opening to insert the stint, we are back where we started. Please talk with Drs. Pranikoff and Hines to see if they feel remotely that the pneumonectomy could be attempted with some degree of possible success. If they decline, I would appreciate your checking with other major hospitals (Johns Hopkins, M. D. Anderson, Mayo, etc.) to see if someone there might offer a ray of hope or attempt a similar surgery. Kevin is comfortable and seems to be adjusting to the oxygen well with his left lung strengthening. I'll wait to hear from you. Thanks, Wayne

I was definitely not going to sit on the sidelines and watch Kevin slowly dwindle away. I began vigorously searching for alternative and homeopathic remedies. If modern medicine could not provide a cure, natural remedies might be the answer.

July 31, 2005

Hi Ken,

The doctors have virtually given up on helping Kevin, although he feels good. I have been researching several alternative homeopathic possibilities including Chinese Tian Xian capsules and liquid, flax-seed oil with cottage cheese and Essiac tea. I thought you might have some thoughts to share on these or other herbal possibilities. They are formulated in many cases for bone cancer as well as other related cancers. Hope to hear from you. Wayne

I was away at a retreat just as I received this and had done a bit of research but had failed to send it to you. The things you mention below sound like you are on track. There is also a mushroom that has recently shown a lot of promise in slowing tumor growth. It is called Agaricus blazeii and is from Brazil. It was offered on some of the web sites I visited.

Another thing that came up during my workshop was the difference between curing and healing. Curing as defined by Alberto Villoldo in his book *Shaman, Healer, Sage* is remedial and involves fixing whatever the problem is. Surgeries, chemotherapy, etc. are aimed at curing. Healing is broader and more complete. Healing transforms one's life but doesn't always produce a physical cure (though often does). "Healing success is measured by increased well-being, a sense of newfound peace, empowerment, and a feeling of communion with all life." I am sure that Kevin has experienced this kind of healing through his spiritual life. Paulo Roberto, a Brazilian healer, says that we can reach this kind of healing thru prayer, sacred music, and study. These three things must be done every day, the more the better. Practice of meditation, bio-feedback, visualization or any practice that allows us to empty our mind of thoughts (and fears) can open us up to Divine Healing.

I will try to keep myself open for other suggestions and continue to hold a special place in my heart for Kevin as well as yourself. Many blessings to you, Ken

We always had faith that God's hand was on Kevin. Now, it was time for some additional hands. Several people had given me prayer clothes, tiny handkerchiefs which had been prayed over by prayer warriors. I had placed them on Kevin's chest and prayed for him many times. A local church up the road invited us for a prayer service. The minister asked, "Who has a need and wants to be prayed for?" Kevin and I raised our hands, and we proceeded to the altar. Intercessory prayers went up from numerous church members, whose hands were placed on Kevin. The prayers were fervent. All of us were crying as we returned to our seats.

The pastors at our home church, upon my request, asked deacons and elders to come forward on another Sunday evening, anointed Kevin's head with oil, and prayed unwaveringly. I voiced part of the prayer, trying to hold back tears, but they came anyway. It was cleansing. It was coming before God's mercy seat with no holds barred. It was putting our faith into action.

August 1, 2005

Hi Wilma and thanks for the e-mail and phone message earlier. I had prostate cancer surgery in June and other than some bladder problems, I'm ok. Kevin feels pretty good but carries oxygen with him since his right lung is blocked by a tumor. I am trying to get hooked up with some herbal or homeopathic cancer medications.

He has been prayed for at several churches (anointed with oil by deacons and pastors). I take one day at a time and try to help him enjoy each day. Doctors advise he may have only weeks or a month to live, but we had rather expect a miracle. I am taking some time off to care for Kevin. We would love to have you visit. Call me sometime. Tell everyone hello, and I miss you guys very much. Wayne ☺

Jim,

I appreciate your willingness to assemble the deacons along with Craig for prayer on Kevin's behalf. As a father, I will do anything to keep Kevin with me just as long as possible, not just for myself, but for the powerful witness his life continues to be for so many. If anyone deserves to have a divine healing, I feel it is Kevin. I pray each night for his healing and in obeying the Scriptures as we did tonight. I feel we must believe that his healing is already in progress. I continue to research novel approaches to help improve his condition. I'm also looking into essiac tea, a Chinese remedy, and a bone cancer collection of herbal drugs from another web site. Again, thanks for your prayerful support. Kevin and I love you very much. Wayne

Hi Tom.

Hope you are well. Kevin is doing very well and is adjusting to the oxygen. He has been to church several times and had a number of band rehearsals. He is planning on attending the local Relay for Life this weekend and a band concert, too. He gets winded easily, but his disposition is very upbeat.

Not to be outdone, he has been prayed for in two local churches and anointed with oil. I am researching the holistic approach and have downloaded several e-books on the subject. He is currently on the anti-cancer diet of Dr. Johanna Budwig (flaxseed oil with cottage cheese four times daily). I have ordered an anti-bone cancer mix from natural remedies along with essiac tea. He is coming to Winston-Salem Wednesday to meet with a chiropractor/holistic doctor to discuss options (no cure, just enhanced life style). I see no degradation in his condition yet except a little cough occasionally. I have other holistic options which I may purchase (HaeLan-95, Immunocal, cantron, Hansi AT). In short, we (he) is still fighting.

Any word yet on a possible pneumonectomy? I wish in retrospect that we had (if anyone there would have done so in good conscience) removed those nodes in April or May. We perhaps could have gotten on Panzem later. I sense that most folks felt that the Panzem (if it worked) would be a better choice than surgery, since it would have been just a quick fix. I need some help working through this one.

Kevin will probably not attend college this fall. I need a letter stating that if he chooses to attend at some point that a diminished number of courses (not eighteen hours, maybe six or so) would be a reasonable pursuit to still grant him status as a full-time student. If you or someone could send me a letter to that effect, I will forward it to the college. It is needed to keep him on our insurance policies since he is now eighteen. Keep in touch as I will with you, and please let me know if there is anything in the offing for him (surgery or treatment options). Take care, Wayne (and Kevin).

Tom Pranikoff and Mike Hines are planning to get together tonight to review Kevin's scans again and discuss the pneumonectomy. I think it's still a possibility, depending on what they say, and if you and Kevin are willing to accept the risks. The letter will be no problem. I'll call you as soon as I know anything (likely tomorrow). Tom

I kept trying to secure new and novel therapies, which we could at least discuss with Tom. I ordered numerous anticancer medications from as far away as China. I always checked with reputable hospital Web sites to be sure there was some anticancer properties in these medications.

August 6, 2005

Introgen Inquiry

My eighteen-year-old son, Kevin Triplett, has battled bone cancer over five years. He had an osteosarcoma tumor removed initially from his right tibia, but it became metastatic with additional tumors and subsequent surgeries involving a lobectomy and paratracheal lymph node removal. He currently has mass suppression in the upper right bronchus due to an additional tumor which makes surgery risky if not impossible. Medically, oncologists at Wake Forest University Baptist Medical Center have exhausted efforts to do more.

I am interested in him enrolling in an introgen clinical trial (advexin, INGN 241, 225, 234). If you require additional information our oncologist Dr. Tom McLean can fill you in or send CT scans, etc. He may be reached at tmclean@wfubmc.edu. We are looking for anything that might impede the growth of the tumors. I hope to hear from you soon. Thank you, Wayne Triplett

August 7, 2005

Kevin,

Hey man, I just listened to your band's two songs on pure volume and it was really cool. It reminded me a lot of 12 Stones and Staind. I wish you the best of luck with Taking Up Arms and everything else. Peace. Ryan

August 8, 2005

Dear Wayne and Kevin,

I just returned today to find your e-mail. I am so sorry. You are in my thoughts and prayers. We have no way of understanding the blows this journey can serve up, but I do know God provides support, in ways, again, that we do not understand. I think sometimes it's like cushions, big, fluffy cushions being placed under us to help soften those blows. I have landed on them many times myself, and it is my prayer that many such cushions of strength and support will come your way. Kevin, I love you, and I am so thankful for the opportunity of having you in my class last year. You are certainly a fine young man. I will continue to think of you both. Love, Paula

August 10, 2005

(Letter to the Ukraine)

My eighteen-year-old son, Kevin Triplett, has been battling osteosarcoma (bone cancer) over five years. He has had five surgeries (right tibia, lobectomy, paratracheal lymph node removal) and now has what appears to be an inoperable tumor (lymph node enlargement) around his upper right bronchus. Conventional therapies have bought him more time, but no cure has yet been realized.

I was intrigued at the hope which Ukrain (C/T) might offer him. If you could e-mail or call and fill me in on the costs, I would be grateful. Do you think it would be beneficial? My current oncologist perhaps could coordinate its usage since it is administered by injection. I hope to hear from you soon. Wayne Triplett, USA (North Carolina)

Hi Tom.

In addition to the Ukraine (C/T) therapy, I'll mention the Coley's toxins approach (raising the body's temperature) which was pioneered years ago. Any thoughts on either of these two approaches? Thanks ... Wayne.

I just did a Google search on both of these and did a little reading. My honest opinion is that neither is likely to help shrink the tumor, and both may cause toxicity (not to mention expense and time away from home and the activities he's enjoying now). So, I cannot endorse the use of either. But good for you, as always, for exploring other options. Tom

One of my teachers at Mt. Pleasant School, Carol Baker, was familiar with alternative medicines. Carol and her family, especially her daughter Crista, would soon endear themselves to us. Moreover, she secured an appointment for Kevin with a medical doctor in this field. Kenneth Crouse, a local nurseryman (botanist) and friend, was very knowledgeable on this subject and shared a host of alternative remedies. The race was on, and after a month on a strict homeopathic regimen, Kevin was improving.

August 15, 2005

Sure enjoyed visiting with all of you last night. I forgot to send the squash home with you. I think Crista is planning to come over so I will send it with her. She said that she was planning on making pancakes, but she did not realize that I had asked Todd about them and he says no wheat products at all, so that rules out pancakes, bread, and biscuits of any kind. She is bringing other "legal" stuff instead. If you can dig out your George Foreman, she can cook up the squash, and you will be set with some good veggies for a few days. Carol

Hi Tom,

Kevin is seeing Todd Smith, a Winston-Salem homeopathic/alternative medicine doctor. I'm currently giving him 28 different herbal supplements daily (66 pills once we reach maximum dosage levels). He is feeling good. He has gained maybe five pounds (mostly in the face), and I wondered if this could be some type of fluid retention? Also, he is desiring to cut back some on his oxygen, as he feels that he is fine without it for short intervals. I have ordered a Chinese herbal blend to be delivered later this week. This product, Tian Xian liquid, has been tested at Sloan-Kettering and does possess some anti-cancer tendencies (increases proliferation of mononuclear cells and T-lymphocytes, increases cytotoxic activity of NK cells, increases phagocytic activity of macrophages). Again, is cutting back on the oxygen advisable, and does he need to be seen in clinic regarding his slight weight gain (puffy cheeks)? The battle continues. Thanks, Wayne.

Yes, that does sound suspicious for fluid retention. Is he urinating well? Perhaps it is a side effect of the dietary supplements. I doubt that his kidneys are being directly affected by the tumor. We are available and willing to see him any day, if you'd like to come by. I am in clinic Thursday. I think weaning the oxygen down, perhaps even off, is a good thing. As long as he's comfortable breathing. FYI, I will be on vacation 8/20–9/5. I hope to be checking e-mail perhaps once a week during that time. I will keep Kevin in my thoughts and prayers. Keep in touch. Tom

Tom had a keen interest in the medications I had been giving Kevin. His physical condition had improved, and some air was entering his right lung. Tom was writing a paper on alternative therapies and asked for a list of Kevin's supplements to include in it. Here is that list:

July 2005–August 2005

Kevin Triplett
Herbal/Homeopathic Medications/Supplements
Daily Dosage: Almost 70 Pills Plus Liquid Supplements

Tian Xian Liquid (14 herbal blend liquid from China ... 4 vials daily)
Bone Cancer Regimen (Bla-Cansema Bloodroot from Montana)*

Cottage Cheese/Flaxseed Oil Diet (Dr. Johanna Budwig ... one-half cup three times daily)
Noni Juice
Immunestasis (corioles, shiitake mushrooms)
Vitamin E
Melatonin
NAC (nacetylldysterine)
Manganese
Vitamin C (dose escalation 1,000 to 10,000 mgs daily)
Immunofin (shark liver oil)
Alpha-liproic acid
Salymarin (milk thistle)
Poly-enzyme 021
Zinc Caps
Carotenoids
Quercetin
Echinacea
Essiac Tea (chapparal, sheep sorrel, Indian rhubarb)

*Contents of BC Regimen above (bloodroot, cat's claw, slippery elm root, burdock root, nettle, fenugreek, yarrow, sage, plantain, bla-cansema blood root, oat straw)

Mushroom Supplement Support
(beginning late January 2006)

Immune FX ... potent blend (capsules) of extracts from six medicinal mushrooms
agaricus blazei, cordyceps sinensis, maitake, shiitake, coriolus versicolor and reishi

Recovery ... functional food (capsules) with anti-inflammatory and anti-catabolic
effects containing Nutricol (bioflavonoid complex).

For more info: www.biomedicalabs.com/immune_fx.htm
                 www.biomedicalabs.com/recovery.htm
                 www.teamdrugs.com

Current M. D. Anderson Cancer Center Interventions
September 2005

High-Dose Methotrexate
Samarium-153 (Quadramet) Injection
Gemcitabine
Avastin

IMRT (intensity modulated radiation therapy) to head mets site (10 sessions)
External Beam Radiation Therapy (general area low dose spread to chest tumor sites) (10 sessions)
Proton Beam High Dose Radiation Therapy (tentative Summer/Fall 2006 to tumor sites)

August 16, 2005

(Note to Kevin's WCC professors)

Hi everyone.

Thanks for including Kevin in your on-line courses. Kevin has been battling osteosarcoma (bone cancer) over five years. He has endured seven surgeries (five major ones). Through it all, he has remained a fighter and an inspiration to young and old alike. This week, I have been able to get him possibly enrolled in a cancer protocol at M. D. Anderson in Houston, TX. We will fly out on Sunday night (8/28) and hopefully return by Wed. (8/31). This is for tests and a consultation. If he is accepted, we may be flying or driving there once a month.

He is currently turning in work via the Campus Cruiser. I ask for your understanding in light of recent developments if his work is occasionally late. He will make every effort to be on time with it. He was looking forward to your "on campus" classes, until the tumor growth occurred.

I am sending my latest update on his progress. I have an extensive e-mail list (about 200 recipients) to keep his many friends informed. I will be happy to include you if you'd like.

Again, thanks to each of you for working with us as I endeavor to keep Kevin's quality of life at a high level while seeking that magic bullet which may stop this dreaded disease. Feel free to call me if you have questions. God Bless, Wayne Triplett

Although Kevin was awarded several college scholarships and had registered for a full class load, his declining health prevented him from attending class in person. He chose the online course option for a while, until he began intensive cancer therapy. His health issues were pressing, and college would have to wait.

As you might imagine, word spread through our community of Kevin's pending passing. As friends came to visit, I would excuse myself to research possible new therapies online. I found a potential cancer vaccine available at the M. D. Anderson Cancer Center in Houston, Texas. After inquiring, I found out the vaccine was not ready, but a new doctor on the pediatric team, recently recruited from the Mayo Clinic in Rochester, Minnesota, was willing for us to visit.

"It [Kevin's condition] looks grave, but if the family is willing to come down, we will see if we can offer him any options," stated Dr. Pete Anderson.

Ironically, Dr. Anderson had only been at M. D. Anderson a few months, and short of a miracle, Kevin was out of options. The rest is history. MDA became our second home for the next fifteen months. Dr. Anderson embarked on a quest to restore to Kevin some QOL (quality of life) which he had been missing. By combining traditional chemotherapies with external beam radiation and nuclear medicine (samarium/quadramet), he had achieved remarkable results with other patients. Soon, Kevin would begin a seven flight marathon to MDA, where his therapies would include samarium, gemcitabine, methotrexate, and radiotherapy.

The following e-mails document a turning point in Kevin's hope for survival. The M. D. Anderson connection was about to be launched.

August 17, 2005

Hi Tom.

In my research I ran across an ostersarcoma cancer vaccine which is used with some pediatric patients at M. D. Anderson. The doctor who possibly could fill you in is Dr. Cynthia Herzog. If they have any possible treatment option for Kevin, we would be interested in pursuing it. I would appreciate it if you could put in a call there, briefly fill them in on Kevin's cancer progression, and see if our coming for a consultation would be advisable. Thanks, Wayne. (Hope you enjoy your vacation).

I just spoke with Dr. Cynthia Herzog. She does not have (or know of) a vaccine trial, however, she has a colleague (Dr. Pete Anderson, who is currently out of the office), who may know of a trial Kevin may be eligible. I will send them both a medical summary this evening. As soon as I hear anything, I'll let you know. I hope to check my e-mail at least once a week during vacation. Tom

Cynthia,

Thanks so much for speaking to me today about my patient Kevin Triplett, the 18 y/o young man with refractory osteosarcoma, and for providing me with Dr. Anderson's name. I will attach a current medical summary. If either of you have any suggestions or know of an appropriate trial that may be of benefit for Kevin, we would greatly appreciate your thoughts. The family is willing to go to Houston for a personal consultation if that would be helpful. Because I am leaving on vacation after tomorrow (8/19/05), I will also cc Kevin's father, Wayne Triplett, on this e-mail, so that he may see your response if you "Reply to All." Thank you very much for your advice. Best regards, Tom

August 25, 2005

Hi Tom.

I have been in touch with M. D. Anderson and we will be flying there Sunday night (8/28) for a possible three day series of tests (bone/PET scan, CT, blood work, pulmonary tests) in preparation for his possible inclusion in Pete Anderson's samarium (quadramet) and gemcitabine trial. This would involve from what I understand at this point a ten minute infusion of the radioisotope with a thirty minute next day followup of gemcitabine (repeated once a month). Some bone marrow fortifications may be necessary but not anticipated. An abstract detailing with a similar adult female case was e-mailed to you as an attachment.

I will be picking up a CD detailing Kevin's treatments to date tomorrow (Friday). I talked with Diane Samelak today about this, although she was unsure of the particulars you included in the

Indianapolis version. Dr. Anderson wanted whatever we could procure for him regarding Kevin.

Kevin has gained nine pounds, rarely uses the oxygen, and I am beginning the Tian Xian liquid which I purchased from Manila. Overall, we have another ray of hope. We essentially are a band of gypsies globetrotting to and fro in search of the magic bullet. Thanks again for your direction in this quest and for leading the way. Enjoy that vacation! Wayne

Dr. McLean (and Triplett family),

Sorry for the delay. I just got back from a two week trip (and now you are on vacation!). Although Kevin's history is extremely discouraging, I saw a similar case, and she has done much better than expected with samarium plus gemcitabine. If the family is willing to come to Houston, I can discuss this further. This woman's case history will be submitted as a draft version enclosed. Pete Anderson

August 27, 2005

Kevin's Medical Update

Hi everyone.

Kevin seems to be doing ok. He currently is off the oxygen, but I keep it on standby. With the dismal oncology report last month, I have opted to continue an alternative/homeopathic/herbal treatment approach for him. He is taking almost 30 types of meds daily (60+ pills). In addition, I have him on an anti-cancer diet of cottage cheese and flax oil. Last week I started him on a Chinese herbal blend (Tian Xian liquid).

I spend a lot of time researching his options, blending his medicines and taking care of his appointments. I have taken a leave of absence from school for a while. Hospice is working with us, but to see Kevin, you would think he is fine.

In my reseach last week I came across a new protocol at M. D. Anderson in Houston, TX. This involves the use of a radioactive chemo drug, samarium 153, paired with a new drug called quadramet (10 minute IV administration). This would be followed on day 2 with a 30 minute infusion of the chemo drug gemcitabine. Results have been encouraging with several other patients.

The lead oncologist at M. D. Anderson has agreed to see Kevin. We will be flying there Sunday afternoon (8/28) for three days of tests and possible first administration of the drugs. Corporate Angels has secured us a flight on a Duke Enterprises corporate jet from Charlotte to Houston. Each time we go on one of these "quests" we seem to encounter a hurricane (Indianapolis ... Dennis, Houston ... Katrina)! We are looking forward to the possibilities we may find there.

As usual, we are globe hopping trying to find what might work. I am recovering from prostate surgery and still have some bladder issues (it is manageable). Kevin and I occasionally get to a movie, and he has a girlfriend. He is making music and attending church. He is taking four on-line courses as WCC.

Your prayers and support continue to be felt. I will keep you posted on any further developments. Love, Wayne and Kevin

Mr. Mayes shared his e-mail from you regarding Kevin. Please add me to your e-mail list and keep me posted on his progress. I've added Kevin to our prayer list at my church! Thanks! Patricia

August 31, 2005

Kevin's Medical Update

Hi everyone.

M. D. Anderson Cancer Center in Houston is ranked #1 in the world for cancer research and novel therapies and for good reason. Kevin met with Dr. Pete Anderson this afternoon and there is encouraging news. The doctor feels he can help Kevin with a three-fold approach to his treatment. Thursday he will receive the nuclear medicine chemo drug samarian (quadramet) and for a few days be literally "radioactive." On Friday, he will receive a dose of gemcitabine (chemo) which works well in tandem. This will be repeated monthly with weekly blood counts being drawn at Baptist in Winston-Salem. If that doesn't produce positive results, our next option is methotrexate (high dose) and proton radiation. Doxil is another possibility. In short, we have additional hope for stopping the cancer's growth and/or shrinking the tumors somewhat. An additional tumorous area was located behind his tongue with the very precise PET scan.

To celebrate, we visited the Hard Rock Cafe and tomorrow evening we hope to attend Lakewood Church (Joel Osteen's new facility) just fifteen minutes from the hospital. We hope to be home Saturday, and I will update you more precisely as the chemo is delivered and as we monitor his white blood count which could temporarily drop.

"As long as there is life, there is hope," Kevin says. This is the place to be when your life is on the line. Take care and all our best to you. Wayne

Tom,

Kevin appears quite healthy and his one lung has 62% predicted PFT's! I really enjoyed this family and providing samarium's "Rays of Hope." I think Kevin may also benefit from Proton Beam RT at MDACC in the future (sometime 2006) when response has plateaued. I will arrange for this consult when we have completed four cycles of samarium + gemcitabine (probably early 2006). A brief summary and some images are enclosed FYI. Kevin has a calendar and will see you on Thursdays for count checks. Pete Anderson MD, PhD

September 2, 2005

Hi Nancy,

Kevin, his mother, and I have been at M. D. Anderson Cancer Clinic in Houston, Texas all week (Sunday thru Saturday) this past week. I e-mailed Kevin's oncologist at W-S and also sent an e-mail to MDA regarding the possibility of them including him in a cancer protocol. I received confirmation last Thursday that an osteosarcoma specialist wanted to see Kevin.

In short, we came to Houston for a consultation and were able to get a treatment protocol set up (samarium/quadramet and gemcitabine). He had his first treatment this week. We are scheduled to come to MDA once a month indefinitely to repeat the procedure if things look promising.

We left home with an herbal approach and with hospice already on the scene. We return tomorrow with a renewed spirit that the specialist at the #1 rated cancer hospital in the world has an approach that may make all the difference!

Kevin has been working all four courses on line and was up-to-date until his absence from home all this week. I would appreciate it if you could find out if his instructors want him to play catch up (some assignments may not be accessible now), or whether they prefer him to work on current requirements.

He is feeling good and if he improves, ultimately he would like to become a day student. It may not be feasible now with the potential of his white blood count dropping in a week or two.

Thank you for keeping in touch and for working with us to keep Kevin caught up as much as possible.

Houston and M. D. Anderson have been a Godsend for Kevin. They have the mindset that cancer not only should be treated, but that it can be beaten (much the same attitude Kevin possesses). Please keep me informed and thanks for all that you do for us. Wayne

Our elation spilled over in the form of e-mails to our new found friends in Houston. It had been a trip to death's door and back. With renewed optimism, MDA became our regular destination.

Kevin had been given a reprieve. I felt in my heart that Kevin actually had a fighting chance to live.

September 4, 2005

Hi Peggy,

What a joy to meet you last week! We are so excited about our new association with MDA, you, and Dr. Anderson. I am attaching two photos (one for you and one for Kevin's nurse). I'm sending Dr. Anderson a separate e-mail. I am adding you to Kevin's Special Friends list and you should receive an e-mail from me later this week. Again, thank you for everything. All our best, Wayne, Kathy, and Kevin

Dr. Anderson,

What a delight meeting you last week! We are so excited about the possibilities which lie ahead for Kevin. You, Peggy, and the entire MDA staff are wonderful! Thank you for all that you do for so many to not only treat cancer but for helping make it history. We look forward to our next visit. I am attaching two photos for you and I will add you to Kevin's Special Friends e-mail update list. You should receive this health update later this week. Again, you are a Godsend. If we can be of help to you to further your research, you can count on us. God bless, Wayne, Kathy, and Kevin

PS ... Kevin thinks you are really cool! (Me Too)

Thanks for the note and pictures. I look forward to future visits, too.
Pete

September 6, 2005

I am so excited that you have found hopeful treatment for Kevin. I
applaud his spirit. What an awesome young man you have raised. I
have sincerely prayed for your family and will continue to do so. Bud
Mayes, HIS 121 and HUM 121, will work with Kevin and whatever
timeframe Kevin can manage this semester. Kevin just needs to do
his assignments as he is able, and let Mr. Mayes know through e-mail
when he is ready to take the test on the 1st unit. Mr. Mayes will devise
a test that Kevin can take on-line without coming to campus. I have
e-mailed Kevin's other instructors with requests to do the same. They
are out of county and state, but I should get a reply to the e-mails
today. Please keep me advised on Kevin's progress as you are able.
Nancy

September 7, 2005

Kevin's Medical Update

Hi everyone.
It is always darkest before the dawn is a saying I have heard for
many years. The events of this month affirm the truth of that statement for Kevin and me. In July, I mentioned that the possible stint
insertion to open up Kevin's right lung was a "no go" due to the
tumor's location and size. Faced with an inoperable tumor and with
hospice already on the scene, we were not content to just sit and wait.
With the help of a friend, I contacted a homeopathic/herbalist doctor in Winston-Salem, and Kevin went for a consultation. As a result
of that visit, I placed Kevin on a "natural" program to health which
included 30+ types of vitamins, etc. with him taking over 60 pills
daily. This included the anti-cancer diet of cottage cheese/flaxseed oil,
a special anti-cancer mix from Montana, and a special herbal blend
from China (Tian Xian liquid). He seemed to feel better after several
weeks on this regimen.
As my research continued, I discovered via the internet a possible
bone cancer vaccine in development at the M. D. Anderson Cancer
Clinic in Houston, Texas. I immediately contacted Kevin's oncologist,

Dr. Tom McLean, at Baptist Hospital asking him to please forward my interest in this trial to a doctor at MDA. He did that, but the trial was not ready. The doctor gave him Dr. Pete Anderson's name who is one of the top osteosarcoma doctors in the world and mentioned that he might be interested in working with Kevin. That interest was confirmed via e-mail, and I immediately began preparations for our visit to MDA.

It is miraculous how things sometimes work out. Dr. Anderson had just begun his practice there in late May. Moreover, the Corporate Angel Network was able to secure a free flight there for us on a Duke Energy corporate jet from Charlotte to Houston on Sunday night (8/28). I had just scheduled Kevin's two days of tests for 8/29 and 8/30 there. The Corporate Angel Network of top U.S. corporations are true unsung heroes who readily fly cancer patients to and sometimes from their treatment destinations as time and space allow. Thanks Duke Energy! As we flew on Sunday evening, we could see the ominous, approaching image of Hurricane Katrina as we approached the Gulf area.

After two days of tests and determining that he had cancer in his chest (mediastinal area), shoulder blade, and base of the tongue, Kevin received the radioactive drug samarium-153 (quadramet) via iv. For a short while, he was "radioactive" as the counter vividly displayed. On day five, he received gemcitabine (chemotherapy) which helps to sensitize the samarium. Several other patients have made progress with these two drugs in tandem. Plans call for our return visit to MDA later this month with weekly blood counts being taken at Baptist in W-S. If his white count drops, he may require additional immune system support (Neulasta). If Kevin responds well, Dr. Anderson envisions additional chemotherapy (high dose methotrexate) along with proton beam radiation. Other agents may be used later (doxil/avastin). We plan on flying to Houston at least once monthly initially. MDA is huge (over thirteen thousand people work at the center) and even larger is their capacity to make out-of-towners feel welcome. As the #1 cancer clinic in the world, they truly deserve that distinction by offering hope to the seemingly hopeless.

We did manage some R-N-R. We attended an inspiring service at the country's largest church, Lakewood Church (Joel Osteen's church), on Wednesday night (8/31). Many displaced people from New Orleans were in attendance. Those folks stood, the congregation reached out to them, and had prayer for them. It was a great experience. The church (a renovated stadium) is magnificent! Many of our cab drivers mentioned having loved ones in New Orleans, many of which had not been heard from in days. We saw many buses, since the hospital is only two miles from the AstroDome.

We attended the Houston Astros home game on Thursday evening. Without tickets, we approached the gate where an elderly couple wanted to rid themselves of three tickets (a steal at $5 each). We sat near them, chatted about our reason for being at MDA, and were shocked as they handed our money back! The folks in Texas have really big hearts, too!

As we left the hotel one morning, Kevin spotted a neighbor of ours, Maurice Templeton, Singing News publisher and owner of Templeton Tours, standing nearby. He helped make possible Kevin's Make-A-Wish trip several years ago to Alaska with Dr. Charles Stanley. Knowing me, I snapped a quick photo of them, and to my delight yesterday found that Maurice had placed it on the Singing News website where he had solicited prayer for Kevin from all his avid readers. This magazine reaches thousands of homes nationally and abroad. Members may access this news release and photo at www.singingnews.com. Maurice had a great checkup at MDA as well! We love you, Maurice!

Kevin and I are greatly buoyed by these recent turn of events. There are many unanswered questions, but a course has been charted. Our lives have been enriched by each of you who have been in prayer for him and have continued to support us. In fact, I have my own prescription for a possible cancer cure (patent pending), take advantage of the newest cancer therapies available, add a good helping of nature's own herbal supplements, form a network of family and friends for long-term support, cultivate this mixture with fervent, daily prayer for healing, and lastly, hold to that spirit of "I can make it, I am determined to live strong and make everyday count."

You can count on that spirit of dogged determination from Kevin. I (we) have seen it time after time. You can be sure that Kevin will be in the midst of the fight, and that his dad will be there, searching. We love you, Wayne and Kevin.

Our many friends flooded my inbox with messages of praise and marveled at this miraculous turn of events. Just when it looked hopeless, everything seemed to turn around. To God be the glory!

> My love to you both. I just read your message. I am speechless, but my heart is praying and my tears are flowing. I hope that it is okay for me to forward the e-mail to my sister, my sister-in-law, and my friend Ann. They each have you and Kevin on prayer lists at church and support groups. Please stay in touch and come by soon. Love, Debbie

> I am in tears as I read this. Not tears of sorrow, but of hope, of inspiration, of gratitude. I'm not sure that I have ever known greater heroes than Kevin and his Dad. I'm not sure I have ever been moved so much as I have heard about your continual plight for life, for the hope you inspire in others, and for the light of Christ that shines through your situation.
> Thank you for sharing your story, your life, with those around you. You are more of a blessing than you may ever know. God bless you, Wayne and Kevin. As always, you are in our prayers. Charles

> You are encouraged! This was an encouragement to me! Thanks so much for sharing your news! I am still amazed at God's power, and that He is in charge of everything! May I have permission to share this e-mail with the folks in Student Services, Kevin's advisor, and my church? Thanks for the update! Patricia

> Hey Kevin!
> School is not cool anymore because all the cool people like you, Jordan, and Conley left. Well, I'll ttyl. Love ya, bye. Killing Loneliness

September 8, 2005

This is truly wonderful and inspiring. I would never have dreamed that there was so much more out there, but trust you to find it! My brother-in-law did the homeopathic/herbal route (with surgery, radiation, and chemo) for a huge tumor in his neck. He had to have food and herbal stuff through a feeding tube. He is fine now, two years later. I so hope the same for Kevin. Very best wishes, Jenny

Dear Wayne and Kevin,
Your message really brightened my day. I'm so thankful the trip to
Houston turned out so well! You both are truly inspirational. I will
continue to pray for both of you. Love, Frances

Frances forwarded your e-mail to me. God is certainly good, isn't He?
I have prayed for you both many times. It's awesome that you were
able to attend a service with Joel Osteen. I've seen him several times
on TV, and he is a powerful preacher. I just wanted you to know that
my thoughts and prayers are with you both. May the Lord continue
to strengthen and guide you daily. Blessings, Karin

You are such an inspiration. I have said many times that I wonder if
I would have done all that you have done if I were in your shoes. I
probably would have taken the doctor's word and said "we have done
all we can do." If I ever need a supporter, researcher, or just a listener,
I know you would be at the top of my list to call. I mention you at
church every week and ask everyone to keep remembering you and
Kevin. They are all amazed as well as to your fight and faith. You are
truly a blessing to us as Christians and hopefully more so to non-
believers too. Please keep in touch. Cheryl

Pat always forwards us news of Kevin. I just read your latest update
and wanted to drop you a congratulations note. It was great seeing
you and Kevin at last month's Relay for Life and both of you have
been part of my daily prayer list for years. It is amazing to be a witness to the power of prayer and how our Lord works in the lives of
those we know.

I also wanted you to know personally that as inspiring as Kevin
has been to all of us as he has fought so hard over the years, you are
just as inspiring. Your continuous dedication and untiring work to
seek out new therapies, experimental treatments, and pull together
resources to travel and help Kevin overcome this disease is just out
and out amazing to me. Someone needs to do a news story, TV show,
or Lifetime movie on your work for Kevin and on your own battle
with the disease. You are a model parent and an inspiration to all
those who are fortunate to know you.

Have a great day and know that both you and Kevin will continue
to be in our prayers everyday. And as always, if there is ever anything

we can do for either of you, please do contact us. May the blessings and miracles continue! God Bless, Mike

It's great to hear that things are looking up. We all continue to keep you and Kevin in our prayers. I enjoyed seeing both of you at Mt. Pleasant when we had Carol Baker's birthday. Everyone at school misses you, but understands that you need to be off right now.

I know several people who have been very impressed by M. D. Anderson. A family member from Michigan was diagnosed ten years ago with a very aggressive late stage lymphoma. The doctors in Flint didn't give him any hope at all. He somehow ended up in Texas and received extensive treatment and a bone marrow transplant. He was disease free for several years. When it appeared again last year, he headed back to Texas. He had a stem cell transplant. Today, he is still under their care but is doing fairly well. Take Care. We'll keep praying! Becky

Your e-mail and pictures warm our hearts and inspire us to be more appreciative of every day and what friendship really means. Wayne, you write so well and your devotion and commitment to your son is the epitome of a father's love. Sometime, when you have the time, you must write a book and include your correspondence or at least some of them, because I am sure there are hundreds. I lost my father to cancer several years ago and just reading about your search brought back those memories, bittersweet, but while they gave him a year, maybe three, he beat it over ten years and for almost all those years had an unbelievably healthy quality of life. My love and prayers continue for you and Kevin. Love, Linda

Thanks for sharing with us all the victories, setbacks, hopes, finds, and moments of Kevin's journey through this illness. Not only do we love you guys and want to share in this as friends, but some of us may need this information for ourselves or other members of our families. I know this is a surreal time for you and many people would be so frightened, they would simply come apart at the seams. I appreciate the fact that you and Kevin have found the strength and wisdom to cope with the situation in the way you are doing so. I can see and hear God's power working in both of you, and it makes me very grateful to know you have His comfort. He will see you through all of your trials.

This recent journey has such a positive note to it. Let's "keep on the sunny side." Please continue to share with us, and always know you are in our daily prayers! Love and Best Wishes, Sherry

How bad is the treatment on Kevin, not physically but emotionally? I know it is not my place to ask, but I do wonder if he is ok! I know I shouldn't, but I do! Seeing him Monday, after not seeing him since my birthday, was a revelation, but he seemed different! I care, Wayne, and I don't want to see him hurt, and I don't want to be in his way! I don't want to cause him more burdens than he already has! I just want him to be happy and content! I love him, Wayne! You may not understand that, but I do and, after Monday, I don' t think I will ever be able to stop! Please keep me updated! I worry when I can't be there for him, even as a friend. Larisa

I have delayed responding to you since this morning, thinking that I would come up with something to say. However, words don't seem adequate. I want you to know that I am truly inspired and blessed by the faith you and Kevin have shown throughout this journey. I do not know if I could have endured as you both have. You and Kevin remain in my thoughts and prayers. Please let me know if I can help in any way. Larry

I have read your e-mail and am again amazed at Kevin's determination and faith. I have a son, Zach, who will turn eleven years old on Monday, and I know I would do the very same for him as you are doing for Kevin. There is no greater love than the love a parent has for his/her children. Sharing your updates with those of us on your e-mail list is very much appreciated. I think of Kevin quite often and wonder how he is doing. Receiving your updates means a lot to me and to everyone at Dr. Jordan's office. I also keep my Sunday School class updated. Please tell Kevin hello from me. He doesn't know me, but I am just one of many that are praying for him and love him! Please let me know if there is ever anything I can do to help. Take care, Jhonda

That's great news. It's still going to be a tough fight but like you said, Kevin's done it before and he can do it again. I forwarded your message to Andrea, since she has been asking about Kevin. I'm sure she would love to hear from Kevin. If there's anything we can do, please let us know. Kevin is always in our thoughts and prayers. Kevin is on our prayer list at church, and our youth always request a special prayer for him. We had a miracle in our family once, and I am praying that you will be blessed in the same way very soon. Allen

Kevin had begun the new cancer treatments in Houston and at Brenner's. Once, during his band practice, Kevin began spitting up a small amount of blood. After calling Dr. McLean, I rushed him to Baptist. It was just a capillary rupture and not a major arterial bleed. This was always a constant worry. I filled a prescription of Amicar (anti-hemoptysis drug), measured the correct portion, and carried it with me in a bottle wherever Kevin went, just in case of another bleeding episode. His vitals had to be closely monitored, and I stayed in very close e-mail contact with both Dr. Anderson in Houston and Dr. McLean in Winston-Salem.

September 10, 2005

I spoke with Wayne today. Because of hemoptysis (after coughing) and location of tumor (near some high-priced real estate in terms of big blood vessels), I recommended:
1) keep platelets >30,000 with transfusions
2) if bleeding is major, ok to give NovoSeven (fVIIa) 1 vial-4.8 mg iv push
3) ok to place on Amicar (1 gm 4–5 x/day) if Kevin has additional minor hemoptysis
Thanks, Pete

I had taken Kevin to see the group Alter Bridge (formerly Creed) some months earlier, and he loved the experience. I managed to get tickets for Kevin, Crista, and me to another concert by them. While we were on the road to see them, however, Kevin became nauseous. We returned home. His health was more important.

September 19, 2005

Hi Carol,
Who could have predicted that Kevin would be sick and not up to going to the concert? Don't worry about the ticket cost. Kevin's blood counts last Friday seemed to be creeping up some. If his counts look

good Thursday, maybe MDA will have us back next week (too soon to tell right now). Kevin has been doing some college work and has two tests at WCC this week. He is consumed with his music and his band has a few dates coming up. Hope all is well with you and your family. Take care, Wayne

I was going to ask Kevin if I could write a paper on him! lol TTY later LK!

The beauty of the Internet is that a patient can readily communicate with his doctor(s). To their credit, Tom and Pete were more than willing to answer any of my questions or offer advice on Kevin's ever-changing condition. They always replied in a timely manner.

September 22, 2005

Hi Pete,

I hope you are safe and sound. It seems that every time we venture out of state for treatments a hurricane is somewhere close by. Kevin's counts have been steadily increasing (faxes should have been sent to you via Tom McLean). His latest counts today (9/22) indicate that his platelets are at 196 K and his ANC is 1,296 (all within acceptable ranges). No Neulasta was needed, and he has not incurred any fever. I know the weather may play havoc with scheduling, but we are ready next week to come for another treatment cycle if you feel likewise. We will work with you on whatever time frame you suggest. When I get the "go ahead" from you, I will look into getting a flight out.

Kevin had no further problems with spitting up blood after the one incident two weeks ago. His small cough persists, but he is on augmentin as of today for a minor sinus infection. Looking forward to seeing you soon and be safe! Wayne

Wayne, Kathy, and Kevin:

I will let you know when it is safe to return to Houston. Alternatively, if it is "awhile," I can help arrange cycle #2 in NC. I am currently safe in Vancouver, but it's bound to be an interesting return. I look forward to Kevin's #1 Storm song. Pete

September 26, 2005

I recently ran across this site and thought you might be interested. It's related to the Anthroposifical Society which is based on the research/ theories of Rudolph Steiner. I have read a fair amount of Rudolph Steiner's work and have been pretty impressed with the breadth of his knowledge, everything from sound therapy and biodynamic gardening to Waldorph education. Hope Kevin, as well as you, are doing as well as possible. Ken

Thanks for the update on Kevin and yourself. We are still praying for the both of you. I am sending you something I saw in a church bulletin, and I thought of you and Kevin. Don't give up, someone really loves you. Don't give up, someone really cares. Don't give up, someone really loves you, and that someone is the LORD. Keep the faith. We love you, too! Your friend always, Bill

It was important to keep tabs on Kevin's blood work and relay this information to Pete at MDA. These labs were done weekly, reports faxed to me, and in turn I would send it to Houston. These results determined the medication dosages and frequencies given at Baptist. Both medical centers worked together to give Kevin the best of care.

September 29, 2005

Hi Pete,
Hope you are well. Here are Kevin's lab results for today (9/29/05).

9/29/05 (today)	9/22/05 (last week)
ANC 1848	1296
Platelets 135,000	196,000
(the platelet number has been steadily climbing until today's count)	
RBC 4.70	4.37
Hemoglobin 15.2	14.1
WBC 4.4 (4,400) 3.6	(3,600)
SEGS 42%	36%

As you can see he is within the acceptable range for another 2-day treatment. I can get a flight out Tuesday afternoon (10/4) and be in clinic at MDA on Wednesday and Thursday, (10/5–10/6) if that will work for you. If you need the complete CBC, I can fax that to you. I will confirm the flight after hearing from you. Thanks and take care. Wayne

Sounds like a "go." Peggy, let's schedule Wed. a.m. appt. (counts and alk phos), 153 Sm-Wed. p.m. and gemcitabine Thurs. Thanks and I'm looking forward to seeing Kevin. It's okay with us if he brings his guitar. Pete

October 3, 2005

Hi Terri,

Great hearing from you! We were set to return to Houston for treatment #2 last week until Hurricane Rita blew in and Kevin's CBC was fluctuating. We will fly out from Charlotte tomorrow afternoon (10/4) for MDA in Houston. We hope to return home Thursday evening.

He has had the persistent tumor compression cough and has for a week had some sort of ear ache. Dr. Wofford prescribed augmentin last week, but I took him to Dr. McLean this morning. He could find no evidence of infection, and he is not taking antibiotics now. I think his jaw or ear pain may be coming from the osteo sight behind his tongue. I'll mention it to Dr. Anderson on Wednesday.

He continues to make music with his band and played at the 5th Quarter high school gig (FCA event) after Friday night's game. He and his band hope to play Saturday in town at a Katrina relief concert. He is in good spirits, but his appetite is not great and sometimes he has trouble sleeping.

I will know more later this week. He is not due for scans until about a month from now. Samarium and gemcitabine are what we are again going out there for. Keep in touch. Thinking of you guys often. Love, Wayne

Kevin's jaw pain was becoming more frequent. I called MDA before leaving for the airport. Within a few minutes, while we were on our way to the airport having just left home, Pete called back stating that he had already set up a head MRI for Kevin. Since our flight had been changed, we no longer had our hotel reservation. Not to worry, because Pete had found us somewhere to stay if we needed it. No one could ask for any more caring than what he offered.

October 4, 2005

Wayne (and Kevin),
Welcome back to Houston. I've arranged a head MRI to look at the
area causing ear pain. Kevin's MRI is in the Clark Clinic Bldg, 3rd
floor, Rose Zone. He should report at 7:30 for IV placement; scan is
at 8 p.m. Tues. 10/4/05. Then, we will re-group in clinic tomorrow.
Please call me when you get in and confirm you got my e-mail and/or
phone message. If you rent a car, I may also have found a place for
you to stay, too. Pete

As our plane landed in Houston, the hotel called me confirming we had a
room. Dr. Anderson's "place for us to stay" would have been in his own home.
His generosity was overwhelming.

October 6, 2005

Kevin's Medical Update

Hi everyone.
Just a quick late night update. Kevin, his mom, and I flew to
Houston (MDA) Tuesday afternoon poised for a two day visit. That
has changed. Kevin has for a few days now been experiencing pain
above his left ear. I was suspicious that the small osteo tumor located
between his eye and brain could be growing. Last night's MRI revealed
this to be true.
Our stay now will be two weeks. He will be receiving daily small
dose radiation treatments for this (10 weekdays) along with high
dose methotrexate (chemo). This will put his regular treatment on
hold until week after next. He should not have too much trouble with
this, no burns, etc., but possible mouth sores from the chemo.
He is feeling good except for his ongoing tumor compression
cough. His mother will return home tomorrow or Friday for a few
items before returning to MDA. Houston is beginning to feel like our
second home. Just know that all is well here, we are in good spirits
and no hurricane to deal with this time is truly a blessing! I'll keep
you posted. Wayne

October 7, 2005

Pete,

Just a note to say "thank you" for the tremendous effort you are making for Kevin. He has no head pain at all after just two RTs and the methotrexate infusion. The one-two punch of chemo and RT seem to be a viable approach.

With that in mind, I'm reminded of Kevin's breathing pattern, and it sounds as if his right lung capacity has diminished. His coughing persists and seems a bit tighter and on occasion labored. If you feel it is advised, I ask if a chest x-ray could be scheduled for Monday (10/10) to see if the tumor compression should be addressed now. Knowing that you and Dr. Mahajan have consulted on this two-fold approach, both of you might have a more definitive diagnosis with this x-ray there for analysis.

Again, we continue to be most impressed with MDA, the Peds Staff, and with you for all that you are doing to make cancer history. Thanks for having us! Have a well-deserved, relaxing weekend. Wayne

Great minds think alike. We have already ordered the chest x-ray for Monday. If that is worrisome in any way, we can F/U with chest CT and RT treatment planning. In the meantime, it's ok to keep track (log) of symptoms, so Dr. Mahajan and I can have a better idea of better vs worse Monday. Pete

October 8, 2005

Hi Terri,

We left home last Tues. for a 2-day trip to Houston. That has now turned in to at least a 2-week stay. Kevin had been having some pain above his left ear for several days. This was one of the osteo hot spot areas A ten day low dose radiation plan was developed. After two treatments he has no pain. He also received high dose methotrexate Thursday. He has hardly eaten since then. His night breathing seems to be more labored, and I think there is some tumor obstruction causing it, although last night's chest x-ray looked much like the one in August. I feel that Dr. Anderson will order a CT tomorrow and possibly develop a compatible external beam radiation/chemo approach for his chest cavity.

I ordered tickets for the Houston Texans game today, but he feels lousy, and we will not be going. It's like the old days, we packed for 2 days not 2 weeks. I hope today to get a shuttle from the hotel to Target. We were lucky enough to get an extension on our room until 10/20. That date may be moved to even later if a chest radiation plan is developed. He breathes heavily at night and has the usual MTX problems.

In short, it's been a challenge to get through this. The doctors, etc. are great, but Kevin seems to be truly tired since Tuesday. Take care, Wayne

Give Kevin a big hug for me. I know how much I worried when Aaron had radiation (10 treatments in 5 days). I think it worried/scared me more than the chemo. Maybe it was that by the time he had radiation, chemo was just normal stuff. Anyway, I hope he does well. Radiation zapped Aaron's appetite and energy rather quickly. He did receive total body. It's tough when you plan for a day trip or even two days, to find out you're there much longer. We also had several of those. It's so unexpected. Always know that we love you all and hold you in our hearts and prayers. Right now, I know that's what you need. I just wish I could give you all a big hug! Let us know how things are going. Give Kevin our love. Terri

October 11, 2005

Kevin's Medical Update

Kevin hoped that his doctors would pursue an "aggressive treatment plan," and that seems to be the case here in Houston. After arriving on 10/4 prepared for a 2 DAY stay … it has now turned into a 3 WEEK marathon. Kevin's headaches were coming from an osteo area (previously noted on PET scan) between his nose and brain. An immediate 10 day radiation plan was designed for him. In addition, they have also designed a low dose radiation plan for his chest tumors (10 more days). These treatments will overlap and only take thirty minutes or so each day. He received high dose methotrexate last Thursday and was zapped until last night (no appetite, nausea). He was fitted with a portable liquid infusion bag for a few days to keep him hydrated. He will be receiving his usual chemo (samarium and gemcitabine) along with avastin later this week.

His recent chest x-ray shows little if any change from the late August impression which is good. Perhaps the September meds are working to suppress tumor growth. Doctors here believe that a multi-level approach (chemo-radiation) works best and each enhances the other. His headaches have been few and far between. Doctors know where Kevin's tumor sites are and plan to address them one-by-one.

We have just completed our first week here this trip and things are going well. I had tickets for the Texans/Titans game, but Kevin was too sick to attend. I think all the Astros playoff tickets are gone and attending would be a long shot at best. We can see Reliant Stadium from our room. We just missed seeing Lance Armstrong who was here 10/3.

Kevin's mom may fly home for a few supplies, although I made it to Target after day six. We had a free flight courtesy of Corporate Angels out here, and Duke Energy has again scheduled us a free flight back on 10/25 (if that schedule holds).

Plans call for weekly trips to WFUBMC for blood checks and to receive avastin there once every two weeks. We are scheduled to return to Houston after Thanksgiving.

Kevin had filet mignon last night (first meal in four days) to celebrate finishing up the methotrexate. He has little pain. I'm getting plenty of cardio-vascular exercise from wheeling him around this large complex in a wheelchair. His spirits are good and I feel that this is the best treatment plan I could find for him anywhere. I do not have my extensive e-mail list with me here, so you may forward this update to those who you feel would like to see it.

In closing, it would be easy to say that it took a long time, maybe too long to get here. Those of you touched by cancer know that it is always by pursuing available options when presented that possibly down the road you may get lucky and find an effective treatment plan. Our hopes and prayers are that this plan is now in full swing. We are doing well and as always, thanks for your support. Love, Wayne and Kevin

Updates on Kevin, both to and from Dr. Anderson, were vital to keep us on track with Kevin's treatment plan. Each time we were in Houston, Pete drafted a calendar to cover the upcoming month to six weeks.

October 30, 2005

Hi Dr. Anderson.
Kevin and family made it safely home to NC last Tuesday evening.
Kevin's mouth soreness is no longer a problem, but his appetite is
recovering more slowly. He has not had a BM in several days, and I
am using a mild laxative to help things along. He has no head or jaw
pain, although he does have some sinus drainage and an intermittent
cough (not as intense as his pre-visit cough). His breathing is relatively clear. I'm supposing the cough may be a side effect of the mediastinal RT. He is continuing the medications you prescribed for him.
Hopefully his energy level will be rebounding soon. He did manage
to get in a brief practice session with his band on Saturday. Thanks
for everything! Be safe, Wayne

Tom,
Kevin's dad gave me an update; what a great family! I realize you used
Avastin before, but here's some additional info on VEGF blockade
during RT and chemotherapy. It may be helpful for understanding
why. If you have any questions, please call anytime. Pete

November 12, 2005

Kev! Dude you tore it up tonight, man! Tomorrow will be fun. See
ya, Joe

November 14, 2005

Pete,
    I saw and have discussed with Wayne your e-mail regarding Kevin
and the possible use of infliximab to perhaps improve his cachexia
and either metoclopromide or erythromycin to improve GI motility. I don't have experience with infliximab for this indication but
am certainly happy to give it if you think it would be the best. With
his weight going up, however, with G-tube feeds, I wouldn't mind
holding off for a bit longer and continuing to use either Megace or
Marinol. And his GI motility I think is OK at present. I worry about
the potential side effects of these meds being worse than the symptoms we're treating. Having said all that, I would be happy to treat
him however you (and Wayne and Kevin) think best. Let me know

how I can help. I will post Kevin's CBC from 1/12/06 below. He also had a CXR that day which showed a small amount of disease progression compared to 11/28/05, but was otherwise stable. Thanks for your continued help. Best regards, Tom

November 18, 2005

Hi Pete,

Hope you are well. Kevin has played two gigs with his band since returning home! His energy level is still quite diminished and he has lost a few more pounds. His mouth sores and radiation burns have cleared up and his appetite is slowly returning to normal. He has been taking prednisone since 11/5 (10 mg initial dose, current 20 mg daily dose). I am also continuing his MG Plus caplets and the weekend dosages of bactrim. I occasionally give him a morphine or ativan tab as needed (not on the same evening). His port-a-cath has been flushing and drawing back on occasion! Avastin given at WFUBMC ... 11/10, avastin (scheduled) ... 11/28. Other observations include: No dyspnea,no hemotysis. Intermittent yet persistent dry cough (occasional sputum productive), Symptomatic for pneumonitis (suggest exploring his candidacy for right lung endobronchial laser therapy). No right lung air flow yet ... he's still trying.

Other than lack of energy, the cough is his main issue. It is suspect for tracheal/bronchial tumor compression or perhaps just the post RT syndrome. I think he is making progress (no head pain, no labored breathing, port again operational).We are scheduled in clinic at MDA on 12/8/05 (I already have the proposed schedule). Have a great Thanksgiving, and we continue to be blessed with our association with MDA and you. Love, Wayne and Kevin

Thanks for the F/U. Good news is always welcome. Peggy can scan your e-mail into the record. Nice F/U! Ok to try to get darbopoietin to get Hb even higher, but >12 H is probably not the reason for tiredness. Another is sleep apnea, obstruction during sleep you don't know about and keeps you tired chronically. If you want to look into the sleep apnea, check this out with Dr. McLean. Otherwise, we can schedule a consult here. And there is always coffee, too! Also, we will schedule Scott Evans/Pulmonary to see Kevin on the next visit for the lung(s). You all also have a great Thanksgiving. Pete

Hi Tom.

Hope you are well. Below you will find an update on Kevin I sent to Dr. Anderson as well as his response. Pete mentioned that Kevin might benefit from taking darbopoietin. I'm unsure whether he was going to prescribe it or if perhaps you could call that in to our local CVS pharmacy.

Kevin's main issue is the persistent cough. If you feel comfortable prescribing something, please do. He is currently taking only Delcym cough syrup and the prednisone. Do you think we need to look at the sleep apnea issue? We will be in clinic on 11/28 around 8:00 AM for the avastin since Kevin has an appointment at 11:30 with Dr. Matt Hough (psychiatry). Thanks for your help and have a great Thanksgiving! Wayne

I made it a point to have my video camera and/or digital camera with me on most occasions. I took hundreds of pictures of places we had been including MDA. On Thanksgiving, 2005, I decided to interview Kevin at our home about his ordeal with cancer. I drafted some questions and ran them by him. My persistence paid off, and he granted me an interview. Although Kevin wasn't feeling well and was coughing, he agreed to answer the following questions for me.

November 24, 2005

Thanksgiving Questions and Answers

How did you feel when you were first diagnosed with cancer?
Bad (we both laughed). I was in shock.

What is your greatest fear in having cancer?
That it can ultimately kill me.

What are some times you remember that were real bad?
Chemotherapy and stuff. My cough has been bad these last few months.

How have you been able to deal with chemotherapy, radiation, and not going to school?
I just deal with it. I just go on.

What are some things that you can't do that you miss?
Go out, go places and drive.

What things have you enjoyed even though you had cancer?
Playing with my band.

Did your mom and I divorcing bother you that much?
It didn't seem to.

Are there particular doctors that you really liked?
I like them all, Dr. McLean and Dr. Anderson especially.

Did you like going to Indianapolis for the new drug?
It was ok.

What are your thoughts about going to Texas (M. D. Anderson)?
It's fine, if it will help me.

What has been a favorite place you've been to even though you were sick?
The beach.

How has your faith and going to church helped you through this?
I know God is with me.

Do you pray a lot?
Not as much as I used to, because I get tired easily.

We went to several concerts. Which ones did you like?
I liked the Cornerstone Concert, Chevelle, and Alter Bridge. My favorite was probably Cornerstone.

People seemed to think you would keep getting cancer. How did you deal with that?
I never really thought about it much.

Do you think about death?
Everybody dies. I'm planning on living.

Who are some of your more special friends?
Gwyn, Adam, and Brandon.

Who are the important influential people in your life?
Jesus Christ.

What advice would you give others with cancer?
Have a good attitude and keep going.

What are your plans and what do you want to do?
Play in the band.

What are you most thankful for?
To be alive.

What do you think is your biggest accomplishment in life?
I guess helping others.

How would you want people to remember you? He was a nice guy, a
good guitarist, and a good Christian?
Yes, all the above.

How do you feel about your struggle right now?
It's just rough.

Do you think M. D. Anderson can help?
Yes, that's why I'm going down there. I have faith in them.

I made many inquiries on alternate therapies. One day, I received an e-mail,
and later a packet from a clinic, unfortunately with no treatment for osteosarcoma. That was fine, because we had the best team, anywhere.

November 28, 2005

(Response to Inquiry from the Burzynski Clinic)

Dear Mr. Triplett,
    Thank you for your interest in the clinic. We have sent an infor-
mational package to the listed address in your request. It should
arrive by mail in 4 to 5 business days. Unfortunately, our therapies

are not helpful for osteosarcoma at this time. Although we have treated patients with osteosarcoma, traditional therapies are usually more effective for treating primary bone cancers. However, the doctors can discuss your son's case in more detail at the consultation in Houston, if he decides to come to meet with our physicians to discuss treatment options. At the consultation, they will present your son with a personalized treatment plan based on his medical history and physical evaluation. Your son may choose to proceed or to find other therapies that may be helpful for him. If your son is not interested in pursuing therapies at our clinic, you may want to get in touch with an organization called People Against Cancer. What they will do is send out Kevin's medical records to various alternative therapy hospitals and clinics across the nation to see if they can find a suitable therapy for him. Their website is www.peopleagainstcancer.com. In addition, there is another helpful resource you may want to contact. His name is Dr. Ralph Moss. Basically, he writes comprehensive reports for all the possible therapies for any type of cancer, alternative as well as traditional. Each report is categorized by the type of cancer so there is one specifically for osteosarcoma. His website is www.cancerdecisions.com or www.ralphmoss.com. We wish we had a more positive response for you and wish you and your son the best at this time. Please feel free to contact us if you have any other questions or concerns, and thank you for your interest in the Burzynski Clinic.
Kind regards, Frances

MDA is the hub of cancer treatment and research. On Kevin's Make-A-Wish trip to Alaska, he met many talented musicians. Roger Bennett, pianist for the gospel quartet Legacy Five, was one of those individuals. Roger had been fighting a form of leukemia over ten years, in and out of remission, and had numerous stays at MDA. Knowing that he was there, somewhere, I sent an e-mail of support to him. Sadly, cancer claimed him in 2007.

Hi Roger,
My son Kevin Triplett and family traveled with you three years ago on the Dr. Charles Stanley Alaska Cruise. His Make-A-Wish cruise was the greatest! He has been fighting osteosarcoma (bone cancer) since April 2000. After numerous chemotherapies, five surgeries, and cutting edge therapies, we made our way to MDA for our first visit in August. Oncologists at Wake Forest (Winston-Salem) had given up

on him due to a large mediastinal tumor restricting his breathing. In fact, we are here now at MDA at the Rotary House.

We met you on the cruise with Legacy Five and have been keeping up with your medical situation. MDA has given Kevin a reprieve, although surviving long-term is a long shot. Maurice Templeton, our neighbor about two miles from us in Millers Creek, NC, was here in August, and he published a photo I took of Kevin and him on the SN web site requesting prayer for Kevin. We meet with Dr. Pete Anderson on Monday to discuss Kevin's progress. He is really struggling with a persistent cough, weight loss, and lack of energy. He is lucky to still be with me, and I am blessed for that.

If we can help you in any way, please don't hesitate to call. As we know, a person must go through the seemingly endless trials of cancer to really know what it is like. One good day can sometimes lead to another. I myself recently had prostate cancer surgery. It is my hope that even now the Lord's hand is upon you and Kevin, and that both of you will experience a healing. I covet your prayers for him, and know that we are praying for you. God Bless You, Roger. Wayne Triplett

Kevin,

The show at the Bassment was awesome. I can't wait to see more. I looked for you at Wal-Mart on Friday night, but I never could find you. Nathan

December 5, 2005

Kevin's Medical Update

Hi everyone.

We arrived in Houston on 11/30 for Kevin's third trip to MDA. This week's scans show some tumor necrosis (tumor kill), so I feel that the chemo/radiation regimen has had a positive impact. His lung function has decreased some in part due to the radiation. Kevin has lost almost 25 pounds since October, and his doctor is determined that he cannot lose anymore. Plans call for him to have a bronchoscopy tomorrow and the insertion of a stomach feeding tube later this week. This tube will be his main source of nutrition for sometime. In addition, he will have three courses of chemo next week. We plan on leaving Houston on 12/23 if all goes well.

Overall, I am encouraged with what I hear. These next few weeks will be a challenge, but once he gets some nutrition, he should begin to feel better. Later this spring, we hope he can receive the new proton beam radiation therapy here. We have a comfy hotel room, supplies from Target, and a television, so things are manageable.

As we prepare to celebrate Kevin's 19th birthday here Wednesday (12/7), I continue to be thankful for the marvels of modern medicine, for the gift of having him with me another year albeit in another state, in a hospital. With luck, we can be home for Christmas! After all, home is where the heart is. Merry Christmas, and we love you. Wayne and Kevin

December 7, 2005

Hi, Wayne and Kevin,

Glad for your safe arrival and for some encouraging news. I'm also pleased to hear about the bronchoscopy. While this raises another issue, thankfully it will provide needed nourishment.

We continue to pray for the both of you and think of you more than once during the day. You have been an inspiration not only to me but to hundreds of people. Though you are paying a great price, God is using you to teach us many lessons that can only be learned the hard way. Hope to see you before Christmas! With our love and prayers, Jim

Dear Wayne and Kevin,

As always, I thank you for including Charlie and me on your update list. We continue to pray for you, as we have for five years. Our church is faithful in their remembrance of you both in prayer as well. I pray that the feeding tube placement ensures better nutrition, Kevin, and that you get stronger with each passing day. The news of the tumor kill is just wonderful! I hope you get to come home for Christmas, but as you said, home is where the heart is, and wherever we are with loved ones, we can celebrate God's goodness. Many wishes for a good trip at MDA and blessings to you both for a Christ-filled Christmas. Tiiu P.S. Happy Birthday, Kevin!

First, a very happy birthday to Kevin. Wayne, I can remember when you gave us the news that a baby was coming to your family. We gave you a baby shower in celebration of this wonderful baby boy to come, and now he has grown up to be a handsome young man, so talented and courageous. May God bless him and heal him. Thanks for writing to us and keeping us posted on all your doings. Hope to see you soon at church. Best wishes, Audrey

When Kevin was able to be home, he always asked about practicing with his group, Taking Up Arms. Often, I would load up several canisters of oxygen, his guitars, and his amps and head over to Charlie and Jim's house where the band would practice in the basement.

"Dad, Adam just called and the guys want to practice tomorrow afternoon," he would say.

"Great, Kevin, if you feel up to it. I'd be glad to take you over there," I would always say.

When we arrived, I would video the group using all types of special effects. Sometimes, after practice, they would load up and come over to Kevin's to watch their sessions. They especially enjoyed watching their live performances in front of an audience. Kevin would watch the tapes over and over.

December 9, 2005

Kevin,

Hey! I haven't ever left you a comment, so I thought I would. Ok, well, thanks a lot for giving me your pick at the show at Celebration Church. I'm sure you've heard this a million times, but I'm going to say it again. You and all the guys in TUA are simply amazing! I can't wait to see you and those boys play again. =) Stephanie

Chemotherapy and radiotherapy left Kevin with a low energy level. Another by-product was tumor necrosis factor (TNF), a condition where the patient loses his appetite due to the rate of tumor kill (necrosis), and the body resorts to nourishment from accumulated body fat. Kevin lost significant weight and rarely ate anything for almost three months. Dr. Anderson suggested the insertion of a feeding tube into his abdominal wall if he kept losing weight.

Kevin, without an appetite, candidly remarked, "Bring it on. I'm ready. I probably need it anyway."

I began feeding Kevin a nutrient called Isosource, using a bag and feeding pump. This initial eight-cans-per-day regimen usually took twelve hours to administer (day and night), but the additional daily three thousand calories soon improved his weight status. Several weeks prior to our flight, I would order the nutritional products and oxygen to have them ready upon our arrival. The pump, pole, and nutritional products had to be packed in luggage and carried with us to Houston each time. I usually took five large pieces of luggage with numerous medical supplies.

December 20, 2005

Kevin's Medical Update

Hi everyone.

We are looking forward to our return flight home on Friday (12/23). We have been in Houston since 11/30 (almost a month). Kevin has had numerous procedures this trip: upper GI, flexible and solid bronchoscopy, insertion of a feeding tube (G tube) in his stomach, three different chemotherapies, a radioactive injection, laser surgery on the left bronchus, and day/night feedings over the past two weeks. He also had a complete battery of tests. I sent some formula home via UPS earlier this week and bought an extra piece of luggage to bring his pole and fluid pump. His weight has fluctuated but has held steady around 137 pounds this week. Since he hardly eats anything, I will be feeding him using the pump at night and the gravity bags once or twice daily. He needs to put on at least twenty pounds before we return to Houston in February.

Overall, his cough has improved and even though his right lung blockage could not be opened yet, he is getting some air into it. His left lung was 10% blocked and that was taken care of using the laser. The therapies seem to have slowed the tumor growth (not as bright on PET scan), and that is good news. His doctor wants him strong for the new proton beam radiation therapy later in 2006. His doctor and I think we made progress this trip. He has suggested Kevin read a book which he requires all his medical students to read, *Anatomy Of An Illness* by Norman Cousins. It details the benefits of one's inner, positive mindset which is needed to successfully fight a life-threatening illness.

This Christmas is unlike any other. Although we missed out on the shopping, hustle and bustle of the usual holiday season, Kevin's continued progress has more than made up for anything wrapped with ribbons and bows. It is a truly special Christmas. May each of you have a great holiday season. You are special! Love, Wayne and Kevin

It is so good to hear from you and we pray for you daily. We should be encouraging you, yet I feel encouraged each time I hear from you. I hope you have a wonderful holiday, and I look forward to hearing from you again soon. Nancy

Very good to hear from you yesterday on the speakerphone! You sounded great, and I know that you're looking forward to getting back to Wilkes County. Yesterday at the meeting, the HS Gang and the Central Office Gang wanted to "chip" in on the money that Elem. Council collected last week. Therefore, I am adding an additional $305 to the previous amount. As you instructed, I'm putting the whole amount in the regular mail today. Best of luck and please come up to school to visit when things slow down. Merry Christmas and a Happy New Year! Jim

December 23, 2005

It is always good to hear an update on you and Kevin. I do think of you guys often and want you to know what a strong support group you have in your Wilkes County colleagues. They care about you deeply. My prayers continue to be that the Lord will stop this disease in its tracks and heal you and Kevin completely. If we believe, it can happen. May you both find time this Christmas season to laugh and enjoy the wonder. Love to you both, Kaye

Dear Wayne and Kevin,
I thought you'll probably have at least hundreds of e-mails on your computer, but I'll just add another. I know I haven't written lately, but you have been on my mind every day. Thank you so much for remembering us on the 12th. It's been particularly difficult for me this year. I know we also missed Kevin's birthday, so late Happy 19th, Kevin!! Those month long hospital stays are tough. I plan on calling you in a few days. Your messages are always so inspirational, Wayne. I hope your Christmas is everything you want it to be. Being home, with Kevin, is the greatest gift of all. Let Kathy know I think of her often, as well. I'll be in touch soon, and again, Merry, merry Christmas. Love, Terri & Steve

Kevin,
Can't wait for you to get back so we can play some shows. Adam

December 25, 2005

Kevin,
I think I saw your dad at Bojangles. I'm glad you're back home buddy.
Merry Christmas! Chelsea

CHAPTER 9

THE
M. D. ANDERSON
CONNECTION ... 2006

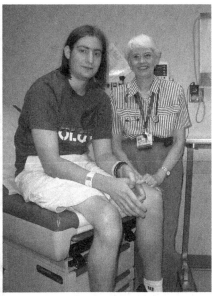

The dynamic duo from M. D. Anderson were Dr. Pete Anderson and his chief nurse
Peggy Pearson.
They became our family while in Houston. Together, they gave Kevin the best of care.
Pete's knowledge of cutting-edge osteosarcoma therapies and the Lord's grace gave Kevin
fifteen extra months with us. Like Kevin, we will always love Pete and Peggy.

A Duke Energy jet gave us a free, luxury flight to Houston on several occasions.
Other times, we flew commercial.

After winning the regional Battle of the Bands, Taking Up Arms presented Kevin with the trophy.
Jim, Charlie, Adam, and Joe honored him, even though Kevin was unable to attend the competition.

A favorite pastime of Kevin was sitting on the front porch at home watching the squirrels, birds, and neighborhood kids at play. He was content enjoying the simple things that life offered.

The cool, crisp air of autumn on the ACB patio in Houston was refreshing.

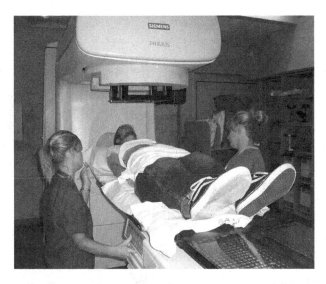

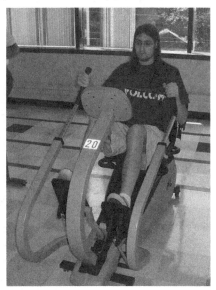

External beam radiation was a way of life for Kevin.

Ringing the victory bell was traditional as each series of radiation was finished. Kevin rang it many times. He holds the mask worn during his brain tumor radiation sessions.

Part of his pulmonary therapy at the Sticht Center included the NuStep machine.

Kevin loved his long hair, but it became difficult to manage during the later stages of his illness.
He made the sacrifice and donated thirteen inches of it to Locks of Love for cancer patient hairpieces. Katie Broyhill, Kevin's stylist his entire life, does the honors.

Kevin sometimes wore his four-wheeler helmet and rekindled memories of days gone by, when he would ride his Arctic Cat 250.

On one trip to Houston, we attended a service at Rev. Joel Osteen's Lakewood Church. Kevin presented Dr. Stephen Laws, superintendent of Wilkes County Schools and friend, a gift bag from this wonderful church.

Maurice Templeton, a cancer survivor, and his wife, Marsha, became good friends. Our neighbors in Millers Creek, North Carolina, we were often at M. D. Anderson at the same time.
Maurice partnered with the Make-A-Wish Foundation to help make Kevin's cruise to Alaska possible.

Kevin and I were honored to carry the banner for his last Relay for Life event in
August 2006.
Two cancer survivors, Kevin and me, supporting each other through thick and thin.
Just over three months later, Kevin would be moving to his heavenly home.

That if thou shalt confess with thy mouth
the Lord Jesus, and shalt believe in thine heart
that God hath raised him from the dead, thou shalt be saved.
Romans 10:9

Treatment at M. D. Anderson had been a lifesaver for Kevin. Dr. Anderson, upon first meeting Kevin, was amazed at his stamina and resilience given the years of cancer therapy he had endured. Ninety-nine days in 2006 would be spent in Houston. Although the trips meant staying four to six weeks each time in a hotel room, this was something Kevin knew he had to do. He was often exhausted, but he believed his treatments were making a difference.

"They have already helped me. As long as I'm improving, I want to keep going," said Kevin.

Kevin's cough was gradually getting worse. His right lung was blocked, but drainage from it continued to be a source of bacterial infection. My heart ached for him as he would cough for hours, even though I had given him suppressants. After several courses of potent antibiotics at MDA, his coughing subsided somewhat, but the infection still lingered.

We had our daily rituals. Every morning, Kevin took numerous medications. He also used the inhalants albuterol and Advair. He would visit the bathroom to brush his teeth; put on deodorant and rinse his mouth; let me get him dressed; get into the wheel chair; and I would load our M. D. Anderson bag with medicine and supplies, and head over to the clinic.

In the evenings, I again gave him medications; cleaned around his G-tube with hydrogen peroxide and disinfected it with ointment; hooked up a new bag and added multiple cans of formula to it on the pole; used a syringe to mix meds and/or chemo with rubber gloves; injected this into his G-tube; attached the tubing to his chest with tape; flushed it, and started the pump. It was our way of life.

I remember thinking, "No one, especially my Kevin, should have to endure this and live this way. Will it ever end?" I meant no harm. I wanted Kevin to get better and rid himself of the shackles which bound him. The answer to that question would come later this year. It would end, but not the way I wanted.

January 3, 2006

Hi Sandy,

We made it home from Houston late on 12/23. Being home was present enough after almost a month at MDA. I have been feeding Kevin eight cans of formula through his G-tube (about 3000 calories) daily. I use the pump at night for a 12 hour feeding and then finish up with 4 hours more through the day. It takes about 16 hours to complete this cycle every day. He is eating only a few bites daily, but this is somewhat normal considering all he has been through. He has what is called cachexin. This condition results when the body has battled a major illness for some time and is due in part to our progress with the tumor kill. The body basically uses fat and muscle and literally feeds on itself to keep going and repair damaged tissue. This hopefully will improve over time, as he gradually eats more. Unlike starvation, a patient has no sensation of being hungry, although the body is in great need of nourishment. His weight is still hovering around 137 pounds (not losing any at this time). This is why he must continue to get this supplementary formula indefinitely. He is also using two inhalers (Advair and albuterol) to improve his breathing.

He rarely leaves home, although I did take him to a movie over the holidays. We go to Baptist once a week to monitor his white blood count and platelet level. Plans call for our next trip to Houston in mid-February.

All things considered it is a manageable situation. Our main goal is getting his appetite turned around, gaining some weight, and resting up for his next Houston trip. Please keep in touch and I do miss you and everyone at MP. Have a great 2006 and you are welcome to visit anytime. Love, Wayne and Kevin

January 7, 2006

Hi Tom,

Kevin began experiencing intermittent sharp pains in his right rib cage area late Thursday (localized to mid-costal side region). This occurs only when he is moving or coughing, not when he is reclining or resting. I am giving him hydrocodone or morphine as directed. This pain may be due to his moving around a lot Thursday, or perhaps there may be some pulmonary fluid build up due to the TNF. He has no fever. Usually, he will vomit a little after the tube feeding during the day. I saw a small amount of what appeared to be blood yesterday. It may just be sinus drainage residue. I will continue to monitor this and if it becomes more intense, I will call health on call. I will bring him to the clinic Monday morning, unless you feel he needs immediate attention. Thanks, Wayne

Kevin's friends were concerned and meant well when they e-mailed or called him. They were totally unaware as to how serious his condition had become. Nonetheless, he loved hearing from them.

Usually, the first thing he did when he returned home was ask this question, "Did I get any mail today?" Early on, he received literally dozens of cards daily. I would stand them up in our breakfast nook area for weeks at a time. Holidays were especially plentiful.

Kevin and I would always prepare a special card to mail to our special friends. Sometimes, it would be a recent photo of Kevin. In 2005, Kevin and I posed before one of his concerts, and Crista took a photo of us, which turned out great, for the card.

In 2006, I ordered a special CD with Christmas music and had a special inscription added which read, "Have a Merry Musical Christmas. Celebrate the holidays with faith, friends, and family. Love, Wayne and Kevin." I ordered and mailed over one hundred of them.

January 10, 2006

Hey Kevo,
   I'm glad you're home and I do hope you start feeling like yourself again soon so you can start playing your music again. I missed you. Love ya, Kevo. Larisa

Kevin T!
   What's up? I haven't seen ya in a long time! How's the band doing? You should come to church cause everyone is wanting to see that darling Kevin's face! Lol ttyl! Meredith

Yo Kev,
   I haven't seen you or talked to you in forever it seems. I hope you're doing well. I'm praying for you. Joe

January 12, 2006

Hi Pete.
Hope you had a great holiday season!

	12/29/05	1/5/06	1/12/06
White Blood Count	2.60 L	12.20 H	8.60
Red Blood Count	3.25 L	3.23 L	3.15 L
Hemoglobin	10.10 L	10.30 L	9.90 L
Hematocrit	29.60 L	30.20 L	29.00 L
Mean Cell Volume	91.00	93.50	92.20
CV of MCV	17.00 H	18.20 H	20.40 H
Platelet Count	83 L	114 L	150 L
SEGS	83%	74%	60%
ANC	2,158	9,028	5,160
Weight	137 lbs.	140 lbs.	142 lbs.

Mean Cell Hemoglobin 31.60 H (1/12/06)
Mean Cell Hemo Conc 34.20 (1/12/06)

General Observations
    Although Kevin has gained five pounds, he still is eating only on occasion in very small amounts. I continue his night pump (5 cans) and day gravity drip (3 cans) feedings of Isosource 1.5 (8 cans = 3,000 calories daily). Typically, he has some nausea with most feedings (using kytril, zofran or ativan prior to feedings). He tires easily, but I am encouraging him to become more active (walking). He has developed a cough due to post-nasal drip, allergies, etc. He uses oxygen intermittently due to this cough. His oxygen level has been checking from 93 to 95% weekly. A check x-ray revealed stability with no fluid accumulation. I am continuing meds. as prescribed with occasional Delcym and Benadryl for cough.
Concerns
    His RBC and hemoglobin counts continue to dip. *Anatomy Of An Illness* by Norman Cousins (prescription filled at Barnes and Noble and in progress). Take care and thanks for all you are doing for Kevin.
Wayne

January 13, 2006

Thanks for the update. Nice to see improvement in counts and weight (~1 kg/week!). When do you see Dr. McLean next? Issues to discuss: a) use of inflixiMAB (anti-TNF antibody) as means to reduce reason for Kevin's cachexia. Same dose as for arthritis (5 mg/kg), b) means to increase bowel motility to make feedings more comfortable: low dose erythromycin vs metoclopromide. c) Cough and "post nasal drip"-symptomatic control (pseudofed) Pete

The following e-mail from Tom really caused me much concern, until I read Pete's follow-up to it. Our network of specialists hashed out many problems.

Wayne,

First, you should know that Kevin's CXR from 1/9/06 shows what appears to be disease progression. I will paste the report below. I did not know this until I just looked it up. I have not yet seen it myself but will do that soon. Kevin's tumor has always been slow growing, and I think that continues to be the case, but this is obviously a bit concerning. It seems that it may now be growing again after shrinking some after the Houston therapy. As to Dr. Anderson's recommendations, I don't have a lot of experience with infliximab or erythromycin for the indications mentioned. I would be willing to try them, but I don't want to do more harm than good. I will call you after I've reviewed his CXR with a radiologist. We can discuss the other things then. As always, feel free to call me anytime. Tom

Chest x-ray is a relatively inaccurate means to assess a mass like Kevin's, but thanks for the heads up and sharing your concerns. Unless Kevin has more symptoms, we will wait until his next PET CT and compare. If he has more symptoms, he should see Dr. Evans sooner. If feeling full from the feeds is the biggest QOL concern, then the low dose erythromycin to promote gut motility may be helpful. Pete

Well wishes and prayers kept coming our way, as well as ideas for additional therapies. Soon, we would discover a different kind of therapy, hands-on holistic medicine. A woman from across the country, a doctor well versed in hands-on healing, was in the area and agreed to see Kevin. She moved her hands up and down his body with him sitting in his wheel chair for almost thirty minutes. He seemed to feel better afterward. Even Tom participated in a healing session.

Afterward, and with the advice of our good friend Ken, we did several sessions at home and in Boone with a more regional healer. These sessions were relaxation sessions with Kevin lying down, while soft, healing musical chants played in the background. Each of us received a crystal, which we wore as a necklace around our necks. I ended up hanging one from each of Kevin's bed posts.

January 16, 2006

I prayed for you and Kevin this morning. I will be praying that he will start eating some. How is his energy level? Is he able to have company? Do you need anything? Please let us know if you do! Tell Kevin that I love him, and I'm praying for him. In Christ, Craig

January 17, 2006

I hope Kevin is feeling well. Would you be so kind as to e-mail me a list of the complementary and alternative therapies you are giving Kevin (past and present)? I am working on a paper relevant to this topic, and I would appreciate reading the list, so I can learn some more about them. Thanks, Tom

January 21, 2006

Ken,

Thanks for the great information on Immune FX. I ordered two bottles of the capsules from Team Drugs in Canada this morning. In addition, I will share this information with Kevin's oncologist at Baptist this week. I am including the website for Sloan-Kettering's (NY) review of herbal/alternative cancer therapies. Take it for what it's worth. Many thanks, Wayne

January 23, 2006

Hi Tom.

Based on talking with my landscaper, who is an avid devotee to alternative medicines and quite well-versed on the subject, I have ordered two mushroom products from Canada. I plan to start Kevin on them when they arrive later this week. The special blend in the Immune FX contains possible anti-cancer components while the Recovery product doubles as an anti-inflammatory (anti-TNF type) supplement. I added both products and their websites to Kevin's Herbal Profile for you. Looking forward to Wed. afternoon, and thanks for hooking Kevin up. Wayne

February 4, 2006

Here is the contact info for Deborah Larrimore, who practices healing touch here in W-S. I personally know her and she is a delightful person. I can also get you Boyd Bailey's contact info, if you want to talk to him about acupuncture. Kathy and I talked a bit more about Kevin. Two other suggestions for you to consider: Coenzyme Q10 (CoQ10) is purported to help the heart (probably would do no harm), and tumeric (curcumin) is sometimes touted as a radiosensitizer (very little data, mostly in the lab only, but you might consider it when he gets radiation (proton beam) therapy again). Hope Kevin is feeling well. Keep in touch. Best regards, Tom

February 13, 2006

Hi Pete.
Hope you are well.
Please note Kevin's recent blood work results:

	1/18/06	1/25/06	2/2/06	2/9/06
WBC	7.3	8.4	8.2	7.5
RBC	3.28	3.16	3.09	3.28
Hemo	10.2	9.6	9.7	9.9
Hematocrit	29.8	28.7	27.5	28.7
MCV	90.9	91.0	88.9	87.7
CV of MCV	20.7	21.9	21.2	20.9
Platelets	244	294	333	339
SEGS	77%	37%	82%	80%
ANC	5,621	3,108	6,724	6,000
Weight	142	146	149	152

<u>General Observations</u>

Kevin has gained a whopping 15 pounds! This is due primarily to the 3 K/day caloric Isosource product via the G-tube. He does eat on occasion very small amounts (favorite popsicles). Minimal nausea with feedings. Declined infliximib. Increased oxygen use (he says it helps him breathe easier and cough less). He may have a slight G-tube infection (some pus). Treating it with low dose augmentin presently. Tube may need to be dialed out a bit. Dr. Eapen requested a consult on this return visit (may be one in the same with Dr. Evans consult). Kevin's persistent cough is the main issue we are dealing with currently. Cardiologist checkup today (2/13/06) revealed increased CHF due to previously diagnosed cardiomyopathy (adriamycin 00/01) and possible mediastinal tumor issues. I asked Dr. Covitz to fax the cardiology report to you He prescribed a diuretic (lasix/furosemide) to dissipate possible fluid retention, which I plan to start tomorrow if you are in agreement. I've ordered Isosource and oxygen products for our stay at the Rotary House.

We are due in clinic on Monday morning (2/20/06), and we will fly in on the 19th. We had several inches of snow here this weekend. Looking forward to skipping the remainder of winter with an early spring in Houston. Take care, Wayne

Thanks for your excellent organizational skills and for keeping me in the loop. Tom

February 27, 2006

Kevin's Medical Update

Hi everyone.

Sometimes it is impossible to go around or jump over an obstacle in our way. Sometimes, as in Kevin's case, you have to go through it. We arrived in Houston at MDA on Sunday, February 19 to begin our fourth treatment session here. We almost feel like honorary Texans! Since late August '05, we have logged over 60 days here. Kevin's first week has been spent with numerous tests and scans (bone scan, PET scan, EKG, Echocardiogram, flexible bronchoscopy, blood work). We received mostly positive news from these tests but some "mixed reviews" as well. The tumor in Kevin's head is no longer there or visible on bone/PET scan!

The tumor in his chest is smaller (less active) and the site in his left shoulder is stable and perhaps a bit smaller. We are so thankful for this great news! On the down side, three new, small tumors were located on bone scan (left and right hips, L1 vertebrae in his mid-spine). These are treatable and we will be pursuing radiation on two of those new sites as well as our fourth course of high dose metho-trexate, samarium-153, gemcitabine, and avastin. This approach was pioneered by Kevin's doctor, Dr. Pete Anderson, while he was at the Mayo Clinic. Now, he has brought his expertise to MDA. Dr. Anderson has shown that radiation and chemotherapy together are capable of delivering a one-two punch to osteosarcoma. Conventional thinking prior to his research had shunned the positive effects of radiation on osteo tumors. Also, Kevin's heart function has decreased since August, and he is suffering from some degree of CHF (congestive heart fail-ure). We are looking at several drugs that may turn this around and strengthen his heart.

Kevin will be having two weeks of radiation and chemotherapy which began today. We hope to leave for home late on March 10 and are due back in Houston on April 23. In addition, Kevin is trying several nasal sprays and medications to get a handle on his inces-sant cough which typically comes and goes around the clock. Dr. Anderson has also prescribed two additional cancer fighting agents available orally when we get home.

We have been in clinic most days from 7:30 AM until 5:00 PM. One night, when he received two units of red blood cells, we left the hos-pital at 1:00 AM for our room. He has gained about 14 pounds due to my feeding him 12 hours daily through his stomach peg or G-tube. He has not eaten a regular meal since October, but this tube placed in December has turned his weight around.

We have been spending our time watching American Idol and the Winter Olympics. I bought a deck of cards from the gift shop. As you know, you play the hand you are dealt. It is remarkable the posi-tive attitude he maintains even after almost six years of therapies. His Christian rock band, Taking Up Arms, recorded a demo CD before we left for Texas, but Kevin was too weak to play.

As Kevin said, "Sometimes I have to make adjustments. I can't play right now, but I want the band to go on, even without me."

It is painful seeing him struggle 24/7 usually from the bed to the wheelchair.

Last week he remarked, "I move like an old man."

He knows that if I could take his pain and suffering away and take it in my body, I would gladly do so.

One night this week, just before going to sleep, he whispered, "Maybe by the time I am 22, this will all be behind me, and I can get back to doing some things I enjoy."

In the quiet of that moment I couldn't help but reply, "Knowing you Kevin, I think I would revise that to age 21 or even 20."

We love and miss you. Wayne, Kathy, and Kevin

Wayne and Kevin,
It was good to hear from you and to hear some positive news. Just hang in there, and lean on our wonderful Father above and remember, you have lots of people who are lifting your names up daily. If we can do anything from North Carolina, just let us know, and we will try and get it done. Love and God's Blessings, Roy and Geraldine

Dear Kevin and Wayne,
It is nice to hear from you guys. I have been praying for you a lot. I am ecstatic to hear about the tumors disappearing and shrinking. Thank you for updating us. I often want to write or call, but I never know whether I should. I have a new cell phone number, so if you should ever feel like talking, you can call. I would love to hear from you again. I will continue to keep you in all of my prayers. Love, Crista

Dear Wayne,
It had been a while since I had heard from you and I have been wondering how things were going. I wish there was something more I could do for you and Kevin in addition to the prayers. I was wondering if Kevin had been given a prayer shawl by anyone? If not, I will ask my mother to make one for him, and I will buy the yarn. She lives in Greensboro, is 78 years old, and is a member of her church's ladies' circle. They crochet and knit shawls and pray a special prayer over them before wrapping them and delivering them to folks like Kevin. They are very soft and comforting (and warm). A copy of the prayer is included with the shawl.

I will remind my Sunday School class, friends and relatives to pray for you two. Remind Kevin that we are pulling for him and love him.

I just called my Mom and she said she would be happy to get a shawl from the group for Kevin if she has not finished the one she is working on by March 10. We are scheduled to go to Greensboro that weekend for a visit, and I can bring it back. I will buy yarn for the group to make another shawl for someone else. Bye for now! Jhonda

I'm so glad to hear from you. I think about you often. Kevin, you are an inspiration to so many people. Keep your positive attitude, and God will help you through this. Love, Christy

It is always good to hear from you guys (even if the news is not always positive). Things do sound promising for Kevin. Mom has kept me up on the latest, and now, I hope with my new e-mail address, you will continue to keep me posted. I am pleased that Kevin's band is in the recording studio. That is very exciting! Tell Kevin that I believe he will be there recording with them very soon. With every new obstacle, Kevin seems to become stronger and face it head on. He is remarkable! Most would give up without a fight or at the very least have a negative attitude. He is lucky to have you and you him. I wish there was something I could do to help. Prayer seems to be working though, and I will continue to do that for you both. It sounds like you have found an excellent doctor, and I do pray that these treatments will continue to bring positive results. Take care of each other, and one day Kevin, you will be 20, 21, 22, and not an "old man." Love you, Denise

Dear Wayne and Kevin,
Words can't express what my heart is feeling. I love you guys so much! You both are such an inspiration to me and a lot of people. I am pray-ing for you as I write. Please know that we are here for you. If there is anything I can do, please let me know. As Paul said to the Colossians, I am absent in the flesh but with you in the Spirit. Wayne, please let Kevin know how much we love him and how much we are praying for him. When we don't see a way, and we don't know what to do, "we simply have to trust." I don't have any answers. I can't tell you I know what you are going through, so all I can lean on is the Lord. Proverbs 3:5–6 says "Trust in the Lord with all your heart, lean not on your own understanding, in all your ways acknowledge Him and He will direct your path." If the Lord has taught me anything over the

last several months, it is that I can't figure out everything, and God's
ways are not my ways. I must Trust and Obey (easier said than done).
I pray that you and Kevin will look to the Lord for your strength. (He
is all we have and all that we could hope for and all we need).
Praying, Craig

Dr. Anderson was not only concerned about fighting Kevin's cancer, he also
strived to give him a better quality of life (QOL). With a vast network of cancer
professionals at MDA, he often enlisted the help of doctors in various depart-
ments. Dr. Scott Evans and Dr. Michael Ewer soon came on board to offer their
expertise.

February 28, 2006

Dr. Ewer,
Thank you for consulting regarding Kevin. His complicated history
is enclosed. Basically, his heart function was ok (EF 45–50%) at the
end of August despite prior cardiomyopathy Now, EF is in decline
(30–35%) and possibly responsible for lack of energy. [I also have
a brief fax from his Peds cardiologist in NC, Wesley Covitz at Wake
Forest, no effect of lasix, no other options offered]. So, it's up to us
to improve things! Please call me when you see Kevin. I'm very interested in improving his QOL. Thanks! Pete

March 1, 2006

Wayne, thank you for the update. Please know that we continue praying for Kevin and for you. Nothing is impossible with God, as you
guys know. Both of you are courageous and brave souls and a witness
to all of us, teaching us many lessons through your life. Praying the
best for you! Jim

Thank you for the update on Kevin. My thoughts and prayers are
with all of you. I am hoping that the proton radiation will help get rid
of this horrible cancer or at least help Kevin have a better quality of
life. He has fought for so long. I hope that if I am ever afflicted with
any life-threatening disease that I have half of his courage. He's my
hero. Love to all. Sharon

Wayne & Kevin,

Thank you for keeping us updated. We have been remembering you in prayer at Goshen, and I'm sure people all over the entire region are praying for you as well.

You are an inspiration to all who know you. I know that one day, when we all stand before our Lord, that you two guys are going to be in for some glorious, eternal rewards. Thanks for being such a blessing to all who know you on this side of eternity. God bless and keep you is our prayer. Charlie & Tiiu

Restrictions on new drug usage was still a problem. If one drug could not be secured, we would move on to another more promising one. I had supreme confidence that Dr. Anderson was providing Kevin with the best of care. He always found a way.

March 14, 2006

Hi Pete.

I submitted your prescription for tarceva to our major medical Caremark Specialty Pharmacy and they denied filling it based on their info that the FDA had not approved this drug for osteosarcoma. All is not lost. I finally reached someone in SD who handles these situations and I think all they need from you is as follows:
Patient Name: Kevin Triplett (TRIKE86)
DOB: 12-7-86
A short paragraph titled: Caremark Appeals, Letter of Medical Necessity

Simply clarify what previous therapy(s) Kevin has had and why tarceva is now recommended for him. Supply your office contact number in the event they have questions. This letter should be faxed to Caremark Appeals. Your original prescription detailed, tarceva, 25mg, 4 tabs daily, 120 quantity, 12 refills. I have already faxed a letter I composed on Kevin's behalf to Caremark. Again, bureaucracy seems to thwart the good that we (you) seek to do, but we will prevail.

Kevin is coughing less, and he received Neulasta today. His counts are low (WBC … 1.9, Hb … 8.7, PLT … 76K), and he may receive RBC and/or platelets if needed on Friday along with the avastin. Dr. McLean stated today that if you preferred, he would pursue getting tarceva for Kevin. He would have to do another prescription, though. Take care, Wayne

March 18, 2006

I appreciate you, Wayne. It is really hard, but you just know they are in the Master's presence. You are a great friend. I want you to know that we all think about you guys a lot. We are still praying. I heard Joel Osteen say last night, "Quit worrying and being stressed out, and just let the Lord have it. He is in control." He is in control of everything and will take care of us. I guess we need to realize that things will be his will. I appreciate you and Kevin. If you need anything, please let me know. Eric

March 28, 2006

Hi Pete,

Kevin began experiencing intermittent pain in his right side this weekend along with a low-grade fever. Dr. McLean prescribed azithromycin (Z-Pac) and oxycodone HCL (10 mg every 12 hours). His chest x-rays (see attachments) reveal less aeration in his right lung than before.

Two explanations seem possible to explain this atelectasis: tumor progression or TNF. The pain corresponds to the time intervals of Kevin's previous courses where TNF was prominent. As you mentioned earlier, typically symptoms become more pronounced initially after treatment. Since the viable tumor area has continued to atrophy, it would seem plausible that the increased swelling (inflammation) could be localized in the bronchus area leading to temporary oxygen restriction. I talked with Dr. Evans briefly today regarding this.

Otherwise, Kevin is doing well and has been coughing less (until recently). We have used some inhaled lidocaine successfully. No word yet on the approval of the tarceva. We are scheduled for avastin tomorrow (3/29). Your thoughts are welcome. Thanks, Wayne.

April 2, 2006

Hi Pete.

I received word Friday that our appeal for tarceva was declined. Please consider the following options. You may call the Caremark physician appeal department as a final persuasive measure. I can try to procure tarceva through my insurance company using this same procedure (no guarantees on approval). We could abandon tarceva and opt for the vinorelbine/oral cyclophosphamide protocol.

Questions: VNR, iv dose escalation approach (15, 20, 25, 30 mg/m)? CTX, oral tablets (25 or 50 mg dosage)? Kevin had two courses of CTX along with topotecan in 2001. Should Dr. McLean manage VNR? Should pioglitazone (which I already have at a minimal cost) be used along with the above new protocol? Kevin's platelets were at 52K on 3/31/06. Another CBC is set for 4/3/06. We are due back at MDA in clinic on 4/24/06 (3 weeks). Thanks, Wayne

I would abandon the Tarceva. I saw info at AACR (meeting I am at) that this medicine can also down-regulate T-cell function, too. Once platelets have recovered to >150,000, let's talk again and plan to start the Vinorelbine/cyclophos. In order to avoid the thrombocytopenia, I would use the 15-25-30 dose and cyclophos at 50 mg daily. If platelets drop <100,000, then stop cyclophos x 1 week and resume at 25 mg if >100,000. Dr. McLean can do. Pete

Pastor Craig kept in constant touch with us via e-mail, while we were in Houston and at home. He looked forward to those special times when he could come by for a visit with Kevin. Often, I would excuse myself, so they could visit and get into the Word of God. Those were truly special times for both of them.

April 4, 2006

Wayne,

Can I come and visit? Is Kevin's strength up for a visit? I have tried to be sensitive and let Kevin regain some strength. So, let me know if I can come. I will be doing some hospital visits. It has been crazy around here. Know that I love you both and pray daily for you. In Christ, Rev. Craig Church

Hi Craig.

You can come over anytime to see Kevin. He usually gets up around 12 noon. Give me a call and let me know which day is best for you. We may go to Baptist Thursday morning for blood work. Thanks, Wayne

I was always on the lookout for special, novelty gifts for Kevin's doctors. Once, I ordered special neckties online. Tom's tie had doctors' office sayings on it, while Pete's was a depiction of the DNA molecule. Kevin and I presented these to them.

April 14, 2006

Thank you for the necktie. That was a thoughtful gift, and I look forward to wearing it. I hope everything went well yesterday. I'm sorry I got called away and wasn't able to catch up with you again before you left. I checked the papers Pete sent us previously. The vinorelbine should be on days 1, 8, and 15, so we will plan on giving him another dose of venorelbine (15 mg/m2, assuming he does OK this week) next Thursday (4/20/06) along with Avastin. The day 15 dose can be given in Houston. Keep in touch. Best regards, Tom

April 26, 2006

Hi Sandy,

We have been in Houston almost a week, and Kevin is still undergoing tests. I will update you further next week.

I do know that the bone tumor sites (large chest tumor, left and right hip tumors, mid-spine, shoulder, and head tumor) appear to be necrotic (dead) and no longer producing viable tumor cells. That is great news!

There are two new areas of concern. His left (good) lung has a small tumor in the lower lobe and his right lung (currently nonfunctioning) has additional diseased areas at two locations.

We see a pulmonologist Friday and a radiologist Monday. I feel he will have two weeks of radiation on the right lung and probably just monitor the left lung site. He currently is not receiving chemo.

Kevin is feeling better and eating some now (weighs 153 pounds). He has not used his oxygen for several days, and his coughing is less. Overall, we are still making progress, two steps forward and one step back.

The proton beam therapy will not be ready here until August at the earliest. If they suggest it, I am willing to fly him to California or Boston to receive that therapy now. We may get back home by mid-May. Take care and keep in touch. Love, Wayne and Kevin.

May 6, 2006

Kevin's Medical Update

Hi everyone,

Fighting bone cancer is much like fighting the recent woods fires in Wilkes County. You put out one fire, and sometimes another one develops, but you keep pressing on.

After two weeks in Houston, Kevin has concluded most of his major tests and scans. The two tumors that were "lethal" (head and chest) appear to be dead (necrotic)! We thank God and all those who have been praying for Kevin for this great news! The bone tumors in his shoulder, head, both hips, spine, and mid-chest appear no longer to be life-threatening.

Kevin's left (good) lung, however, has developed a small tumor in the lower left lobe. Dr. Anderson will monitor this area and perhaps when we return to Houston in late July or early August, that tumor will undergo proton beam therapy or radiofrequency ablation (burn it). His right lung has also developed additional disease in the central and posterior regions. This lung will probably not be functional, but radiation should take care of the additional tumor areas.

Kevin had a great week last week (his best since October, eating, walking around, off oxygen). Wednesday, after his bronchoscopy, he developed chills, a very high fever and nausea. After a chest x-ray, doctors determined he had developed pneumonia and/or a bacterial infection in his right (nonfunctional) lung. He has been in the hospital since then, but he should be released today or Sunday.

This has put us behind schedule, but we plan to start two weeks (10 days) of radiation Monday on his right lung. Also, he will be getting chemo which will take almost three weeks. He will be getting chemo two weeks on and two weeks off in June and July once we return home. We should be home May 25 or 26 if there are no additional setbacks.

While I'm hesitant to proclaim Mission Accomplished, I will venture to say Mission NOT Impossible! We are making progress. The challenge is to continue to closely monitor Kevin's progress and alleviate any recurring tumors (put out those brush fires) before they get out of hand. Your continued prayers and support make all the difference.

"So many things are possible just as long as you don't know they're impossible."
-Norton Juster
Love, Wayne and Kevin

This latest medical update ignited a flurry of well wishes from friends everywhere. Seemingly, everyone was rejoicing with us! God was in the business of answering prayers!

Hallelujah! Amen! Praise God! God is good! I am delighted to hear your news. "Way to go Kevin" for being such a fighter and "way to go Wayne" for not ever giving in or giving up! You guys are two of the strongest I am proud to know! Thanks for the update and I will "still be praying for you always!" There are better days ahead for you both! God bless! Denise

May 7, 2006

Wayne and Kevin,
Thanks so much for the update. Even though I have retired, Becky and I remember you all often, talk about you, your courage, your determination, your faith, your persistence. We pray for you and have been blessed on this rainy Sunday as we prepare for church. Thanks for keeping us on your mailing list. If ever I can do anything other than pray, please let me know. Love, Jim and Becky

I don't even know what to say. Congratulations, happy to hear your good news, blessings and praise, none of them seem enough, when I read of the improvement Kevin has made. This is just fantastic news, even if coupled with some small setbacks. I have no doubt that when everything is behind you and Kevin, and everyone is completely healed and well, you are going to be millionaires with your best selling inspirational books and movies.
Please know that you and your family are always in our thoughts. I've been wondering about you, since I haven't received an update in awhile and was so happy to hear positive news this morning. Keep in touch, Laura

I have been keeping up with you guys since you left Mt. Pleasant. I knew, from the first time I met with you in your office, that you were experiencing life different from most. You just had a compassion when I explained Noah's medical condition and our family life, that was evident. Since then, Noah and I have been praying together nightly for you and Kevin. We will continue to pray. Thank you for the updates you send. My co-worker, Lisa, shares them with me. I never had any peace about Noah until the doctors finally told us that prayer was all we had. Please know that we will continue to pray. Take good care of yourself, too. God bless you and keep you safe. Tina

Wayne & Kevin,

Thanks for updating us on Kevin's progress. Yes, we thank God for those miracles that He sends on His timetable. We will continue to pray for miracles for both of you and hope you will be back in Wilkes very soon. Love you both, Vernon and Brenda

May 13, 2006

Kevin's Thank-You Note to Tyson Foods

Hi everyone.

I have been at M. D. Anderson Cancer Center in Houston, TX since April 23 (three weeks). This is my fifth trip out here. My bone scans look really good, but I am receiving radiation and chemotherapy for new tumor areas in my right and left lungs. I had pneumonia and a staph blood infection last week and spent six days in the hospital. That has gotten me a little behind in my treatment schedule. I hope to be home at least by the end of May.

On behalf of my dad and mom, I want to thank you for all you have done for me over the years. I have had bone cancer over six years, and you have been there for me with your prayers and financial support. That means a lot to me, and I (we) will always appreciate the great Tyson family!

M. D. Anderson (the greatest cancer facility in the world) has given me new hope for recovery. You may remember that last July, I was given only a few weeks or a month to live. I believe that someday a cure for cancer will be found. Until then, generous people like you make the load a lot lighter. You are special. May God bless each of you! Keep pounding! Love, Kevin Triplett

May 15, 2006

Hello Wayne and Kevin,

I was so excited to hear from you. I have wondered how Kevin is doing and have asked Helen every time I speak with her if she has heard from you. I am sorry that more tumors were found, but it's great that they are no longer life threatening. I know you and Kevin will be glad to return home soon. Wilkes County awaits you with open arms.

Where will Kevin go to receive his chemo? I hope that Kevin is recovering from his pneumonia OK and becoming stronger everyday.

I pray daily for you and Kevin, and I know that God will watch over you and keep you safe. I have a book that I want you to read when you get back to Wilkes, *The Anatomy of Hope: How People Prevail in the Face of Illness* by Jerome Groopman M.D. This is a great book and you realize how important faith and hope are to the healing process and to sustain life. May God be close to you always. Donna

Mt. Pleasant School's memory book dedication proceeded in the absence of Kevin and me. We had planned to attend, but Kevin's therapy schedule dictated that we remain in Houston. In our absence, Kevin's mother and grandparents accepted the award and my special message was read in our absence.

May 18, 2006

A Special Message from Wayne Triplett

Dear Mt. Pleasant Faculty, Staff, and Students,

Thank you so much for honoring Kevin and me with this 2006 Memory Book dedication! It is truly a most precious honor. Some of our family members did make it and I appreciate them being here.

Kevin and I wanted to be with you, but we have been in Houston, Texas, for almost five weeks on this our fifth trip to M. D. Anderson, the greatest cancer treatment center in the world. In fact, at this very moment, Kevin is receiving a chest scan.

Last spring, I was diagnosed with prostate cancer and had cancer surgery in June. The worst news came last July when Kevin, after battling bone cancer over five years, was told by doctors that he had only weeks or a month to live. My research led us to M. D. Anderson, and

I'm happy to report that over nine months later, Kevin is still fighting and is making progress! He will continue receiving cancer treatments at Wake Forest and in Houston.

We plan to fly home Saturday, May 27. Believe me, our hotel room seems really small after almost five weeks of living there. I cherish the great memories of Mt. Pleasant, the morning "musical" announcements, the students lunching with the principal and especially the great time Kevin and I had last year at the talent show. You will always be the greatest school, anywhere! I truly miss the many great friends I made here. Your support has really lifted our spirits, and we thank you for being there for us. Always be proud that you are part of this great community and a school filled with caring students and a wonderful staff. Always be proud that you remain close to Kevin and me, even though at times we are far away. Thank you again for this great honor. We love you very much. Wayne and Kevin Triplett

May 25, 2006

Tom,
Doing better. Done with RT+TMZ; port replacement today and home Saturday. Suggested TMZ+irinotecan in ~2 weeks. Wayne will call. We will see him in early August. If stable or better, consider 6 cycles L9NC +TMZ if PFT>50%. If new lesions or progression of bone scan to PET+ in L shoulder, then RT to this one. Kevin seems to be doing better now that we no longer worry about harming the R lung and have provided definitive RX to residual disease there. Pete

Kevin,
Hey man, I hope you're feeling well. Jesus and me love you. Gwyn

Kevin,
What's up man? I hope everything is going well for you. I haven't seen you in a long time. I need to make a visit up your way soon. I've been thinking about doing that for quite some time, but I just haven't made it. Oh well, once again, I hope things are going well, and I hope to see you soon. Take care my friend. I'll talk to you later. Jordan

June 5, 2006

Kevin!

I miss you, man. It seems like forever, since I've even talked to you. Well, I hope everything's going alright. I'll see you soon. Joe

After returning home, Kevin began intensive pulmonary rehabilitation at Wake Forest's Sticht Center, along with additional chemotherapy. The daily walking with close monitoring, stretching exercises, and cardio-machine workouts boosted his energy level.

June 7, 2006

Hi Tom.

I have purchased the temozolomide from my local pharmacy and will bring Monday's dose with me when we come on June 12. I also have emend anti-nausea medication and the loperamide for diarrhea. Kevin has pulmonary therapy at the Sticht Center on M/W/F at 10 a.m., and we will be in the clinic M–F each day by 11:30 AM. The irinotecan dose as prescribed on Dr. Anderson's calendar is 10 mg/M2/dose = 18 mg daily x 5 x 2 weeks. I will get his CBC and electrolyte counts done locally tomorrow (6/8) and bring that info with us. Kevin is becoming more mobile, is eating more, and generally seems to be progressing very positively. Thanks for pulling all of this together. Wayne

July 5, 2006

Hi Tom,

Hope you had a great July 4th! Kevin is doing well, eating more, and continuing to enjoy his pulmonary/cardiac therapy at the Sticht Center. As a reminder, his upcoming chemo regimen at WFUBMC is as follows: July 10–July 14 ... oral temozolomide and irinotecan (TMZ/I); July 17–July 21 ... irinotecan July 22 or July 24 ... Neulasta?

These will be afternoon or mid-day short stay hospital administrations (session 1 ... Monday at 11:30 AM). I will update the schedule when we arrive in short stay Monday. I assume the TMZ will be administered there through your pharmacy. I'll bring some in case we need it. I will get Kevin's CBC locally today and fax that to you. Thanks for all you do for us! You're great! Wayne

Chest CT scans and x-rays were commonplace in monitoring Kevin's cancer. The July report noted additional areas of concern.

Kevin had received a portable chest catheter (Port-A-Cath) in 2000, when he began chemotherapy. This device made infusion of chemotherapy agents less risky and easier to administer. This port was removed several years later when his need for chemotherapy seemed remote. As his cancer kept recurring, a new chest port was implanted in the same general area. This port functioned for several years but became nonfunctioning when the growing pulmonary tumors disoriented it. With little space to work within his chest cavity, Kevin's third port was placed in his lower abdominal region, free from the confines of the tumors.

July 10, 2006

PA AND LATERAL CHEST

FINDINGS: The right lung remains virtually completely opacified with shift of the mediastinum to the right secondary to obstructive process related to large calcified right lung mass. This is consistent with previously identified osteosarcoma. The left lung is mildly hyper-expanded. Examination of the left lower lung field reveals a nodular opacity approximately 1 cm in diameter in the anterior area of the left sixth rib. This area overlies a vessel, and the opacity is not clearly visualized on the lateral view. However, a metastatic process cannot be excluded and careful follow-up is recommended. The placement of a new Port-A-Cath using an inferior approach is identified with termination in the right atrium in the expected position. The previously seen superiorly placed Port-A-Cath has been removed. The bony skeleton appears intact with no significant evidence of meta-static infiltration of skeletal structures. Midline sternotomy wires are again visualized.

CONCLUSION: 1. Persistence of right lung obstructive process and calcified mass consistent with osteosarcoma. 2. Question of new pulmonary nodule in the region of the left lung base as described above. Recommend close follow-up.

July 16, 2006

Hi Pete.

Kevin has made great progress over the past two months. He is eating more; consequently, I have stopped the day feedings (3 cans) and only use the pump at night (5 cans). His weight currently is around 157 pounds. His pulmonary rehab (3 days/week) has given him added stamina and his heart rate has continued to lower as his conditioning improves (May 06—-135-154 bpm., July 06—-118-152 bpm).

His chest x-ray (7/10/06) seems to reveal stability in the solitary osteo nodule in the lower left lung. I will send the x-rays to you in my follow-up e-mail. Kevin has completed the June chemo regimen (temozolomide and irinotecan) and is beginning week two of the July regimen. He has tolerated this routine well.

We are scheduled to fly to MDA on August 6 with our first clinic visit on Monday, August 7. There is currently no data for this on Kevin's MDA calendar. As your team schedules his first week of scans and tests, I assume Dr. Evans, Dr. Shannon, and perhaps Dr. Woo would desire a consult. Please, no upper GI, (Kevin's request … lol). Dr. McLean has been taking good care of him. I continue to be encouraged with the progress Kevin is making, and we look forward to seeing you in early August. Wishing you the best, Wayne and Kevin

Thanks much for the update. Maritza and Peggy will get the schedule worked out with you. Since temozolomide + irinotecan seems so tolerable, it will be interesting to see if Kevin can qualify for something similar, the L9NC protocol. Pete

Sorry it took me so long to get you these images. The radiologist does in fact see a small nodule on the left (I assume this is the same one seen on CT scan). I will paste the report below. I'm sure Pete will be interested in seeing this. Let me know if you want me send it to him; otherwise, I'll assume you will. I hope Kevin's irinotecan and TMZ are going well. Feel free to come by clinic, call, or e-mail any time. Best regards, Tom

July 20, 2006

Hi Peggy,

I have a flight booked and a room reserved at the Rotary House beginning August 6 anticipating an August 7 clinic visit. I have not seen any scheduled appointments posted on the web site for Kevin yet (Dr. Anderson, Dr. Evans ... flex bronch, Dr. Shannon, Dr. Woo, PET, bone scan, etc.). If you would look into this, I would appreciate it. I want to be sure we are on the same page with our upcoming visit. Thanks for all you do and we are looking forward to seeing you soon.
Wayne

My concern over Kevin's continued bronchial complications prompted me to consult with Pete and Dr. Scott Evans. Dr. Evans, like Pete, was extremely knowledgeable in his area of expertise, pulmonary medicine. He took great care in explaining all procedures and findings to us and performed numerous flexible and rigid bronchoscopies on Kevin. Clearly, Kevin's progress was being impeded by this infection. Kevin was beginning to voice that he was not feeling well, so I knew it was serious.

August 13, 2006

Dr. Evans,

Kevin continues to spike a fever at night (100.3, 100.9 ... last two nights respectively). His phlegm production (clear to tan) continues (day and night) and he has frequent nausea. His antibiotic courses of doxycycline and ciprofloxin (in progress) seem to have limited efficacy. Given this six-week long bronchial condition with accompanying foul breath, would a mucus (phlegm) culture be in order or even some hospitalization with more potent iv antibiotics to perhaps put this bug(s) to rest? He has electron beam radiation (5 sessions) this week and we remain at your disposal for a follow-up clinic visit. Thanks for all that you do. Wayne

August 15, 2006

Hi Pete and Scott,

Kevin continues to spike a fever this evening (Mon ... 100.6, Tues ... 100.3). Using his words, "I don't feel good." The tan colored, odorous phlegm production continues, and I just don't think he is responding that well to the two oral antibiotics.

For your consideration, I think a course of more potent iv administered antibiotics over several days would be beneficial. As he says, "I would gladly go to the hospital or day clinic to feel better." He had some chills this evening and this bacterium seems be a difficult hurtle for him to get over. I have tentatively booked a flight home Sat., but I can reschedule if need be. Kevin's schedule is open other than brief daily RT sessions the remainder of the week. Your expertise is most appreciated. Thanks, Wayne a.k.a. Desperately Seeking Relief

August 16, 2006

Wayne,
Thank you for your persistence and update. Please stop by the clinic, and we will get started on iv antibiotics today. Although we do not have the final culture, the predominant organism is gm+ also with some coccobacilli. I think a daily iv daptomycin would be a good idea (better gm+ spectrum than vanco since it will cover both staph and enterococcus), then when you return home, oral linezolid (for 10 more days) should be done (instead of cipro-which is just gram neg). Pete

Kevin's Medical Update

Hi everyone.
Kevin's scans last week revealed no new bone tumors, but there is a new, small tumor in his left lung (total of two there). This week he is having electron beam radiation on those two sites which should take care of them.

We were poised to fly home this Friday (8/18), but he developed a chronic pulmonary infection requiring him to have iv antibiotics for at least six days in clinic. If he improves, we plan to fly home next Friday (8/25). Our schedule seems to change almost daily as does his condition.

I am giving him chemotherapy in our hotel room, mixing it with fruit juice, and injecting it via his G-tube. I also mix his inhalation meds which I administer by a nebulizer twice daily. After that, there is the night formula feeding. Our countertop looks like a miniature science lab. I always knew my graduate concentration in science would come in useful (lol).

Once this bronchial infection clears up, he should feel much better. It has persisted for about six weeks now. I hope to be back in good ole Wilkes County and "on the job" by Monday, August 28. I'll update you again once we get home. Kevin and I appreciate your support and we think of you daily. Thanks for everything! Love, Wayne and Kevin

While in Houston at MDA, I decided to have my thyroid gland checked. The gland was quite large with multi-nodular goiters, which I had kept check on for some eighteen years. After a biopsy which appeared negative, I decided after consultation to have it removed on Kevin's next visit to MDA in November. The nodules appeared to be growing which necessitated its removal.

August 23, 2006

Hi Tom.

We plan to fly home tomorrow (8/24). I'll share his MDA protocol calendar with you. I had my multi-nodular goiter checked here at MDA and on the advice of my surgeon I plan on having a thyroidectomy when we return in November. My surgeon is an associate of yours who readily sang your praises, reflected on your wife and kids, and said to tell you hello, Nancy Perrier. She is a surgeon in the gastrointestinal clinic (associate professor of surgical oncology). Kevin's WBC has dropped some (3.9 today), and he may need Neulasta Monday. I'll get another CBC on Friday in Wilkesboro and e-mail you accordingly. I am planning to work when I'm home to salvage my remaining sick days. It is good to know you are there for us. Love, Wayne and Kevin

Thanks so much for the update. Sorry about Kevin's infection, and I hope the antibiotics are working. I'm also sorry to hear you'll need a thyroidectomy! That's not related to your prostate cancer, is it? What a small world that Nancy Perrier is your surgeon. I think very highly of her. It was a big loss for Wake Forest when M. D. Anderson recruited her away. I will be out of the office Friday (we are going on a family camping trip), but I'll alert my colleagues that a CBC will likely be coming through the fax. I will also put Kevin in the book for an appointment Monday for a CBC and maybe Neulasta. It's cooler here in NC, so hang in there with the Texas heat a little bit longer! See you soon and best wishes to Kevin. Tom

The doctor walked into our examination room at MDA, but we did not recognize her.

"Excuse me," she said. "I have a young patient, a fifteen-year-old Hispanic girl, who needs a G-tube, but she is afraid of having it implanted. Would Kevin agree to talk with her? I know that he has one."

Kevin, looking on, said, "Sure."

"She doesn't speak much English, but I think she will understand you, and I will assist."

The young girl was wheeled in and her wheelchair was parked facing Kevin's.

The doctor began, "This is Kevin, and he has a G-tube. He can tell you about it."

Kevin, lifting his shirt, pointed to the tiny rubber cap jutting up slightly from his stomach. "At first, I was scared to have it done, too," he said. "I wasn't eating at all, and I knew that to survive, I needed food. I told them to bring it on. I was ready. Really, it was no big deal. It didn't even hurt. I have gained a lot of weight, since I got a lot of nourishment through it. I would advise you to get it done. You won't be sorry."

The girl said something. Her doctor translated that she never realized it was such a small button. The doctor thanked Kevin, and they waved good-bye. Kevin had come to the rescue in a most unusual way. I shared what happened to the young girl in Kevin's medical update.

August 27, 2006

Kevin's Medical Update

Hi everyone.

M. D. Anderson Cancer Center in Houston continues to make cancer history, and Kevin continues his battle against cancer. We have just returned from our three week visit to MDA. Kevin's tests and scans reveal no new cancer sites in his bones, but a new small nodule is apparent in his left lung (two left lung nodules total). This area was treated during week two with electron beam radiotherapy. He also had additional complications with a chronic pulmonary infection which ultimately was treated with iv antibiotics for a week.

Now that we are home, I will be administering chemotherapy two weeks per month (2 to 3 cycles) along with alternating weeks of nebulized GM-CSF (twice daily) which should bolster his immune system. The bacterial infection has zapped his energy, but an additional oral antibiotic he is currently taking hopefully will alleviate this concern. We plan to return to Houston for a follow-up visit on November 5.

MDA, the Mecca of cancer research from my point of view, seemed the likely place to have my thyroid gland checked. I have for many years had an enlarged thyroid gland with a multi-nodular goiter. The endocrinologist surgeon has advised its removal (thyroidectomy) due to its increased growth and to avoid future concerns. It appears non-cancerous, although I will have a biopsy in November. This should be a non-eventful procedure with a very short recuperation period. No sense in Kevin getting the sole benefit of their expertise (lol).

Each trip affords us a unique glimpse into how cancer has affected so many people. We met a fifteen year old Hispanic girl who, much like Kevin last December, needed a G-tube for feeding purposes. Her doctor sought us out in the hopes that Kevin might convince her to have it implanted. Kevin raised his shirt revealing his tiny button, talked with her candidly about the advantages and importance of maintaining a healthy weight, and the rest is history. We learned days later that she did have this surgery!

While at the hotel computer, I overheard a young man next to me on his cell phone. He was attempting to find a local mortuary to handle the cremation of his father, who had just passed away from cancer. He seemed very composed even though there was understandable frustration in his voice. I offered my condolences, and he thanked me. These two chance meetings truly put a human face on cancer and the devastation it imparts to young and old alike.

Kevin and I were especially honored to carry the banner in this year's Wilkes County Relay for Life Survivors' Walk. It was very emotional as we each said our names, the type of cancer we had, and the number of years since our diagnosis. Many thanks for the excellent coverage by Frances Hayes of the Journal-Patriot. We flew to Houston before seeing the paper and just yesterday read the article and saw the photo on our return. There are literally hundreds of overcomers in our county who by their presence alone that night inspired everyone to keep on keeping on. Cancer continues to touch so many local families, but we are fortunate to have the love and support of a caring community and county.

Someday cancer will be old news and relegated to a disease that will finally be manageable and cured. Until then, research at MDA, Sloan-Kettering, Duke, Wake Forest, and a host of other cancer medical centers offer the best hope of survival for those afflicted. This six and a half year journey has been perilous but not without its rewards. Our cancer network grows stronger, our resolve to fight it continues, and the hopes of this generation are for a cure. We love you, Wayne and Kevin.

We love you both, too. What a wonderful father and fighter you are and all of your e-mail updates belong in a book. Hang in there. You're still on our prayer lists. Love to you, Greg and Lisa

Wayne and Kevin,

Thanks for the update and for keeping me on your mailing list. Becky and I continue to pray for the two of you. I'm not sure if you know that Becky is a cancer survivor since 1974. She says, "I had cancer, but I don't have it now." Jim

Congrats on the positive reports. It sounds to me like God is using Kevin and his experiences to help others. You have seen first hand of the devastating effects, and we certainly believe we will see cures and treatments soon. You two are quite an amazing pair in my eyes. Jeff

Yo Yo Big K,

Hope everything is well. I've tried to call you a few times but no luck. I've been praying for you. Adam

August 29, 2006

I have read this update over and over and remain amazed at your faith and optimism. I, too, share both, as Kevin continues to beat the odds. I hope and trust you feel the support of hundreds of prayers being said daily. I am glad you are home and blessed to know you and Kevin. Steve

Thank you for sending an update on your son. I, too, believe that cancer will someday be a disease of the past. My mother is a cancer survivor. My father passed away 26 years ago from cancer. It is amazing to me how much the treatments have changed in those 26 years. There is so much hope! Take care of yourself as well. I know how difficult it is to take care of others (we tend to forget about ourselves). I am sending you a prayer that I live by daily. Hope it helps.

St. Theresa's Prayer

May today there be peace within. May you trust God that you are exactly where you are meant to be. May you not forget the infinite possibilities that are born of faith. May you use those gifts that you have received, and pass on the love that has been given to you. May you be content knowing you are a child of God. Let this presence settle into your bones, and allow your soul the freedom to sing, dance, praise and love. It is there for each and every one of us. Keep the faith. Val

Hey Kevin and Wayne,

We are so happy for good, good reports. We will be at M. D. Anderson the first week in November. If you are still there, maybe we can get together. Love to you. Maurice and Marsha

September 8, 2006

Thanks, Wayne! You have set a shining example for Dad's everywhere to follow. My thoughts and prayers are with you. I serve a mighty God who is able to do all things! Christine

Kevin's continual cough was getting worse. Even though we were a thousand miles from MDA, Kevin's doctors were as close as my computer. Dr. Evans came through with some solid advice. The tumor's encroachment in his chest cavity was stressing the function of vital bodily systems. The bacterial infection, in retrospect, was just one complication which was making Kevin's fight for survival very tenuous.

September 20, 2006

Hi Dr. Evans,

We have been home almost a month (NC), and Kevin has completed his linezolid (14 day course). He is taking vantin in conjunction with his oral (G-tube) 10 day per month administration of irinotecan. Nebulized leukine (GM-CSF) is alternated every other week 7 days on and 7 days off (twice per day). He is tolerating the chemo well with fairly stable counts (general fatigue), but he does receive darbopoetin every other week (RBC stimulant). The main problem is his persistent phlegm production albeit clear to slightly tan, very viscous and often draining down his throat. It (mucus) also originates from his lung when he coughs. The cough is not as chronic as before, but he frankly is a "phlegm factory" and has grown quite pessimistic about this chronic pulmonary issue. There is usually no (or relatively slight) fever accompanying these episodes. Phlegm production may be advisable (at least getting rid of it), but would a cough suppressant be in order, something that might block the coughing impulse? He begins pulmonary rehab locally on Friday. Many thanks and we will see you in November hopefully for a consult. Wayne

September 21, 2006

Thanks for your note, Wayne.

If Kevin is a "phlegm factory," then I agree with your subsequent comment that "getting rid of it" is advisable. That is, his cough is appropriate.

If we are adequately managing infection, as it sounds is the case, then we should consider the other likely causes of the cough. The most likely non-infectious cause here is chronic airway irritation by the tumor. The receptors in his chest that are supposed to tell his brain to cough are almost constantly irritated by the sharp, rock-like lesions in the distal trachea and right main stem bronchus. This is being treated the best known way by Dr Anderson. Notably, the possibility of us getting a new micro debrider seems even more likely than on prior discussion, so that option may be available soon as well. But for now, aside from trials of anesthetic agents (like the inhaled lidocaine we tried) or surgical/interventional radiology approaches to sever/destroy the nerves (which I do not advise), there are not many additional interventions.

If not tumor-irritation of thoracic nerves or postobstructive bronchopneumonia, what else could it be? Certainly, Kevin is just as susceptible to common causes of chronic cough as the non-cancer population. In non-smokers, these prominently include asthma, gastroesophageal reflux, and post-nasal drainage. We have no spirometric evidence of asthma, nor is the pattern suggestive of an episodic process. GERD is possible. I don't see that he's on an acid blocker now, though I thought he was in the past. This does not necessarily need to be associated with heartburn. Your comment about draining down his throat makes me wonder more about whether we're missing some nasal symptoms as we focus on his chest. We once tried intranasal Flonase and intranasal Atrovent. Did these ever seem to help, and is he still using them?

In terms of non-specifically suppressing secretion production in the chest, we have few good agents. We've tried to import some so-called anticholinergic medications from anesthesia practice into the pulmonary world in recent years, but this has had little benefit acutely (during a bronchoscopy) or chronically. A trial of inhaled Atrovent helps a few people but not most.

Returning to cough suppression, as stated, he probably has an appropriate cough and needs to clear the secretions to avoid worsening problems with infections. However, if he can't sleep due to persistent cough, we should at least provide some narcotic-containing cough syrup to allow him to get some rest. You may best get this through your local doctor, as I don't know if North Carolina will allow me to phone in a prescription for a controlled substance. Please let me know about the nasal therapies. Also, did you ever determine whether Tessalon seemed to help at all? We still have the option of inhaled lidocaine again, though I hesitate to use it with all the sputum he's producing.
Scott E. Evans, M.D.

September 22, 2006

Scott,

Thanks for your thoughtful reply. I saw Kevin today in clinic and gave him a prescription for Hycodan tablets to use as a cough suppressant, although I think he's less bothered by the cough as he is the mucus production. From your comments, it sounds like Robinul would be unlikely to help him. His psychiatrist wanted to get your thoughts on Xanax (and one other anti-anxiolytic, the name of which I can't remember). I can't find any contraindication for this in terms of pulmonary function. Is Xanax OK for Kevin to try from your standpoint? Finally, we are giving him 2 units of blood today (Hb 8.7). Hopefully, this will make him feel a bit better. Best regards,
Tom

Tom,

Thank you for the follow-up and for handling the narcotic prescription. You correctly surmise that I think Robinul would provide little benefit. I strongly endorse the use of necessary anxiolytics, as directed by his psychiatrist. I have no concerns that moderate doses of a benzodiazepine should result in hypercapneic respiratory failure, though caution should be used when combined with the Hycodan.

Please let me know if I can provide further assistance. Scott

Wayne & Kevin,

As always, our prayers are with you both. I know you are encouraged by what sounds like at least some good news about Kevin's long ordeal, and we will continue to believe that soon this difficult time will be only a memory. Ron

Wayne & Kevin,

I pray both of you are doing well. I have been on vacation and hadn't heard how you are doing. I know you were sick when you first returned from Texas and I was waiting to hear back to see when I could come by. So please give me an update, and let me know if you are up to company. I saw your picture in the paper last night as I was going through the pile of papers from being on vacation. Please know that I pray for you both often and love you both. I was praying for you this morning, and I couldn't get this word off my mind "perseverance." Paul, throughout his epistles in the NT, spoke of this word and lived it. It means to continue a course of action in spite of difficulty and opposition. You both are an encouragement to me and many others. Keep fighting. Keep looking to Jesus. He will see us through. In Christ, Craig

September 28, 2006

Kevin,

Hey man, I stopped by to see how things are. I hope it's good. Get back at me, man. It's been forever. Jim

I continued to provide regular updates to Pete at MDA. All types of data was needed to analyze Kevin's condition, which I provided in my correspondences: prescription updates, chemotherapy timetables, vitals such as weight, blood count results (CBC), and general observations. Keeping in touch with Kevin's doctors, albeit in two different states, was vital to his progress. Kevin's rehab gave him added strength, but the bronchial infection lingered.

Sometimes my medical updates to Pete were quite lengthy. Kevin's was a complicated case and merited reporting all the facts.

October 7, 2006

Hi Pete.

Kevin has been in pulmonary rehab several weeks now and is feeling better. He does have clear to currently brownish sputum accompanied with occasional coughing (somewhat odorous). I suggest either another course of linezolid 600 mg po q 12 hours for 14 days (I have 2 refills remaining) or perhaps vantin 200 mg po q 12 hours for 2 weeks. I suspect gram + bacterium to be an issue again in its formative stages. PLEASE ADVISE.

<u>Med. Change</u> ... discontinued zoloft and wellbutrin XL (per pediatric psychiatrist)

prescribed clonazepam (1 mg po daily ... anxiety), improved psychological state

<u>Irinotecan</u>
8/14/06–8/18/06 ... 8/21/06–8/25/06
9/11/06–9/15/06 ... 9/18/06–9/22/06
Omitting 10/9/06–10/13/06 ... 10/16/06–10/20/06

<u>GM-CSF</u>
8/14/06–8/20/06
8/28/06–9/3/06
9/11/06–9/17/06
9/25/06–10/1/06
10/1/06–10/15/06
10/23/06–10/29/06

<u>Darbopoetin</u>
8/9/06
8/23/06
9/7/06
9/21/06 + RBC (2 units per Dr. McLean)
10/5/06
10/19/06
11/2/06

<u>Neulasta</u>
None administered (Aug.–Oct. 06)

	8/25/06	8/30/06	9/11/06	9/13/06	9/27/06	10/5/06
WBC ...	4.9	4.2	4.1	3.6	5.5	3.7
RBC ...	2.87	2.59	2.69	2.76	3.30	2.68
Hgb ...	9.8	9.2	9.7	10.0	11.2	9.3
PLT ...	230	183	125	135	166	164
GR% ...	87.2	76.7	76.6	80.7	88.7	76.7
LY% ...	10.4	13.6	17.1	17.3	6.4 1	8.8
GR# ...	4.2	3.2	3.1	2.9	4.9	2.8
LY# ...	10.4	0.6	0.7	0.6	0.4	0.7
MO# ...	0.1	0.4	0.3	0.1	0.3	0.2
Segs ...	85	71	72	70	78	80
Sodium ...	134	135	133	140	136	136

<u>Kevin Triplett's Current Meds</u>
enalapril ... 10 mg tab daily
digoxin.... 37 mg (1 & 1/2 tabs) daily
clonazepam (klonopin) ... 1mg tab ... b.i.d.
lexapro ... 5 mg/5 ml solution ... 2 tsps ... o.n. (G-tube)
bactrim (sulfamethoxazole w/tmp susphit) ... 2 tsps ... b.i.d ... (Sat./
Sun., G-tube)
zofran ODT: 8 mg tab GSK ... (as needed for nausea)

Weight ... 146 lbs (10/6/06)
Kevin is due in clinic at MDA on 11/6/06 ... desire consult w/Dr.
Evans (possible flex bronch.) and Dr. Shannon (CPF). Have a safe
flight to Europe and back home again. Wayne

The information I learned while at MDA not only benefited Kevin, but others as well. Dr. McLean was eager to hear about the new techniques, some of which had implications for perhaps implementation at Brenner's. Friends back home were faced with their own medical dilemmas and often turned to me for advice on what MDA possibly had to offer them. Others were benefiting from the M. D. Anderson connection.

October 16, 2006

Hi Wayne,

Hope you and Kevin are doing great. I need your expertise. My husband has been diagnosed recently with stage melanoma. He will have surgery next week. As far as we can tell, it is only in his neck and has not progressed to other parts of his body. His cancer specialist is discussing sending my husband to Duke for treatment after the surgery, since it is an unusual cancer and the doctors locally are not as knowledgeable. Have you and Kevin had experience with Duke? If so, did you find them as knowledgeable and accommodating as Anderson in Houston? If we decide on Houston, we may need your knowledge on places to stay and determining if there is alternate transportation instead of commercial flights. Thanks for your help. Please let us know how you and Kevin are doing. We keep you in our prayers and ask that you do the same for us. Nancy

Hi Nancy,

Our best to you and your husband. A positive, upbeat attitude will serve him well and make a world of difference in coping. We did not try Duke, since treatments there were much the same as at Wake Forest (bone cancer). M. D. Anderson has been wonderful and has saved Kevin's life (+ prayer) to this point. I would suggest your contacting MDA on line at www.mdanderson.org and then clicking on the Patient Referral tab in the middle Cancer Professional Section (takes you to another page where you click on Patient Self-Referral) on the left margin. A doctor can also make a referral by clicking Patient Referral and then on the Referring Physician tab. MDA personnel will contact you usually within 24 hours by e-mail and/or phone. Just fill in the basic referral form on line. I have referred several people to MDA.

We stay at the Rotary House which is a hotel owned by and connected to MDA. There are other hotels in the immediate area. I have a brochure detailing the area if you would like one. Rotary is around $130 per night including taxes. The main advantage is that you can go to and from MDA at any time without going outside. You can use the tram, wheelchair, or just walk in case you have an emergency.

We fly typically with Continental Express (around $330 round trip each). The Corporate Angels network also provides free flights there and back subject to their business jet schedules www.corpangelnetwork.org.

Duke is a very reputable and highly rated medical center. If I can help in any research relative to the melanoma, let me know. I would definitely discuss options of treatment facilities with your husband's doctor. Kevin and I recommend MDA. It is a relatively short, just over 2 hour flight from Greensboro or Charlotte. They even put your appointment schedule on-line, and you can access it once you become a patient. We return to MDA on November 5. Please keep us in your prayers and we will you, too. Keep Pounding and LiveStrong! Keep in touch, Wayne

Nancy's e-mail reply closed with a favorite scripture quote of hers, which seemed to sum up Kevin's life and struggles as well. I chose that scripture quote to be etched into Kevin's memorial stone.

Hi Wayne and Kevin,
Thank you so much for the information. My husband and I certainly send our prayers and best wishes for you both on November 5. We firmly believe in prayer and God's amazing grace. We go to a head and neck cancer surgeon on Friday. We will know about surgery after that appointment. My husband is very positive and upbeat, as is his nature anyway. For I consider that the sufferings of this present time are not worthy to be compared with the glory which shall be revealed in us. Romans 8:18, Nancy

October 20, 2006

Kevin loved his family very much. He especially respected his cousins, Barry and Gary Shew. Barry, a youth minister, had enlisted in the army and was in the midst of basic training away from home. Kevin hoped to see him at Christmas and wrote the following letter to him, his last letter before departing on his final trip to Houston.

10/20/06

Dear Barry,
    This is your cousin Kevin
Triplett. I hope you are doing well.
From pictures, I have seen you seem
to be doing good. You look good and healthy.
I enjoyed watching your graduation video.
I thought it was interesting. Maybe in Texas
things will be easier on you.
    As for me, I continue to struggle
daily with my health. Some areas do seem
to be getting better though. I just try
to live a simple life and take one
day at a time. I will be back in
Texas soon and I hope they can really
do something that will help me. They have
already done so much and I am thankful
for that.
    I miss you. I hope to see you
around Christmas. I love you. Stay
strong in our Lord and Savior Jesus
Christ. He is with you always.

                        Keep Pounding,
                          Kevin Triplett

Kevin, being a true American, wanted to participate in the political process. Knowing we would be in Houston in November, he felt strongly about the upcoming election, especially with a judicial election being on the ballot. A member of our church, Michael Duncan, was a candidate, and Kevin wanted to make his vote count. When the results were in, Michael had won.

October 23, 2006

Hi Alice,

Kevin has typically been either in the hospital or too sick to vote. He is nineteen, and last week I took him to the county offices to register to vote for the first time. We discussed that to have a voice in who is elected we must cast our ballots accordingly. Knowing that Michael is running for judge, we decided that even though we will be out of town in Houston on election day, we plan on voting absentee ballots for Michael.

These are just two votes of hopefully many for him, but much like a shut-in, Kevin's effort counts for a lot. I just wanted you to know that Kevin felt it was the right thing to do, even if he didn't feel up to par. In a sense, the more normal things he can do, the more he feels like everybody else. Thank you for your continued prayers and support. My best to you and your family. Wayne

Hi Tom,

Kevin has taken vancomycin (vantin) for 10 days and the staphylococcus aureus (culture confirmed last week) issue still persists. This seems to be a recurring infection possibly due to bronchial/tracheal post tumor compression or additional midchest pulmonary issues. In short, he has this persistent bacterial issue intermittently. I refilled a vantin prescription and plan to continue it an additional four days (14 days total). I also have refills for linezolid (zyvox), which he took for 14 days in Houston. It also seems to be effective against gram + bacteriums as is staph aureus. If his sputum discoloration and odor continues into late next week, do you advise beginning a course of linezolid? Kevin will return to Brenner's on 11/2 for darbopoetin and to MDA on 11/6. Thanks for all that you do for Kevin. Take care, Wayne

Kevin,

Just wanted to say, what's up man. Dude, where have you been. Man, I haven't seen you in forever, not even in town or anything. Well, I hope you're doing good. Holler back at me some time. Eddie

November 4, 2006

Hi Maurice and Marsha,

Kevin, his mother, and I are flying to MDA tomorrow afternoon (Sunday … 11/5). We will be staying at the Rotary House, if you'd like to get together. Hope you have received another clean bill of health. We will be praying for you. Love, Wayne and Kevin

Hey Kevin. I just thought I would drop by and say hey and see how you are. I hope you are doing great. Man, I haven't talked to you in like fifty zillion years lol. Well, I'll ttyl. Love ya, bye. Killing Loneliness

November 9, 2006

Kevin and Wayne's Medical Update

Kevin, his mother, and I are in Houston again (7th flight). I had a thyroidectomy yesterday to remove my over-sized gland with no complications. The nodules appeared to be noncancerous, although the pathology report will not be available until next week. I am sporting a new three inch scar on my neck, though.

Kevin's scans revealed four additional tumor areas (right/left hips … right/left lungs). We will meet with the radiologist next week to possibly schedule RFA (radio frequency ablation to burn one of the tumors). The other sites will possibly receive external beam radiation. His doctor will be scheduling a new chemotherapy approach soon. He is currently receiving iv antibiotics for his lung infection.

We are doing well, remaining upbeat and in good spirits albeit a bit groggy from yesterday's "happy juice." I will update you later with a more comprehensive e-mail after we get a calendar developed. I assume we will be here through Thanksgiving.

We did see our neighbor, Maurice Templeton, today. He is at MDA for a checkup. He will be seeing Dr. Charles Stanley next week and will mention Kevin to him. We met Dr. Stanley on Kevin's Make-A-Wish cruise.

We remain thankful and blessed to have such a great network of friends like you. Your thoughts and prayers continue to reach out to us across the miles. We love you. Wayne and Kevin

Thank you for the update, as always. I hope you and Kevin are both up and on your feet again soon. I will certainly pray for you both. Please let me know if there is anything else I can do for you. Sincerely, Tom

Dear Wayne and Kevin,
I got your e-mail today and so good to hear from you all. We can compare neck scars, Wayne, next time we see each other. Sure thinking of you both and waiting to hear of your calendar and plans for the next few weeks. Don't worry about writing me back personally, you have so many wanting to hear. I'll wait to see the next note you send to us all. Please know you are in my thoughts and prayers everyday. You both have been an important part of my life in the past. My, has it been 8 years or so? The picture you gave me from our "Walk" at MCIS/MCPS back when you were in 8th grade, Kevin, that picture is on my desk at MCES! Take care, and know you both mean a great deal to a lot of people. Love, Fran

Wayne and Kevin,
We will continue to remember you in prayer, believing that all this will soon be only a distant memory. In the meantime, try to lay off the "happy juice." LOL! Ron

November 16, 2006

I am thankful for Wayne and Kevin Triplett. Kevin for his will to live and Wayne for his unwavering optimism. Steve

Hi Flatlanders,
Thanks for your e-mail. I hope you are doing better since your surgery. I know you are in good hands at MDA. You have the best of the best working for you. Please take care of yourself and take time out to rest and eat right. I hope Kevin is feeling better and is remaining upbeat. I am sorry that you will be in Texas for Thanksgiving, but I guess that MDA seems a bit like home. You and Kevin are a great source of strength and inspiration. I will continue to pray for good

health for you both. If I can help out in any way, please let me know. Michelle said she misses you and sends her love. May God be close to you, Donna

November 22, 2006

Kevin,

You've been on my heart recently. I was thinking about cutting up together with Gwyn. You are one of the nicest, loving, nonjudgmental people I know. God has gifted you in that department. Over the times of being with the two of you, you taught me something. Love them for who they are on the inside and for the true potential within. I'll remember to pray for you, and thank God for what you've taught me. If there is anything I can do, even listen, call me! Have a good week! Jennifer

You and Kevin remain an inspiration to everyone. While I know there are places you would rather be at Thanksgiving, isn't it nice to know that you are together another Thanksgiving. You both are miracles! Take care. Steve

Kevin,

Marsha and I are praying for you and your family. I pray that this Thanksgiving will be special to you. In 1996, I was at the same place you are today, and we ate Thanksgiving lunch at Lubbies. It ain't home, but we were thankful for our time together. We love you, Maurice and Marsha

I always gave Kevin cards for special days, birthdays, and holidays, as well as get-well cards. Sometimes, I would have them nearby, knowing that he would discover them. He would usually open them right away, read what I had written, and say thank you. I would then give him a nice hug.

November 23, 2006

Text of My Thanksgiving Card to Kevin

Dear Kevin,

Thinking of you makes me smile with my heart! Happy Thanksgiving 2006. Spending it with you is the only way I would want to spend it. You brighten up my and everyone's life. All my love always as you get better. Love, Dad

Happy Thanksgiving, Kev. I hope all is well. Joe

Kevin had been in the hospital six days at MDA for treatment primarily for the bronchial infection. During this time, he also went down for radiation and received chemotherapy in his hospital room. The hospital staff prepared the traditional Thanksgiving meal on November twenty-third for patients and their families. I put together a meal for him; he sat up in bed and enjoyed his turkey leg with trimmings.

Later that evening, Kevin's final battle on earth would begin. Neither Kathy nor I had any idea early on, that this would be Kevin's last night with us. With the typical hospital evening in progress, I sent the following e-mails from Kevin's laptop computer at his bedside.

November 26, 2006

Dear Mrs. Chapin's Class,
    Thank you so much for the beautiful Thanksgiving and get well cards! What a wonderful surprise when Kevin and I opened them on Saturday (Nov. 25). We have them in his hospital room. Kevin has been in the hospital one week being treated with antibiotics for a lung infection. He has one more week of radiation.
    I have a radioactive iodine treatment the first week of December. The doctor put me on a strict diet last week, but Kevin and I both had turkey on Thanksgiving in the hospital. If our schedule does not change, we may be home on December 8. Overall, we are doing okay. We hope each of you had a great Thanksgiving. Thank you for thinking of us and for making our Thanksgiving very special! Love, Mr. Triplett and Kevin

Dear C. C. Wright Staff,
    Thank you so much for the get well cards and for the gift certificate for groceries. What a wonderful surprise hearing from you! We have the cards in our hotel room. Kevin has been in the hospital one week being treated with antibiotics for a lung infection. He has one more week of radiation.
    I have a radioactive iodine treatment the first week of December. The doctor put me on a strict diet last week, but Kevin and I both

had turkey on Thanksgiving in the hospital. If our schedule does not change, we may be home on December 8. Overall, we are doing okay. We hope each of you had a great Thanksgiving. Thank you for thinking of us and for making our Thanksgiving very special! Love, Wayne and Kevin

CHAPTER 10

LIKE SON ... LIKE FATHER

In 2005, Kevin and I had even more in common.
I joined him as a cancer survivor, too.
The 2005 Relay for Life became much more meaningful.

Behold, I stand at the door, and knock: if any man hear my voice,
and open the door, I will come in to him, and will sup with him, and
he with me.
Revelation 3:20

Sometimes the caregiver gets sick and needs a little TLC. After dealing with a rising PSA level in late 2004, two biopsies revealed an aggressive form of prostate cancer in me. The surgeon advised a radical prostatectomy, which he performed in June 2005 using the new da Vinci robotic technique. The cancer was contained in the gland, and I continue to be monitored regularly.

I had been plagued with a multi-nodular goiter for almost twenty years. A biopsy ten years earlier had yielded just typical enlargement. I felt the gland was beginning to grow in size and it seemed natural to take care of my situation and have it removed while at M. D. Anderson. The postsurgical pathology report in November 2006 indicated cancer within the gland, although the presurgical biopsy looked negative. Fortunately, the cancer was contained within the gland. Again, I was lucky. I returned to Houston in December 2006 for a radioactive iodine treatment and in April 2007 for a recheck. I am scheduled for a follow-up visit at MDA in early 2008 with specific monitoring of an enlarged lymph node in my neck. I appear to be cancer free at this time.

Unlike Kevin, I did not lose my hair or suffer any adverse chemotherapy treatments. I was fortunate, since my caring for Kevin always took center stage. My health issues seemed almost insignificant compared to his. I learned a lot from him and his battles with cancer. I even adopted his lifestyle: just take one day at a time and find joy in the simple things.

People seem dumbfounded that in the midst of Kevin's cancer, I developed it, twice, myself. I learned long ago that asking why would yield no answers. It is not for me to know. Disease is a natural part of life, and as long as it did not prevent me from caring for Kevin, it was manageable. Kevin and I now had even more in common.

The following e-mails capture a glimpse of my cancer diagnosis and treatment.

October 23, 2004

Hi Tom,

My three month blood work showed an elevated PSA level (3.5 to 5.9). Could you suggest a WFUBMC urologist whom I might could see? I'm partial to the best in healthcare (WFUBMC). Thanks ... Wayne.

March 11, 2005

Hi Debbie,

Kevin had an uneventful chemo session. My biopsy is not until March 22. Hopefully, I will see you before then. I will have to play catch up at school this weekend, if I'm up to it. I would call you, but episodic coughing would limit my talking with you. Take care ... Wayne

April 8, 2005

Now it's my turn. After monitoring my escalating PSA level since October 2004 and with the second biopsy just in, my urologist has confirmed that I have prostate cancer. I suppose it is Kevin's turn to look after dear old dad! There is no time to feel sorry for oneself. Wayne

Good Morning Wayne,

I was sorry to hear about your prostate cancer. It is very much a worry for men our age. My father had the same procedure that you mentioned this past summer. He is doing well and the recovery time is not bad. In a couple of weeks you should feel much better. You and Kevin remain in my prayers. Ken

Hi Larry and thanks for your e-mail. I will be having the relatively new daVinci robotic laparoscopic radical prostatectomy at Baptist Hospital in W-S on June 13. This technique should allow for a shorter recuperation time, less blood loss, and a return to some degree of normalcy sooner. This technique is only performed in NC at Baptist and at Duke. It's always good to hear from you, and I try to keep my eye on the paper(s) to keep up with your educational happenings. Great job, and Kevin and I consider you a true friend. Wayne

June 14, 2005

Just wanted to let everyone know that Wayne came through his surgery extremely well this morning. He is in Room 1015 North Tower at Baptist. He is on some high powered pain medication, so if you call, he may seem very happy! Please keep him in your thoughts and prayers for a speedy and complete recovery. I know he would love to hear from you. Kaye

June 16, 2005

Hi everyone.
I had a wonderful surprise visit Thursday afternoon from two of our own, Michele and Mike, and they came bearing gifts! Many thanks to each of you for the cash donation and the large fruit basket! I'm going to dig in, as soon as I get off this liquid diet. The surgery went well, but now I'm dealing with the dreaded catheter for 10 days along with no driving. On the positive side, Kevin's summer work load has just expanded! You're the greatest, and I hope you enjoy the attached snapshot celebrating our moment of bliss. Behave in Asheville. Wayne

June 19, 2005

Hi Rosie,
I'm at home on day 6 of 10 with a catheter in place. Needless to say, it limits my movements. I had Kevin drive me to town once, but I was fearful someone would hit us and dislodge it. My surgery on the 13th went well, but it was almost an all day affair with recovery and all. I went home last Wednesday and have been there ever since. I go Thursday (6/23) to have the catheter removed. I hope I can be at school the last week of June to work on the SIP. Most patients take about six weeks off, but if I can remember not to lift anything, I think I will be fine. Keep in touch and thanks for everything. Wayne

June 27, 2005

Hi Debbie,

Glad your biopsy came back negative. Breast cancer seems to afflict so many women these days, and I know the waiting game was like being on pins and needles.

I do feel better without the catheter, but now I'm leaking like a sieve! I bought a dozen, well, pads last Thursday and used them all before nightfall. I've now graduated to Depends (diapers), about six a day, and the nurse says in 1 to 3 months, it should improve. I really have a feel for what you ladies have to go thru. We never know what we may have to deal with one step at a time.

Kevin is working at Wendy's and ready for his DC trip next week followed by his July 11–13 new treatment in Indianapolis. I went back to work today after two weeks (not the usual six weeks) and got a little work done. You are welcome to visit anytime, and I can always use some TLC. I'm pretty docile, since I'm recuperating but up for conversation. I really missed being able to drive for almost two weeks. Kevin has been pretty handy around the house keeping things going. Drop me an e-mail anytime. Got to go, nature calls. Keep in touch. Wayne

October 1, 2006

Hi Brian.

I will be returning to MDA on November 6. My schedule calls for a thyroid ultrasound with BX on November 6 and a visit with Dr. Perrier and an anesthesia consult on November 7. I assume my surgery will be possibly Wednesday, November 8, or sometime that week. Please be sure this surgery is scheduled per our discussion at my visit there in August. I did not see any scheduling of surgery as of yet on my itinerary. I would appreciate an e-mail update. Thanks and see you in November. Wayne

October 27, 2006

Mr. Triplett,

Your surgery has been scheduled for November 8th. You should be able to see it on your on-line schedule within 48 hours. If you have any questions, please don't hesitate to e-mail or call. Brian

November 3, 2006

Mr. Triplett,

Please discontinue use of all aspirin, ibuprofen, naproxen, and vitamin E supplementation in preparation for your impending surgery on 11/8/06. Brian

November 16, 2006

As you know, Wayne had his thyroid removed last week. His test results came back positive for cancer. It is fairly contained in a small area. The plans involve drinking a radioactive fluid to take care of the area. Kevin is undergoing treatments, and they will be in Houston through December 4th. There is a possibility of removing one of Kevin's lungs. This is all I know for now. I know you will continue to keep them in your prayers. Karen

CHAPTER 11

KEVIN'S HOME GOING AND CELEBRATION SERVICE

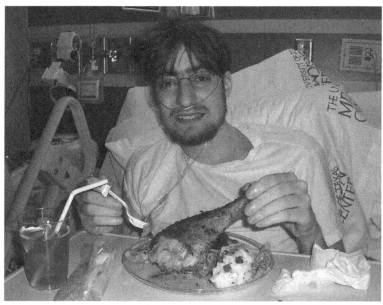

Kevin and his mom posed for this in-clinic photo at MDA on his last trip to Houston. Kevin had turkey on his last Thanksgiving, November 23, 2006, in his hospital bed.

The Lord is my shepherd; I shall not want.
He maketh me to lie down in green pastures: he leadeth me beside the
still waters.
He restoreth my soul: he leadeth me in the paths of righteousness for his
name's sake.
Yea, though I walk through the valley of the shadow of death, I will fear
no evil:
for thou art with me; thy rod and thy staff they comfort me.
Thou preparest a table before me in the presence of mine enemies:
thou anointest my head with oil; my cup runneth over.
Surely goodness and mercy shall follow me all the days of my life:
and I will dwell in the house of the Lord for ever.
Psalm 23

Kevin's seventh trip to Houston was to have been a "tune up" to get his lung infection under control. He would receive stronger antibiotics, as well as repeating the usual scans and developing a treatment plan. Kevin was hospitalized on Tuesday evening, November 21, 2006, due to continued fever and general discomfort. I had been giving Kevin nourishment through his G-tube as well as chemotherapy in our hotel room. He seemed to be responding well to the medications, but he had some puffiness around his eyes. This possibly was due to edema, although he had been taking a water pill.

The hospital staff prepared a Thanksgiving meal for those patients and their families who were there, and Kevin enjoyed the turkey and trimmings. On the Saturday evening after Thanksgiving, he became restless for a while and required some morphine. This happened again on Sunday evening, November 26, and he required more meds. He laid back in bed, and I presumed he was resting, so I took his laptop computer and composed two e-mail updates to my school staff at his bedside.

The evening wore on with his vitals fluctuating and him becoming more lethargic. When the doctor on call came in I asked her, "Do you think he is going to be okay?" She replied, "We've seen this before. Sometimes they make it through the night." Immediately, I felt a shock course through my body. Was Kevin going to die tonight? He was just talking an hour earlier. I don't think Kevin heard her, and I never told him what she said. I just tried to make him comfortable. His mom and I took turns wiping his forehead, rubbing his arms, and holding his hands over the next six hours.

"How are you feeling, honey?" I asked. "Are you okay?" He never spoke but nodded his head up and down. "Is anything hurting you?" I asked. This time he turned his head left and right signaling that he was in no pain. His morphine had been increased, and his oxygen level on the machine was at its highest setting. There was a steady stream of nurses in and out each respecting our privacy. "I (we) love you Kevin, and I'm here for you. I'm not going anywhere. I'll stay with you all night," I kept repeating. I continued holding and caressing his hands. I placed a small cassette player beside him and began playing a taped sermon by Pastor Craig which had been sent to us. I borrowed the doctor's stethoscope and listened to his heart beating. His breathing became more labored, and the oxygen bag attached to his face filled and emptied sporadically.

He looked at me with eyes wide-open as if he was staring past me, and I sensed his time was growing short. I seemed to notice a slight grin on his face as as he stared wide-eyed one final time. It was 4:18 AM CST in Houston, Texas, and Kevin had taken his last breath. I turned to his mother and said, "I think he's gone." I turned him from his side to his back. He looked so serene and was warm to the touch. For the first time in ages, he was in no pain. No doubt, Jesus had just welcomed him home.

I was not scared or panicky. I was there to witness his birth and now in the end, his death. It was a spiritual moment for me. With tear-filled eyes, we gathered our things, and a short time later met with the chaplain around Kevin's bed for prayer. Kevin was an organ donor, and his corneas would help others to see. He would make his trip back to North Carolina on a later flight. Within twenty minutes of his death, I called Kevin's dear friend, Rev. Craig Church. "Craig, sorry to call you so early, but I have some bad news to tell you." "What's wrong? Is it Kevin?" he asked. "Yes, he passed away a few minutes ago," I said through tears. We both cried together for a few moments.

I knew that barring a miracle, cancer would ultimately claim Kevin. He knew it, too, and on occasion stated, "Dad, I don't want to live another fifteen months like the last. I had just as soon go home to be with Jesus." He wanted to live, he fought hard all the way, but he knew the odds of surviving and living a normal life were not in his favor.

He has left me for a while, and even though his life was brief, he made many contributions. Kevin's submitting to cutting-edge cancer therapies paved the way for the potential healing of cancer patients yet to be diagnosed. He not only called himself a Christian, he lived that lifestyle and was a witness for Christ by what he said, by the music he made, and by how he lived. Although cancer was tough, his God was tougher and gave him the strength to carry on. Kevin's life is now an open book and a proven road map on how to navigate the pitfalls and challenges of our lives. He never gave up. He lived strong and kept pounding.

Kevin is never truly gone from those who knew him, for we carry his memory, his hopes and dreams for a cure, and his courage with us. He can't come to me, but one day I can go to him. His life mattered and was a life well lived. May God bless and keep him in His loving care.

Kathy and I, upon returning home, met with the funeral director and made plans for his celebration service. Kevin would be wearing the suit and tie he wore at his senior prom, the suit which originally belonged to me, which I had altered for him. Kathy purchased a new Bible, with his name embossed on the cover, which he would hold in his hands. The casket drawer would contain his keepsakes, pictures, bracelets, and his group's CD. I sent the following e-mail to Kevin's special friends.

Kevin Wayne Triplett

December 7, 1986–November 27, 2006

"A Celebration Of A Life That Matters"

Thursday, November 30, 2006
Mid-day Viewing at Reins-Sturdivant Funeral Home, 1–3 PM
(family not present at this time)

Millers Creek Baptist Church

Celebration Of Life Service, 5–7:30 PM
Family Will Receive Friends, 7:30–9:30 PM

Interment, Scenic Memorial Gardens
Friday, December 1, 2006, 11 AM

Flowers will be accepted or memorials may be made to:
The Kevin W. Triplett Memorial Scholarship Fund
c/o State Employees Credit Union
PO Box 700, Wilkesboro, NC 28697
Acct. #G7296774
or to an organization of the donor's choice

Kevin's Celebration of Life Program follows.

Life's Most Important Things

Everyone has got their view on what they think is most important in life. It's sad that some people get so caught up in drugs and alcohol that they miss what is most important in life.

The most important thing in life is your relationship with God. God has a special plan for everyone. The greatest decision anyone can make is deciding to trust God's son Jesus Christ as personal Lord and Savior and repent of their sins.

Another important thing in life is your relationships with others. We should love others even our enemies. We should treat others the way that we want to be treated. When someone does us wrong we should not hold grudges. We should forgive them and love them. It is better to encourage others rather than bring them down.

An education is very important to have in life. Times have radically changed and without a good education it is hard for some people to find a good paying job. I don't always like going to school. I am a senior in high school and I realize and appreciate more how Blessed I am to have had a good education all my life with teachers that care.

Those are three things that I believe are most important in life. They really impacted my life and always will. It's great to be alive. Enjoy life!

(from Kevin's senior year autobiography)

Memorials may be made to

The Kevin W. Triplett Memorial
Scholarship Fund
c/o State Employees' Credit Union
PO Box 700
Wilkesboro, NC 28697
Acct. #G7296774

This scholarship awarded annually will benefit a deserving West Wilkes High School senior who may be facing medical or financial hardships. It is a fitting legacy to Kevin's noble fight against cancer, to the love he had for West High and to the emphasis he placed on the value of an education.

Kevin Wayne Triplett

"A Celebration Of A Life That Matters"

December 7, 1986 - November 27, 2006

Cancer

I found out about you when I was thirteen.
You made your presence known.
Only God Knows how long you had been
lurking inside of me.
Only He knows how long you had been
growing
trying to take over my body.
I don't know why you came to me.
I guess that's just what was meant to be.
You shook us up,
but we didn't give up.
Things were dark like the night,
but we chose to fight
battle after battle we began to see the light.
You put us to the test
We gave you our best.

by Kevin Triplett

Millers Creek Baptist Church
November 30, 2006
Celebration Of Life Service...5-7:30 PM
Family Will Receive Friends...7:30-9:30 PM

"Amazing Grace"..............................Steve Cardwell
Comments & Poem............Rev. Shannon Critcher
"Laid To Rest"................................Taking Up Arms
Comments and Kevin's Paper...Rev. Craig Church
Song...Rev. David Dyer
Comments..Rev. Jim Gore
"Some Will Seek Forgiveness".........Taking Up Arms
Comments.......................Congregation & Friends
"Jesus Savior Pilot Me"................The Inspirations
Comments ....Wayne Triplett
"For Kevin...Love Dad"...A Video Tribute

Taking Up Arms...Joseph Hutchinson, Jim &
Charlie Coleman, Adam Minton (absent)
Pall Bearers...Gwyn McGlamery, Joseph
Hutchinson, Jim & Charlie Coleman, Matt Faw,
Gary Shew

November 27, 2006

Reins-Sturdivant Funeral Home Obituary
Kevin Wayne Triplett
Born in Watauga County, NC, on Dec. 7, 1986
Departed on Nov. 27, 2006
and resided in Millers Creek, NC.

Mr. Kevin Wayne Triplett, age 19, of Cedar Ridge Drive, Millers Creek died Monday, November 27, 2006, at M.D. Anderson Cancer Center in Houston, Texas. Funeral services will be held Thursday from 5 until 7:30 at Millers Creek Baptist Church with the Rev. Shannon Critcher, the Rev. Craig Church and the Rev. Jim Gore officiating. The family will receive friends following the service from 7:30 until 9:30. A graveside service will be held Friday at 11:00 AM at Scenic Memorial Gardens.

Kevin was born December 7, 1986, in Watauga County to Wayne and Kathy Shew Triplett. He graduated from West Wilkes High School in 2005, where he sang in the West Wilkes Chorus and received the High School Principal's Award. He was a member of Millers Creek Baptist Church where he played the guitar in the praise band. Kevin also played guitar with Taking Up Arms, a Christian alternative band, which he co-founded. He planned to attend Wilkes Community College where he had received the WCC Blanche P. McNeil Memorial Scholarship, the American Cancer Society Scholarship and the Rex and Jestene Templeton Scholarship.

A grandfather, Guy Triplett preceded him in death. He is survived by: his mother, Kathy Shew Triplett of Wilkesboro; his father, Wayne Triplett of Millers Creek; Grandparents, Ralph and Martha Shew of North Wilkesboro and Ruby Triplett of Ferguson.

Flowers will be accepted or memorials may be made to The Kevin W. Triplett Memorial Scholarship Fund, c/o State Employees' Credit Union, P O Box 700, Wilkesboro, NC, 28697 or to the charity of the donor's choice. Reins-Sturdivant Funeral Home is in charge of the services.

Shortly after Kevin's passing, I called our funeral director in North Wilkesboro, North Carolina. They asked if it would be fine with the family if an acknowledgment of Kevin's death could be placed in our local paper. I agreed, since I knew everyone would want to know.

When I returned home, there on the front page was the headline, "Kevin Triplett Dies Today." The color photo of Kevin and me leading the Relay for Life Survivors' Lap just three months earlier appeared below the title. Charles Williams, editor-in-chief, had pulled together a collection of excerpts from former articles detailing Kevin's many years of fighting cancer. What a tribute!

November 27, 2006

Article from the *Wilkes Journal-Patriot*
"Kevin Triplett Dies Today
Nearly Seven-Year Battle With Cancer Ends"

Kevin Triplett, 19, of Millers Creek, known locally for his battle with cancer, died this morning at the M. D. Anderson Cancer Center in Houston, Texas. He was the son of Wayne and Kathy Triplett. Funeral arrangements, to be handled by Reins-Sturdivant Funeral Home, are incomplete.

Long Battle With Cancer

Kevin was first diagnosed with bone cancer in April 2000, at the age of 13 after experiencing pain in his right leg. He at first thought that the soreness and discomfort was a result of over-extending himself, since he was an avid basketball player. When the condition persisted after Kevin began a program of physical therapy, an MRI and x-rays were ordered. They showed a tumor below Kevin's knee, in the tibia bone. A needle biopsy showed that the bone tumor was cancerous.

The tumor was located close to one of Kevin's main veins, and doctors at WFUBMC told Kevin there was a possibility he could lose his leg. He was also told he would have to undergo about a year of chemotherapy and rehabilitation and would likely be on crutches about a year and a half. The physicians said that even after surgery was performed to remove the tumor, it was possible that the cancer could come back in the leg. If the cancer did return, Kevin's leg would have to be amputated. There was also the possibility of a cancerous tumor appearing in one of Kevin's lungs, because the organ is located in a soft, warm, and moist climate.

In June 2000, Kevin underwent a 12-hour surgery at Baptist and the doctors were able to save his leg by replacing the bone removed with a donor bone. By September 2000, Kevin was wearing a knee immobilizer.

Following the surgery, Kevin endured 11½ months of chemotherapy. For the next eleven months, there were virtually no problems and family members were hopeful that the ordeal was over.

As a precaution, physicians ordered a CT scan of the leg every six months and a chest scan every three months. It was during a routine visit for a chest scan in December 2001 that a tumor the size of a pea was found in one of Kevin's lungs. Doctors performed a four-hour surgery on December 31, 2001 and removed the tumor.

Shortly after Kevin was released from the hospital in January, he began another regimen of chemotherapy which lasted until mid-April. Through this process, Kevin missed about two months of school in seventh grade, seven months in eighth grade, and half the school year in the ninth grade.

Osteosarcoma is a bone cancer that consists of malignant cells that produce immature bone. It is the most common type of bone cancer in children and adolescents.

With bone cancer during the first five years there is a high rate of reoccurrence, then it levels off to about twenty percent. Usually this form of bone cancer appears in one limb only, the long bones of the leg or upper arm, and it affects about 200 children out of about a million and primarily affects boys.

Tumors have reappeared in various parts of Kevin's body in recent years, and he and his family made over a half dozen trips to the cancer center in Houston for extended treatments. Earlier this month, scans revealed four additional tumor areas (right and left hips and right and left lungs). The family was to meet with radiologists to possibly schedule radio frequency ablation to burn one of the tumors. Physicians at the time were considering external beam radiation on the other areas, and a new chemotherapy approach was planned. He was receiving antibiotics for a lung infection.

At the same time, Kevin's father, Wayne, the assistant principal at North Wilkesboro and C.C. Wright Elementary, had a thyroidectomy in Houston to remove an over-sized gland with no complications. The nodules appeared to be non-cancerous.

In 2002, Kevin was granted a wish by the Make-A-Wish Foundation. He chose a seven day, Christian-oriented cruise to Alaska to enjoy the beauty of the countryside.

Teacher Comments

Steve Moree, the principal at West Wilkes during Kevin's high school years, commented today, "Kevin was an example of courage which I held up to the student body repeatedly. Everyone knew about his battle with cancer and his classmates and teachers supported him."

"It was easy to support someone as wonderful as Kevin," added Moree. "I never once heard him complain at all. His spirit will live a long time among his classmates. The courage of Kevin and his family has been an inspiration to many people."

Jim Brooks, a teacher at West Wilkes who had Kevin as a student in his Introduction To Cinema class, said this morning that, "The thing that struck me the most about Kevin was the courage with which he faced such a long struggle with cancer. He was not only a role model for his peers but also for the adults around him."

"He certainly inspired so many folks with the quiet dignity and strength that he always seemed to possess, no matter how difficult things were," Brooks added. "He was always smiling every time I saw him, no matter how bad he felt. This is certainly a loss that students and teachers are feeling today."

Kathy Sebastian, who taught Kevin in several classes, remembered him as "very kind and thoughtful. Through all of his ordeal, he never let his sickness get him down. He didn't want people to be burdened with his illness," she said. "He came back to school a week after lung surgery, and he missed fewer days overall than a lot of students."

"Besides all of the courage and all of his other characteristics, he truly was a kind person and so considerate of other students and teachers," Ms. Sebastian said. "He never said a mean word about anyone. It seems so unjust that someone so kind and caring would be sick. I know it sounds like a cliché, but it was certainly true in Kevin's case."

Kevin graduated from West Wilkes in 2005. His honors and activities included chorus and playing guitar in the Millers Creek Baptist Church praise team band. Triplett received the WCC Blanche P. McNeil Memorial Scholarship, the American Cancer Society Scholarship, and the Rex and Jestene Templeton Scholarship and attended WCC.

Kevin said he was able to get through this ordeal by praying and trusting God, and through the support of others, which not only included his parents, but the congregation of Millers Creek Baptist Church, which he attended.

Upon returning home, my e-mail inbox was flooded with heartfelt condolences and words of encouragement. I have included some here, but due to their volume, it was impossible to include them all. I stand amazed and am so appreciative.

November 27, 2006

Kevin Triplett passed away this morning around 4 AM in Houston. Wayne is making arrangements to fly back home either today or tomorrow. There are no other details at this time. I will send more information when we receive it. John

I was so saddened to hear of Kevin's passing. He was a great young man who was full of life. I know your great spirit kept him going, and I know his spirit and yours inspired us all. I will always treasure the time I was around Kevin. He taught me how precious life is and, Wayne, you have taught me to appreciate life as never before. I will continue to treasure our friendship. Please call me if there is anything I can do. Your friend, John

We just heard the sad, sad news. What a battle you guys waged. You were such troopers, and believers, and truly an inspiration to many, many people. We loved Kevin very much, and there will always be very special memories of the times he and Frankie spent growing up together. Our prayers are with you and your family Wayne. Kevin will be a special angel to us all. Much love, the Barger's

November 28, 2006

I spoke with Wayne this morning. He arrived home late yesterday. I know most of you received the e-mail I forwarded yesterday morning. Wayne said he was on the laptop Sunday evening sending e-mails and Kevin went into a "sudden sporadic crisis mode" and things did not improve through the night. He did say everything is "surreal" at this point. Wayne will be returning to Houston on Sunday for his treatment and will be there for 4–5 days. He is not sure if he will return before Christmas break. He sends his love and thanks everyone for their prayers and support. Karen

I cannot imagine all you and Kevin have been through. You are the greatest dad! I am sorry, and I will be in touch with you soon. Take care and God bless is how I end many of my emails. TCGB! Your friend, Charles

Wayne and Kathy,
Roy and I are truly sorry for what the two of you are having to deal with, but we know that Kevin is in a better place now and playing his music for the Lord. God's loving arms are holding you both right now and just hold on. Geraldine and Roy

I wanted to let you know that I am thinking of you, and that I am here for you if there is anything that I can do. I am deeply saddened by the loss of Kevin. He has been such a miracle to care about. He fought so bravely and was at such peace every time I talked to him. He truly is a miracle and a shining example of tenacity and courage. I don't know if you know how deeply he touched my heart. I will forever be proud of him. Thank you for letting me be a part of his life. He has left footprints on my heart that I won't ever forget. My prayers are with you. In His Love, Brook

Wayne and Kathy,
The saying about "it's not what you leave this world with, but rather what you leave with the world" must have been said with Kevin in mind! He's such an inspiration to all of us. He fought a valiant battle and won in so many ways. My prayers and thoughts are with you. Sherry

November 29, 2006

I placed photos of Kevin, his mom, and me in his inside coat pocket and in his casket drawer with these heartfelt messages printed on the back of them.

Dearest Kevin,
You are the greatest person I have ever known. You continue to teach me many things. My life's purpose was to help you get well. I hope to meet you again someday. I want God's will in my life. Neither time

nor death can separate us for long. I love you with all my heart, yesterday, today, and forever. Rest in peace, Little Buddy. No more pain! Until we see Jesus together! All my love, Dad

My Kevin,
You are and always will be the love of my life. We will always be together. All my love, Dad
The Greatest Son

Dearest Kevin,
Your mom and I will love you forever. You're never alone or out of our thoughts. I can't wait to see you again, someday soon I hope. My journey will be to live a life deserving enough to be where you are with Jesus. Until we meet again, you have my heart and love, forever. Love, Dad and Mom

Wayne, words fail me. Ron

Kevin and you really touched our lives. Pete

I will always remember Kevin's courage and sweet spirit. You as parents did such a wonderful job to give him quality time. I will pray for your comfort and healing. Love ... Peggy

I'm blessed to have had the opportunity to have known Kevin. God bless you and be with you. Maritza

I am so sorry for your loss. What a precious son Kevin was, and how blessed he was to have two such supportive parents. I just know he is in heaven playing his guitar. Sandi

Dear Wayne and Kathy,
We were all saddened to learn that Kevin had passed away from sarcoma. He certainly fought the brave battle and did not give in to his disease. Your support of him throughout his battle and your efforts on his behalf were truly exemplary and inspiring to us. We would all like to express our condolences in Kevin's death. We all feel fortunate

that we had the opportunity to get to know him as well as you fine folks. If there is anything we can ever do, please do not hesitate to call or write.
Sincerely,
William G. Ward, M.D.
Professor
Department of Orthopaedic Surgery
Wake Forest University Baptist Medical Center

Our prayers have been and will continue to be with you. I don't have the words, so I'm not even going to try. Please know that many, many prayers are being made for you. Your brother in Christ, Charles

Thank you for including us. Kevin's life did make a difference! Pete

Wayne and Kathy,
God bless you both for being such loving and kind parents to Kevin. We watched him grow up from a tiny infant to an awesome young man. Our thoughts and prayers are with you. He loved those biscuits and gravy. Many hugs, Judy and Ann at Glenn's

I will always remember Kevin's speech at Relay for Life several years ago. I was so moved along with everyone at Relay. Kevin was a powerful strength for so many. I will keep you in my prayers.
Jenny

We are sorry for your loss. Your loss is Heaven's gain. I am sure he is in Heaven with Aunt Marie, Papa, Mama Richie, and Don right now. Kevin was an inspiration to each of us who knew him. He constantly amazed me by his resilience. He fought a long, difficult battle that most would not have been able to withstand. He is my hero. Love to all, Sharon and Brenda

I can't tell you how sorry I am to hear of Kevin's passing. I know you have dedicated the last seven years of your life and his to doing everything possible to help him. You are an amazing person, and I admire all you have done. I have spoken of you often on this subject. I cannot imagine how you are feeling right now, and I hope I never do. Nothing is worse then losing your precious child, no matter what their age. We have a new teacher at school that has just found out her son has cancer. We have been telling her of you and all the wonderful things you had done for Kevin. They have not been given a lot of hope for him, and she is devastated. She was wanting to talk to you about options for her son, and then we received the news from you, and I think it just about did Jackie in. I think the little bit of hope she was holding on to kind of slipped away from her. She received more bad results yesterday, and I feel so sorry for her. Maybe after things slow down with you and you have time to think, I can hook you and her family up via e-mail so that you could give her some pointers. You are as close to an expert as I know. If you do not feel you want to, I understand that, too and I will let her know. Let me know how you are doing. I heard you were not doing well either. Again, keep your faith and hang in there. Kevin is no longer suffering, and he is walking with the Lord. Take care, Cheryl

I am so sorry about Kevin. It has to be a very sad time for you and your family. I know things are more easily said than lived, but try to remember he is in a better place with no more pain and suffering. I lost my daddy fourteen years ago to cancer, so I have a glimpse of what you have been through. Time has helped me, and I have learned to deal with it but haven't gotten over him and never will, because he was worth every tear I shed. I just want you to know our prayers are with you, and may God be you in this time of sorrow. If there is anything we can do, please feel free to ask. God Bless, Colleen

Our hearts go out to the Triplett family. Kevin certainly fought a good fight. I lost a son at age 42, and I can share in your pain. As time goes on, God does have a way to let us remember the blessings that our sons brought to us. Thanks also for the photo. I will have this framed and will cherish it. I am supposed to leave tomorrow for an IN TOUCH meeting in Atlanta, but I am not sure I can make it. I think I have come down with a flu bug. If possible, I will see you today, but if I don't, Ill see you when I get back from Atlanta. Maurice

Kevin's memorial service was a celebration of his life. The music touched everyone's heart, and the words shared by Kevin's pastors brought much comfort to us. Their depth of caring for him was obvious. Comments by his friends and others in attendance will never be forgotten. Our love and thanks forever is extended to them.

November 30, 2006

A Celebration of A Life That Matters
The Memorial Service

"Amazing Grace" was played on the harmonica by Steve Cardwell.

Rev. Shannon Critcher's Comments

Jesus loves me this I know, for the Bible tells me so. Oh, how he loves you and me. Thank you on behalf of the family for coming to celebrate the amazing grace that God has extended to this family through the life of Kevin Triplett, through what he has been able to accomplish in their lives these last three or four days. God has been very good. They want you to know that they celebrate God's goodness. So, thank you for being here, and thank you for praying for the family not only since Monday but over the last five or six years. Thank you very much for every prayer that you expended on their behalf, on Kevin's behalf. Wayne and Kathy were very clear that they wanted today to be a celebration, a celebration of Kevin's earthly life and his eternal life. Both were possessions he held near and dear. You see, Kevin is not laying here before us today. This is just his body. His soul, which is the real Kevin, was something that God gave him when he was birthed into existence, and Kevin became a living soul. Just as he was, you are. That soul is the real you and the real me. This is just a shell that housed the soul. One day, it will be raised. One day, it will be changed, but right now Kevin is in the presence of Jesus because of the relationship that he made in 1999 that he started with Jesus Christ. So, today we celebrate not only the years that we lived with Kevin in this life, but the life that he is now enjoying in heaven with his savior Jesus Christ.

I mentioned in 1999, something happened to Kevin. He met someone that changed him for all eternity. Now Kevin, since that time, wrestled with that decision. He wrestled with whether he was truly a Christian for really I guess it was a year or so. He really struggled with that. I sat in his living room and talked with him. I know he came into my office and in Jim's office and we talked. Kevin wrestled with that relationship wondering if what he had, his salvation, was really secure or not. Would it last? Was that decision valid? Do you know what he figured out with the help of the Holy Spirit? It was. That that happened in 1999 is unlosable. It's something you can't lose one day just by something else. Kevin got that settled. He would talk about frequently driving down a stake. In about 2000 or 2001, frequently he drove down a stake. I noticed in 2004, Pastor Craig did a message on that, and there are a couple of stakes up here dated 5-16-04 when Kevin said, "Yes. I know beyond the shadow of a doubt that my life belongs to Jesus Christ." I wonder today if you could drive down that stake? Do you really know that your salvation is in God's hand? The Holy Spirit gave Kevin that assurance. I know that blessed hope is one of the things, one of the reasons beyond the help of his family and his church and his friends, that blessed hope is what helped Kevin wrestle with cancer with such vibrancy and with such strength. He knew that he belonged to God, and that God was with him. Many of you I've heard mention and I've read in the papers how you never heard Kevin complain. You didn't hear it come out of his mouth. You've talked about how he and his faith in an almighty God were a testimony and a help to you in these last six years. Oh, what a blessing that we were blessed with young men like Kevin Triplett. Praise God that he allowed our lives to be impacted by Kevin. Oh that you and I would be able to face life and the giants of life that come into our lives with the grace and the faith that Kevin did. I hope that's how you want to tackle the things that are happening in your life with the same grace, the same strength that Kevin faced cancer. You see, we can face those giants. The Bible says we should face them with the strength of God. If we would just trust God, trust that he is big, and trust that he is powerful, bigger than all the things that can come against us. You see in the midst of our heartache, in the midst of adversity, in the midst of trials, even in the midst of darkest days and the news of cancer and radiation and chemotherapy, God is good and we can trust him.

In just a few moments, Pastor Craig will be talking about trusting Jesus. I want to encourage you to listen to what the Holy Spirit wants to say to you, that he'd take the testimony of Kevin Triplett's life, and may he take today's celebration, and may he renew your heart. Listen, God loves us. He demonstrated that love on a cross two thousand years ago when he sent his son to die and shed his blood so that our sins could be forgiven. He demonstrated it through the resurrection of Jesus when on the third day, Jesus got up out of the grave. He demonstrates it day in and day out during this pilgrimage of life that God walks beside us.

I know if Kevin were standing here he would want you to hear about Jesus today. He would want you to know that in the midst of the cancer, that Jesus walked with him. From his bedside, Jesus sat there and held his hand. Listen to this beautiful Psalm 23. "The Lord is my shepherd, I shall not want." Oh, Kevin enjoyed the shepherd Jesus. Kevin knew who Christ was, and that Jesus was in control of his life. "He maketh me to lie down in green pastures, and he leadeth me beside the still waters. He restoreth my soul." You mean in the midst of cancer that Kevin was able to restore his soul daily? Sure he was, and so was Kathy, and so was Wayne. I know it's tough at times, but they were able to because of Christ, because he led them beside the still waters. "He leadeth me in the paths of righteousness for his namesake." Do you ever wonder why bad things happen to what we call good people? We know that there are none good. We know that none are righteous, not one. Do you ever wonder why cancer attacks a thirteen-year-old? I do. I don't have a good answer for you, other than it's for his namesake and for his glory. Can God get glory out of suffering? Yes. He can. I believe that beyond the shadow of a doubt that this happened to Kevin for the name of Jesus Christ's sake, and it happened to the glory of God. I believe that he met that, and God's glory radiated through Kevin's life. "Yea, though I walk through the valley of the shadow of death." Kevin did that for six years didn't he? The shadow of death was on his life for six long years. The Bible says that even though we walk through the valley of the shadow of death, "I will fear no evil for thou art with me. Thy rod and thy staff, they comfort me." You see, God and Jesus the shepherd, were with Kevin every step of the way. The Bible says that "there preparest a table before me in the presence of mine enemies." I hope you catch that. I hope that you see that Jesus does not always take us away from our enemies and hide us and prepare a table. Sometimes, he sets the banquet table right there in front of that enemy. I believe that a banquet was prepared for Kevin day after day in front of the enemy cancer, right there in front of that enemy. The Bible says that Jesus "anoints our head with oil, and that our cup can run over." Can you imagine Kevin receiving from Jesus the oil of gladness, the oil of strength as day in and day out Jesus the shepherd will anoint his head? Maybe that's why you didn't hear many complaints. Maybe that's why his cup runneth over. "Surely goodness and mercy shall follow me all the days of my life." You know what? In April of 1999, God's goodness didn't stop following Kevin. It didn't. God's mercy didn't stop following Him. It followed him all the days of his life.

On Monday, Kevin was doing something I can only dream of. He closes this psalm with "I will dwell in the house of the Lord forever" Folks, because in 1999 Kevin met Jesus Christ, he is dwelling in God's house, not down the street, but in God's house forever. And you can, too if you'll just give your life to Jesus Christ. Let's pray.

Lord God, you are good, and Lord I thank you so much for the way that you changed my life through Kevin's life, Lord through his battle with cancer. Lord, I thank you that you changed my life, as I've watched the support that Wayne, Kathy, his grandparents, his family members, and his friends gave to Kevin. I saw something that you accomplished, and I saw your glory. I don't know if there's many people who fought more of a fight than what this family did. God, I thank you that through every mile they've gone to Baptist and to Texas, Lord to every doctors' visit, through every treatment, through everything that you've walked beside this family. You have been their shepherd, and oh what a good shepherd you have been. Thank you for protecting them, thank you for strengthening them, and granting them peace. Father, it's in the name of the good shepherd Jesus that we present this celebration to you this evening that you receive glory. Give us eyes to see your work through this circumstance, through Kevin's sickness, through his death. God, may you receive glory. Lord, as your Word is preached, as songs are sung, as people share, may this celebration be presented to you in the name of Jesus Christ. On behalf of the family, and on behalf of those here, Lord we present it to you in such a manner. God speak, in Christ's name. Amen.

I promised the Lord something a little over a year ago that every time there was a funeral, I would share this. I hope I never fail to that intermingled with all the pain, the heartache and the missing, there's preciousness. The Bible says that the death of a saint is precious in the sight of the Lord. And if it's precious in God's sight, it should be precious in ours. I know it hurts, but family and friends I beg you. Don't miss the glory of God. Kevin knew Jesus Christ. And there he is this precious moment. When he closed his eyes and breathed his last on Monday, it was precious, very, very precious. Don't ever lose that family.

Pastor Shannon then read Kevin's poem ... *Cancer*.
The poem can be found in Kevin's autobiography.

"Laid To Rest" was performed by Kevin's band Taking Up Arms.

Rev. Craig Church's Comments
A Life Well Lived

Wayne, Kathy, and family, I want to say I love you, and I loved Kevin. I hurt with you today, but I also believe that I can celebrate with you. I don't know of a greater example of a family going the extra mile, doing all they could do, waging a fight as noble as you waged against cancer. You are to be commended. I thank you for the example of love, of determination, and of a noble fight. Well done.

Few people have had an impact on my life like Kevin had. Early Monday morning after I had gotten a phone call from brother Wayne, I started praying and the Lord placed on my heart a passage of scripture. That passage of scripture describes Kevin's life. It's found in Proverbs 3:5–6. If I could find words this afternoon to describe Kevin's life, it would be a life well lived. These verses of scripture will explain a life well lived. In Proverbs 3:5–6 the Bible says: "Trust in the Lord with all thine heart. Lean not on thy own understanding, but in all thy ways acknowledge him, and he will direct thy paths." That couple verses of scripture describes Kevin's life. As Pastor Shannon has already alluded to, in 1999 Kevin Triplett trusted Jesus Christ as his personal Lord and savior. As I will read here in just a minute, he said that was the greatest decision he ever made in his life, was to trust Jesus Christ as his personal Lord and savior. We would talk on several occasions of his salvation experience, and he would examine that as Pastor Shannon has mentioned. He would examine that at times, and I want to encourage you during this time, this solemn time we've met together, that you examine your salvation experience. As Paul tells us to examine our faith and see if we have that saving faith that the Bible speaks of. The first part of this passage of scripture says trust in the Lord with all your heart, and Kevin trusted Jesus as his savior. Kevin trusted the Lord with his life, also. In the midst of cancer, he trusted in the unchanging hand of an almighty God.

I can remember one of the last times that I talked to Kevin on a Wednesday night, and our youth here at Millers Creek had gone to see Facing the Giants. I was watching that movie. The movie is really saying that God is able to take you through any challenges in your life, and God is bigger than any giant in your life, and all things are possible with God. I was sitting there, and I was thinking about Kevin as I was watching that movie. I was thinking of some giants in my life, and about that time the phone rang, and it was Kevin. He was calling me from Texas. He didn't do that a lot. It was a special time. I believe it was a divine phone call, because I went outside and I got in the lobby of the theater, and I started talking to Kevin. Kevin said, "Craig, I'm going through a procedure tomorrow, and I just called and wanted to ask you just to pray with me." Kevin was trusting God with his life. It was amazing how the Holy Spirit of God interjected in that conversation and in that prayer. It was probably the sweetest time Kevin and I ever had on the phone. There in the lobby of a theater, God was moving. I said, "Kevin, I will promise you this. God is bigger than any giant that you will ever face in your life." I want to let each one of you know whatever you are going through this day, God is bigger than any giant in your life, and if you trust him as Kevin did, he will see you through. I promise.

Kevin not only trusted in the Lord with all his heart, but the second part of this passage of scripture says lean not unto thy own understanding. Kevin didn't lean on his own understanding. You see, I have a hard time understanding what we are facing today. My mind can't comprehend it. I have a hard time with it, but you see Kevin didn't lean on his own understanding. If he had been leaning on his own understanding, he could have gotten bitter and asked why, why, why instead of what can I do even though I'm in this position that I'm in? He did not rely on his own understanding, he faced it head on. I can stand up here this afternoon and tell you all of the many special times of Kevin's faith, of Kevin's strength, of Kevin's courage, of Kevin's being positive, of Kevin wanting to pray for others more than himself. I can tell you all these times that we had together. He didn't lean on his own understanding. It's hard for us to come in here today and understand why good people have to face things like this. Why do the good die young? I don't understand. Isaiah 55: 9

says: As the heavens are higher than the earth so are my ways higher than your ways and my thoughts than your thoughts. God's ways are higher than our ways. God's thoughts are higher than our thoughts. Kevin understood that. Many times we would talk about that, and we would talk about Romans 8:28, and we know that all things work together for good to them that love the Lord, that are called according to his purpose, not our good but the good of the kingdom. Kevin understood that; therefore, Kevin trusted in the Lord Jesus Christ for salvation and for strength to get him through. He didn't rely on his own understanding. He looked to Jesus and acknowledged him in every way as these passages of scripture said. In all thy ways acknowledge him. I don't know of a young man who has done that any better than Kevin.

We had a special time last night in our youth, just a time of remembering and had a time of sharing just what Kevin had meant to them. I sat there and listened. Brother Kevin was the one who invited me to church here. Kevin was the one who gave me inspiration to do this or to do that. That's what is described as a life well lived, impacting others through the cause of Jesus Christ. He acknowledged the Lord Jesus Christ as savior, as Lord, and as his strength. What a testimony Kevin has left with us. Trust in the Lord with all thy heart and lean not unto thy own understanding. In all thy ways acknowledge Him, and He shall direct thy paths.

Because of a life well lived, Kevin's path was directed. On November 27, a little after 4 AM in the morning, he was directed into the arms of Jesus, a life well lived. Where there is no more, brother Wayne, no more pain, no more cancer, no more treatments. He has conquered his giant and moved to the life everlasting. The testimony of Kevin, a life well lived, trust in the Lord with all thy heart and lean not unto thine own understanding, in all thy ways acknowledge him, and he shall direct thy paths.

What would we do if we could follow after the legacy that has been left in the Word of God and trusting Jesus Christ, a life well lived. In II Timothy 4:6–8 the Bible says: "For I am now ready to be offered and the time of my departure is at hand." The most amazing phone call I've ever received, and I don't even know if Wayne knows this, was two and a half years ago on a Saturday morning, Kevin called me. I can't remember if he was going in to face one of the many surgeries that he had to face, or if he was just getting home. He called me early that Saturday morning and you've got to understand that this was a sixteen and a half year old young man. He said, "Craig, I just wanted to call you. I've been thinking about dieing." I tried to minister to him, and then some of the most amazing words came out of his mouth. He said, "Craig, this morning I was thinking about dieing. I got excited, because I want to see Jesus." I want to let everybody know in this place this afternoon that Kevin got to see Jesus Monday. I don't know about you, but I'm just a little bit envious tonight. I'm just a little bit envious. He fought a good fight as the Bible says in this passage of scripture. It says: I have fought a good fight, I have finished my course, I have kept the faith, and that is what Kevin did. It says: Henceforth there is laid up for me a crown of righteousness which the Lord, the righteous judge, shall give me at that day and not to me only, but unto all them also that love his appearing. We celebrate Kevin's life. We celebrate his home going. He has touched so many lives in this room and in this community, and I praise God for that. I praise God for Kevin's life. He has left a legacy. There are people that live eighty, ninety years, and never leave the legacy that Kevin Triplett has left for us. May we always remember, may we always learn, and may we always lean and trust on the savior that he did. I see this, all this stuff here (wheel chair, three pair of crutches, his cane, medicine pole and pump, box of medications, his shoes, Kevin's stakes of assurance, the cross which hung on his wall in his room), and Wayne and I were in here this morning and all these meds over here. I want you to know that what's on top of this overcomes it all, and that is the cross of Calvary, the shed blood and the risen Savior that we serve. This is the time of celebration! Kevin is with the Lord Jesus Christ! Paul says to be absent from the body is to be present with the Lord! We come into this place sad and hurting, but I praise God that Kevin is in a better place. The cross of Calvary and the shed blood of Jesus Christ saw him through cancer, saw him through death, and now he lives forever with our Lord Jesus Christ. Kevin said in the back of your program, and I want to read that to you. This is what Kevin wrote as the most important things in life. I got to see this in Kevin over and over and over. These are not just words, he lived this.

Pastor Craig then read Kevin's narrative ... "Life's Most Important Things"
The narrative can be found in Kevin's autobiography.

I believe at this time Kevin would want me to tell you how to have a personal relationship with this Lord Jesus Christ that he trusted and gave his heart and life to. I want to encourage each one of you to come by. This (framed display) is Kevin's testimony. As you come by to visit the family later, I want you to read this. This is what Jesus Christ did in his life. These are some verses that he has on this piece of paper, and I feel led to share with you tonight. I want to tell each one of you that God loves you more than anything. The Bible says in John 3:16: "For God so loved the world that he gave his only begotten son, that whosoever believeth on him should not perish but have everlasting life." This is the life that Kevin is enjoying right now. I want you to know that Jesus Christ died for you. The Bible says in Romans 5:8: "But God demonstrated his love toward us in that while we were yet sinners, Christ died for us." I want you to know this afternoon that the only way to heaven is through Jesus Christ. The world will tell you there are many ways to heaven, but my Bible tells me in John 14:6 that Jesus says: "I am the way, the truth, and the life. No man cometh to the father except through me." This afternoon, Kevin would want me to tell you that Jesus wants you to be saved. The Bible says in Luke 19:10: "For the son of man has come to seek and to save that which is lost." The bottom of this plaque reads Ephesians 2:8–9: "For by grace are ye saved through faith and that not of yourself, it is a gift of God. Not of works lest any man should boast." You may be here this afternoon and say Craig, if you were talking about me this afternoon, you couldn't say a life well lived. I don't know this Jesus that you're talking about. Right now, the Holy Spirit of God is speaking to my heart, and I want to know him. Let me tell you what the Bible says and how you can be saved. These are the same words that Pastor Jim in his office spoke to Kevin through the Word and led him to Jesus Christ. It's Romans 10:9: "If thou shalt confess with thy mouth the Lord Jesus and shalt believe in thy heart that God has raised him from the dead, thou shalt be saved. For with the heart man believeth unto righteousness and with the mouth confession is made unto salvation." My Bible says in Romans 10:13: "For whosoever shall call upon the name of the Lord shall be saved."

There may be some here who say this is not appropriate at a funeral. Kevin said it was the greatest decision he ever made. I think he would want me to offer that to you. He would want me to introduce you to the savior that saved his life, took him through cancer, and has led him home. If you're here and you don't know Jesus Christ as your personal Lord and savior, I'm not talking about being baptized, I'm not talking about being on the church roll. I'm talking about a personal relationship with Jesus Christ. You can have that today. You can call on him right now. You can start living that life, a life well lived. Bow your heads with me. David Dyer is getting ready to come and sing a song. I want to encourage you right now that if you don't know this Jesus that I have been talking about, that Kevin knew, and if you feel the Holy Spirit of God speaking to your heart, call on him right now. Say, Lord I'm a sinner, and I know my sin separates me from you. Come into my heart and save me. I believe that you died on the cross and three days later rose again. Come into my heart and save me. Be my Lord and savior. I want to encourage you to do business with the Lord. Examine yourself and make the greatest decision anybody could make, to accept Jesus Christ as your personal Lord and savior. Call on him now.

David Dyer, Kevin's friend, sang … "I Can Only Imagine"

Rev. Jim Gore's Comments

Wayne, Kathy, and family, the hearts of thousands of people as you well know are going out to you this week. I can think of at least eight or nine times since Monday morning that folks have stopped me here and there just to ask about it. Yesterday, I was on the other side of the county and had a tee shirt on that said Millers Creek Christian School. Somebody said, "Are you a part of Millers Creek?" I said, "Well, yes." They asked me about Kevin and you all. I know that county-wide and much further than that, people have been expressing their feelings, their emotions, and their prayer support for you all. Certainly, Becky and I will continue our prayers for you, focusing more on you now as Kevin no longer needs them.

I do want to say, though that you all have shown us how to care for loved ones. Thank you for that. Kevin has taught us how to live in the face of death. I know others thank him for that as well. These are lessons that we all need to know, because the truth is, we cannot live to the glory of God until we are ready to die and meet God, until we have come to grips with the fact that we are going to die one day.

Only then can we truly begin to live the way that God would have us live.

I want to read just two or three verses, and I'm very brief. These are verses found in John 14 and they are spoken by the Lord Jesus just before He was ready to go to the cross. He had been talking with his disciples about his going away. They were having some difficulty with that, and we understand why they would. This is what Jesus said: "Let not your heart be troubled. You believe in God, believe also in me. In my father's house are many mansions. If it were not so, I would have told you." I want to personalize the remaining verse and a half of this. I do no injustice to the text in so doing. Jesus said: I go to prepare a place for Kevin, and if I go and prepare a place for Kevin, I will come again and receive Kevin to myself that where I am, there Kevin may be also. What words of comfort that is to us. We can count on it because Jesus, the son of the living God, said it.

Let's pray. Father, we rejoice in your love and your goodness. And Lord, we come and face times such as this, hard times because those whom we love have been taken from this earth. We know Kevin is with you today by his own testimony by the Word of God. Yet, we know that he will sorely be missed by this family, this church, by the people in our schools here in the county, by teachers, by so many people who knew him and loved him and had such high regard for him. So, we just pray thy comfort Lord on each of our hearts. Thank you that you have prepared a place and that you are for all of us who will trust in you. May we so live that when this day comes for us, as it has come for Kevin, that there will be no doubt in the minds of those left behind that you have saved me and us and that we, too will be with you, in Jesus name I pray. Amen

"Some Will Seek Forgiveness" was performed by Kevin's band
Taking Up Arms.

Comments from Kevin's Friends

I want to say on behalf of the group Kevin was in, Taking Up Arms, that Kevin was one of the greatest guys I've ever met. We started out, and I can't believe he is here. He walked in and said, "Hi, do you want to start a band?" I said, "Yeah, my brother and I both will do it." We started playing. It seemed like every practice when Kevin came in, he touched all our lives by the way he was. Everyone knew what Kevin was going through. You never heard him complain, even if he was in pain or anything. He just went through practice and had a great time like always. I appreciate Wayne for all the help that he gave us through the band. I appreciate him and his family so much, because they meant so much to all of us. We all will miss Kevin so much. God bless Kevin and his family. We love you. Charlie

I just want to talk about Kathy. I love her. Wayne's a good man and a good father. Kathy is a private person, and she hasn't been like a lot of people to share things. She shared them with the people she works with. We worked with Kathy at Tyson through the years. We watched her go through the pain. She suffered a lot alone, and loving her child so much she couldn't stand it. We watched her bravery over the days and suffered along with her. We love Kathy very much, and I don't want us to forget her dedication to her son. Susie

I'm glad to be here in honor of Kevin. Even if I had a bad day, I'd talk to him, and he could be in such high spirits like nothing, nothing bothered him. There is not one word that you can think of that would describe Kevin. All I know is that he holds the stars above me, and he earned his wings, and he proved that to every one of us. He was a true angel on earth. I'll always love and miss him very much. Cyretha

I first remember Kevin when he was in my five-year-old Sunday school class. I haven't talked a lot about that. He was such a sweet little fellow. He had this shy little grin on his face all the time. He was one of the hardest ones that I ever had to get to talk back to me. He was extremely shy then. It was a joy to watch him grow in the Lord as he matured here at Millers Creek. He was such a blessing as he became a teenager, and he was such an influence on those around him as he struggled with this cancer. I talked to him quite a few times. He always had the sweetest spirit. I just really think that Kevin, he was amazing like this. My words can't express the sorrow that I have. I know that Kevin is in a better place now, and he is hand in hand with Jesus Christ. There's no better place to be. He will be greatly missed, and we love him. Marlayne

I had the opportunity to be Kevin's principal and that was a real honor. One of my favorite movies of all time is called *Brian's Song*. In that, those of you that are sport's fans, will remember that the announcer said to remember Brian Picolo for the way he lived, not the way he died. I think everyone here that knows Kevin will take that with them. I will remember about Kevin's passing, but I will always remember the courage by which Kevin lived. I've heard it said that we don't seek greatness. Sometimes greatness is thrust upon us. Greatness was thrust upon Kevin, and he didn't seek it. Kevin sometimes wondered what we were all fussing about, because he was just doing what he could do. He lived a life courageously. Many times I held Kevin up as an example to other students who were upset about something, too. I hope that we all can live as close as Kevin did. Steve

Wayne and Kathy, I just want to say that I loved Kevin. I was just drawn so much to Kevin, and at that time I did not know why. I knew he was going through a terrible battle. A few weeks later, my grandson was diagnosed with a brain tumor, and it was also cancer. The first time I saw Kevin in the hospital, I was there with my grandson. Craig and I came by to see Kevin as he was taking his treatments laying in bed eating a cheeseburger, just as nonchalant as could be. His dad was with him, and we just had a nice conversation. After Adam had his surgery, Kevin's grandmother lived right across the road, and Kevin came over and visited with Adam and encouraged him, and it cheered him up. Kevin helped give me courage to get through that, and I will be forever grateful. We love you so much. We love you both. He was such a wonderful young man. Louise

I don't personally know Kevin. I've worked with Kathy for two years. I know the strength in that family was just phenomenal. We should just pray for them. The Lord showed me that Kevin was in a robe of white, he's cured, and in no pain. Our loss here on earth is heaven's gain. I can guarantee that angels are rejoicing now. He's in no more pain. Abbie

I'm Kevin's grandfather. I feel like I'm sitting here quenching the spirit. I don't want to do that. I read some material that Kevin wrote and it was about what he thought of me. I walked up to Kathy and I told her that we need to turn this around. We all loved Kevin. He was a kind, generous, loving boy. I'm going to miss him. Ralph

I'd like to stand for my brother Wayne, Kathy, and Kevin. They have been an inspiration to us. I think of my brother. I talked to him, but not as much as I should have. I stand for my mom. She couldn't be here for health reasons, but Kevin was the light of her heart. She was a prayer warrior, and she still is. She wanted Wayne to know she is here, her love is here, and she loves Kevin dearly. Jill

When I got to West Wilkes, I didn't know Kevin. I didn't know much about him. As you're going through a football season, you don't pay attention to a lot of things other than what you're looking at sometimes. After about a year and seeing Kevin around, a lot of kids they've got something wrong with them, they want to tell you about every single day. They might walk around the halls and if they've got a hang nail, they're going to let you know about it, but never Kevin. I had no idea until one day I had not seen Kevin for a long period of time. I set down in the office a minute, and they let me know what was going on. Kevin was such a great student and last year during football season, I talked with the football players about courage. I used Kevin as an example. The kids wanted to sign a football for Kevin. I had it for a long time until Wayne and Kevin got back from Houston. I wanted to go by and visit them at the house, but I just put it off. I got some reports from Steve that Kevin wasn't doing very well. It was a Friday night, we were out there on the field getting ready for the fifth quarter. The band had this huge ribbon at there on the track. We were going to walk it. I had that football up in my office. We were getting ready to walk, and on a football field you don't want the kids to be distracted too much. I saw they were getting ready to play some music. I could hear Kevin playing. I had never heard him play at a football game. That was the thing about Kevin. He wanted to influence others. He wanted and had a message for others. A lot of kids would have been selfish with their time and would have wanted to spend time with their family. Kevin really had a message to get out to the kids. That really stuck with me. Luckily, my coaches, the team, and I were able to give that ball to Kevin. Football is an important part of their day, but I think the kids really wanted to spend some time with Kevin. I'll always remember that about Kevin. He wanted to spend some time with others. Tim

A friend of mine told me that Kevin had just passed away. It was such a shock. My favorite memory with Kevin was our eighth grade prom. Jenni had brought him as a date. I remember I was always a wall-flower and still am. I was sitting over there, and Kevin came up to me and asked me to dance. It was my first dance ever. He was such a won-derful guy, and he just laughed. He was just so happy. He was always such an inspiration to me. On Monday, I was in class and asked my professor if I could leave, and he said yes. It was so unlike him. It must have been from God. I went back to my dorm and opened my Bible and sat there for hours and prayed. I just knew that something inside, I didn't actually cry that much, for some reason, and I was just so happy, because I knew he was not in pain anymore. He was such an inspiration. I thought how that if that happened to me would I be that faithful? Could I fight that long or would I just have given up? I thank him for his testimony for everyone. He was just a terrific indi-vidual. It just makes me want to live for Christ. Ashleigh

Probably you know me. My name is Joe, and I was the singer for the band Taking Up Arms which Kevin was in. I only knew Kevin for a little over a year, but in that year I'd have to say that he probably impacted my life and inspired me more than anyone else that I have ever met, because of the way he handled things and what was hap-pening despite his current situations. I remember one time when we were over at Charlie and Jim's house, and we were practicing. We were in the back yard for some reason. We found an old speed limit sign in the brush. We pulled it out. We were just messing around with it and stuff and Kevin says, "Wow, it's not everyday you see one of these." We were like, "Yeah, thanks Kevin." Kevin was just an amazing person. He really just inspired me to pattern my life after him. Joe

You've heard them talking about Kevin's band. Early on right before they started it, Gwyn, Zeb, and me, we used to play. We were all over at Kevin's house one time. We were jamming around and just playing. Taking Up Arms hadn't been formed yet. They didn't have a group right then. Kevin looked up at us and said, "You know guys, I really admire you. What you do. I'd just love to do that more than anything in the world." The three of us were there. Gwyn, Zeb, and I just looked at each other. We all knew there was no reason in the world for Kevin to look up to us. At the time, we were in high school, and we were playing music in front of people, and we were real proud of what we were doing. Everything he said that day changed our whole perspective, because Kevin was dealing with so much more, but he didn't see it as anything special. He just thought he was doing what he thought he could. I don't think he ever realized how he played, too, not like he was. Kevin never saw himself as an inspiration. He never saw himself as anything more than a kid that had something to deal with. He had a dream like the rest of us did. He just wanted to get in front of some people and play some music. I don't think any of us can ever do it again without thinking about him. One of the happiest night's I've had at a show was when Taking Up Arms and Tethered had gotten together, and Kevin and they had come to a show. He always came. He came whatever and did whatever he could to be there. There was a little time before hand and Kevin talked to Gwyn or something and said, "Do you think we can play?" He said, "Sure, go do it." I don't think I have ever seen a group of kids more involved. I don't think anybody was looking at anybody else. When it was all over, Kevin just lifted his hands up, and I think a few people in the crowd cried. I've never seen anything more intense in my life. I have a hard time playing anything anymore. I wish I could do it with that kind of emotion. Brandon

I didn't want to get up. I figured if I'd start talking, I'll cry, but Kevin and I were more like brothers than friends. I went through a lot with the man. He took me to Alaska with him. I went to the beach the first time with him. I shared right up there with him playing with the praise team. He was there, and I was over there somewhere. There were a lot of shows I got to share the stage with Kevin. It was great. I'd go over to his house. We'd get loud, and Wayne would scream at us. He'd want to know what was going on upstairs. I laughed a lot, too. He'd love riding around in that blue Mustang of his. He thought that was the greatest thing in the world. We were all over this town. It was great. I called Craig. It was Monday morning, and I had to work third shift. I didn't even go to sleep. I called him just wanting to talk. I could tell something was up. I said what I had to say. He said, "I have some bad news." I was like, "Well, it can't be that bad." He said, "Kevin passed away." My reaction to that wasn't the best in the world. He had cancer and that's bad, of course. I guess you do have a chance to die, but I thought he was doing better. It hit so hard. This week has been crazy thinking about the small stuff, riding four-wheelers. When Wayne was the principal at the Career Center going over there and setting up amplifiers and playing all day long for no reason, just to play. He was the best friend I have ever had. I doubt if I find anybody like Kevin again. I loved him. I do love him. It's kind of hard to say stuff in the past tense as if he's gone. I caught myself this week getting ready to talk about him like he was here. It hurts. It hurts a lot. Wayne knows I love him. Kathy and all you guys have done a lot for me, and my prayers are with you, and my love is with you. I thank you all for what you have done for me and what Kevin did for me. Gwyn

Wayne, Kathy, and friends, I remember Kevin when we first started participating here at the church. We were having evaluations to see how our kids were with their musical abilities. The thing that sticks in my mind the most is what Kevin told me. "I'll do whatever you want me to," he said. And he always would. I remember at first it was a struggle with hours of practice. It seemed like we were only learning just one or two songs. Kevin would say, "Just keep on going. We're getting better. We're getting there." I never will forget the first time we ever went anywhere besides the church to sing. It was at the Relay for Life. Folks, that was something Kevin wanted to do. At the time, I didn't really think we were prepared for it, but I said Kevin wants to do it, so we're going to do it. What an inspiration he was for me, just persevere, just keep on going and do whatever is necessary. Chris

When Kevin was in the eighth grade after he had been diagnosed in the seventh grade, that was also when Justin Eller passed away. Both those young men have been a light to this whole community. The school decided to try to raise money in honor and in memory of them and donate it to Brenner Children's Hospital. The only thing I want to say is, I love Wayne and Kathy, and I appreciate you so much. You two, as Kevin has, have been an inspiration to all of us. At Baptist, at the new cancer research part on the fifth floor, they have a wall dedicated to contributors who have sent a donation. We raised just a little bit over ten thousand dollars. For that much or more, you were recognized on the wall. There are plaques on the wall and ours isn't large, but to me it means more than anything. It's safe to say that a lot of us will be going to that part of Baptist Hospital. If you have time and it will take you a while, but look for it. That is a testimony to Justin and Kevin. They mean so much to this community and touched so many lives. Fran

I'm not sure which year it was that Kevin spoke at our Relay for Life at the community college. I think it was four years ago. I was so impressed with his speech. I'm not a cancer survivor, but I've lost family members to it. I will never forget how moved everyone was, especially the survivors. I keep my thoughts and prayers with the family. Jenny

I'll try to get through this the best I can. I'm Kevin's cousin. What do you say about somebody that truly all of you already know? You know, we can't keep him a secret anymore. He was our golden child so to say. Kevin wasn't dealt a fair hand in life, but it's not what you're dealt, but what you do with the hand that you are given. I know myself, I could never have done what Kevin did. He is the strongest person, not only physically but mentally, that I know, and that I have ever met. The only thing that Kevin wanted to be was normal. He just wanted to be normal. He wanted to be treated normal. I think sometimes with somebody that has cancer or a disability, you don't know what to say to them. You don't know how to act towards them because you're not experiencing what they are experiencing. I'm ashamed on my part that I didn't do more small things for Kevin, that I know I'm able and I could have done. I don't know what to say about him besides that he will be truly missed very much, especially at Christmas. There is one thing that has never changed in twenty-six years of my life. On Christmas eve, I will be at my grandmother's house. That was one thing that my brother and I looked forward to doing, seeing Kevin at grandmas. There will be a void there, but I know he got the best Christmas present anybody in this room could ever get. Kevin, I love you, and you will truly be missed. You made me want to be a better person, but also a better Christian, so that I could have something to look forward to, and I will see you again. Gary

Let me have seconds on that (Kevin's grandpa speaks again). I think I'm over my crying right now, and I want to say something that's important. Kevin loved West High. He went to elementary school, and he loved it. He had lots of friends. He loved them all. He loved this church. He loved to play with his band. He loved those boys. He was bright. A lot of people are bright when it comes down to when you are so bad off, but Kevin knew. You didn't have to tell him, he knew how things were going. He knew they had done about all they could do. I want to thank this church for praying for Kevin. A lot of prayers went out here, I know. I appreciate it. He talked about Craig. He talked about you boys and always gave you a good word. Thank you. Ralph

"Jesus Savior Pilot Me," a recording by the Inspirations, was played.

Kevin Wayne Triplett
A Celebration of A Life That Matters Eulogy
(delivered by Wayne Triplett)

It's a celebration of the life of Kevin! I can do all things through Christ who strengthens me, but sometimes I get by with a little help from my friends, Mr. Lexapro and Ms. Ativan (anti-depressants).

Imagine you're sitting on the sofa at home and your expectant wife says, "it's time!" I had rehearsed this scenario countless times, but I dropped and spilled the "it's a boy" candy cigars all over the floor, and Kathy was shaking like a leaf. It didn't stop there. The squeak, squeak, squeak of the hospital basinet heralded Kevin's arrival for his three times a day feeding, or was it ten times a day feeding? Little did I know that years later that same squeaking sound would come back to haunt me as I pushed Kevin's IV pump and pole from bedroom to bathroom.

It isn't often that a child can be someone's greatest teacher, but for me Kevin was that person. Kevin was born on December 7, 1986 (Pearl Harbor Day). As his dad, his birth remains the most significant event of my life. You dads in the delivery room know what I'm talking about. Of course, you can get yelled at there, too. I remember being in the delivery room and catching a quick smile from him as he was born. My life was changed forever from that moment on.

As a child and toddler, we were inseparable. Our lives revolved around playing with blocks, riding in the stroller, making baby formula, and looking for Ninja Turtle characters all over several towns.

We took our nature walks, played in the newly fallen leaves, and made great snowmen. I loved seeing him play with his friends next door, Frankie and Christopher Barger (yes, they were small boys too at one time, roller blading, biking, sword fighting). What fun we had! Those were great days! Ask Ray or Ricki about the Ravenwood Olympics. You should've seen Ray wrapped like a mummy and covered with shaving cream!

In elementary school, Kevin truly enjoyed tee-ball, baseball, and basketball at the Y, as well as being on the school basketball team (undefeated). I have precious videos of many of those special moments, some of which I'm going to share with you.

When osteosarcoma (bone cancer) struck him in his seventh grade year, we were devastated. Kevin and I left Dr. Bennett's office and sat in the front seat of my Rav4 crying, anticipating the year that lay ahead. For not one but almost six and a half years, he fought this deadly disease valiantly (chemotherapy, radiation, two leg surgeries, three lung surgeries, lymph node surgery, on crutches eighteen months, experimental treatments, hundreds of trips to Baptist Hospitals Brenner Children's Hospital and ultimately on to Indianapolis, and finally to the number one cancer clinic in the world M. D. Anderson in Houston, Texas). Yes, I have no doubt that Kevin had the best of care and as you know, I constantly searched for that magic bullet, that magic cure. As his surgeon said, "He went in a child but came out a man." This was true of Kevin. He never complained and saw his predicament as God's will for him that the new cutting edge cancer therapies, many of which pioneered by him, would ultimately benefit many other people. Even in death, he gave both his corneas so others might see the light of day. We will never know the silent agony he endured, facing days at West High with crutches and a cane, spending long days and nights with that persistent cough (a spit bowl in every room and in every vehicle), and facing life without the assurance of a bright future of college, marriage, and grandchildren. Kevin and I considered ourselves fortunate to greet another birthday, another Thanksgiving, another Christmas, not knowing if each would be his last. The harsh reality of his situation is a quote from a wonderful friend and West Virginia mom, Terri Scott, who lost her son, Kevin's friend Aaron Scott, to cancer just a few years ago. She stated, "People try to help, but in reality they are clueless." It is true. Kind words and empathy help, but until you as a parent are faced with the roller coaster existence of watching your child go from 225 pounds to 108 pounds, enduring countless chemo regimens, fighting back each time surgery lands him in the hospital for days or weeks at a time, dealing with the constant specter of old man death over his shoulder; those things cannot be conveyed to you by mere words, they must be lived, and I pray that no one else here has to face that. Life, with its uncertainty, became much more precious, because we knew that at any given moment, it could be taken away. At each grave report or as we called it, at each death sentence, Kevin fought back, he gained a reprieve. He seemed almost invincible.

It isn't supposed to be this way, a father standing over his son, but death is no respecter of persons. We are powerless to choose the day, time, or order of our loved one's passing. After all, this last trip to Houston was to be a checkup or tune up for him. Now we, his family, are left to pick up the pieces of our lives, broken without him, and put them back together again in some fashion. Indeed, I told Kevin many times that I would gladly trade places with him; I would take the disease if it were possible. Even though I have battled cancer twice, it's nothing, nothing compared to the daily agony of what he faced. You see, Kevin had a lot of living yet to do, a lot of music yet to perform. Kevin was a giver, not a taker. Many times he got out of bed before dawn for the ride to Baptist for chemo or surgery. Many times I loaded his guitar for his praise band practice or performance since he was too weak to lift it, and Taking Up Arms (his band) couldn't feel his pain from the months of coughing, chemo, and radiation. Kevin seemed to draw strength from these series of unfortunate events, and as they say he would keep on keeping on, never complaining about his state in life, the cards he had been dealt.

Don't be mistaken, Kevin had a rich, rewarding life, given the fact that his battle with cancer forced him to grow up much faster than most. He loved West High and his many friends there. His part time job at Wendy's brought him many new friends, not to mention the hundreds of burgers he cooked which many of you ate. This church was his life's blood, and girls, if he seemed a bit distant, he liked you, too. It's just that his life was consumed with medical issues and his music. And did he ever love his music! Taking Up Arms (his band) was the realization of a dream come true. As long as he had the strength, he lived to play with the guys in that band. From his early practice sessions upstairs in the bonus room with Gwyn, to The Edge, and finally to Taking Up Arms, music was his therapy, and he was great at it! And when TUA won the county battle of the bands competition last month and brought the trophy by and gave it to Kevin, he just beamed. What a great group of Christian musicians. He loved his long hair, but with more time spent over the spit bowl than his guitar, his hair just got in the way. None the less, he found a way to give. It went to the Locks of Love for other needy folks.

At Baptist Hospital during his many surgeries, Pastor Craig's presence brought him comfort. Pastor Jim and Shannon would frequently visit bringing him news of what was going on at church. In Houston, his frequent calls to and from Craig gave him encouragement. Craig, there was a special bond there. You were good for each other. Thank you so much.

Speaking of great times, Kevin may have told you about our Make-A-Wish trip to Alaska. Kevin's best friend, Gwyn, somehow got lost in port, or I thought he did. Being a good surrogate dad, I found him and unloaded, the old finger in the chest routine. Kevin stood back and had a great big laugh over it. Gwyn didn't, and don't ever repeat what I said to you. We had great trips to the movies in Elkin, too. Kevin's Mustang was his pride and joy, and he had hopes of trading up to a GT.

I have met many noted people in my life, but Kevin is the greatest person I have ever known. He touched so many lives in a positive way and was an inspiration to hundreds of others by his perseverance, even in the face of overwhelming odds.

He was an inspiration spiritually to his peers with his active involvement in this church's youth programs and of course the praise band. He was even the keynote speaker for the local Relay for Life cancer fundraiser. Numerous articles and interviews detailing his battle with cancer were published in the local newspaper. He took all of this in stride and was very modest about it. I knew that his story, his battle with cancer, could and did become a comfort to many others.

To have a normal life again was not in the offing for Kevin, but through it all he had his faith, his music, his church family, his great sense of humor, support of his doctors, and most of all, his dad, and Kevin was fine. I can't count the hours late at night I spent looking for special protocols, treatments that might buy him more time with me. He was and is my inspiration and took what early on could have been a death sentence for many people, and made it a beginning.

This beginning carried and still does carry with it the hope for a cure, and the promise that whatever happened in his life that he would be fine, because he was in God's hands. This acceptance gave him an inner peace which escapes so many people. I want that, and I challenge each of us to follow his lead, if we haven't, and claim it. Even in death Sunday night, he was calm, nodding that he felt okay, no pain. His mother and I never left his side the entire night, stroking his hair, and holding his hand with Pastor Craig's message recorded two weeks earlier softly playing on the recorder near his pillow. Thank you, William, for sending those tapes. His breaths, though heavy, grew closer and weaker almost like gasps, and then with eyes wide open, looking at us, he breathed his last few breaths. The small air bag emptied like a deflated balloon, and I looked at Kathy and said, "I think he's gone." A strange peace fell over the room as if something spiritual had occurred. He looked so content, without pain, warm to the touch, and almost to the point of a slight smile beginning to break. I'll never forget it.

It was said when Abraham Lincoln died that now he belongs to the ages. Now ... the memories of Kevin belong to me and to you. I pray that we will take the faith, courage, and compassion with which he lived, take from it what we will and hold it in a special place in our hearts. I miss him. I was a single parent ... now ... I'm a senior citizen. And I know you hurt and miss him, too. That's normal. Yes, Kevin was a model for us all. He belonged to us all as his name was lifted up daily in many of your prayers. He taught us all many of life's lessons ... lessons which hopefully you will continue to ponder in your heart. Your wonderful words of recollections and personal encounters with him just affirm what we knew already: that he was one great human being. Kevin, after all, means handsome and gentle.

His life and struggles continue to be life's greatest lesson for me. Kevin no longer is tethered to the leg braces, crutches, wheelchair, spit bowls, cane, and using nine or more boxes of tissues every week, and oxygen which made moving around difficult for him. He said, "I don't want to live the next fifteen months like the last fifteen. Don't worry about me. I'll be fine. I'm ready." He said, "My birth date and death date don't mean a lot. It's the line in the middle connecting them that matters. After all, life is only a vapor." Uncommon wisdom, wouldn't you say from a teenager, priceless. My most precious gift, my son, has been called home, and even now I have a greater longing to go. His race down here is run and no doubt God needed another guitarist in His praise band in heaven. I live with that hope that one day we will be reunited and absent from each other for just a short while. Kevin's healing is now complete!

I encourage those of you who feel so moved to make a donation to the Kevin Wayne Triplett Memorial Scholarship Fund which will be used exclusively to benefit a deserving graduating senior from West High, who may be facing physical or financial hardship. And I encourage you to drop me a note or e-mail if you'd like to share a special "Kevin moment," as I hope to share our experiences ultimately in the form of a book, *Kevin's Journey ... A Young Man's Battle Against Cancer*.

I can't begin to thank all the people, churches, and schools who have helped us along the way for fear of leaving many names out. I want to thank you for honoring Kevin today with your presence and for your years of prayerful and financial support, your visits, your cards, your phone calls, and e-mails. You never let us down, you were always there for us, and we love you for that.

My video tribute to Kevin was a labor of love, something I felt compelled to compile. I appreciate Harold Ferguson and Adam Minton for their help in editing. At an hour and fifteen minutes in length it shares a more personal side of Kevin, one which you have not seen. If you can stay, Kevin would be honored. If you need to leave or go to the restroom, I understand. Kevin often asked me, "Dad, why are you always taking pictures and videos?" I would just say, "You know Kevin that you are always glad I did when the band gets together and we watch your latest performance." I knew in my heart that one day the photos and videos would be a source of comfort for me, a way of keeping Kevin close, watching highlights of his life all over again. Two years ago, when his prognosis was also grim, I thought I had completed it, but Kevin's fighting spirit gave me the gift of his presence another year and I reopened it last summer. Other than his Heavenly Father, I had the most intimate glimpse into his life. It is my gift to you, and I share it with the hope that you will leave today knowing just how special his life was to all of us. Kevin, my mentor, my teacher, my little buddy, my son, of whom I could not be more proud. For Kevin ... Love Dad.

Kevin's video tribute played as his family received friends.

December 1, 2006

Mausoleum Chapel Service
Rev. Craig Church's Comments

On behalf of Wayne, Kathy, and the family I want to thank you
for coming as we continue our celebration of Kevin's life. I want to
reiterate to you this morning that this is not the end. There is no end
in Jesus Christ. He is eternal, and I praise the Lord for that. Family, I
want us to look at some scripture to bring you comfort this morning.
It says in II Corinthians chapter four starting at verse sixteen, and I
will read some in chapter five as well. The Bible says, "for which cause
we faint not for therefore we do not lose heart because Jesus Christ is
eternal." It says, "but though the outward man perish, yet the inward
man is renewed day by day." It says, "for our light affliction which is
but for a moment worketh for us a far more exceeding and eternal
wake of glory." By the way, I just saw the sun come out. Kevin is in
the Son. Amen. While we look not at the things which are seen, but at
the things which are not seen. For the things which are seen are temporary, but the things which are not seen are eternal. In chapter five
it says, "for we know that if our earthly house of this tabernacle will
dissolve or destroy, we have a building of God, a house not made with
hands eternal in the heavens." It says, "for in this we groan earnestly
desiring to be clothed upon with our house which is from heaven." It
says in verse four, "for we that are in this tabernacle do groan being
burdened not for that we be unclothed, but clothed upon that mor-
tality might be swallowed up with life. Therefore, we are always confident knowing that while we are home in the body, we are absent from
the Lord. For we walk by faith and not by sight. We are confident, I
say, and willing rather to be absent from the body and to be present
with the Lord." I want to assure you that Kevin is in the presence of
the Lord Jesus Christ this morning. There is comfort in this passage
of scripture, but there is also a challenge for us. The Bible says in I
Corinthians 15:51, "Behold I show you a mystery. We shall not all
sleep, but we shall all be changed in a moment in a twinkling of an eye
at the last trump. The trump shall sound and the dead shall be raised
incorruptible, and we shall be changed. For this corruptible must put
on incorruption and this mortal must put on immortality. So when
this corruptible shall have put on incorruption and this mortal shall
have put on immortality, then shall be brought to pass the saying

that is written." This is why we celebrate. "Death is swallowed up in victory. Oh death, where is thy sting? Oh grave, where is thy victory? The sting of death is sin, and the strength of sin is the law. But thanks be to God which gives us the victory through our Lord and savior Jesus Christ." May we, family and friends, that are gathered here, it is going to be hard. We are going to miss Kevin. There are going to be times when we are hurting, but I want you to know Kevin has won the victory. Kevin is with Jesus Christ. I want to challenge each one of you in this passage of scripture in verse fifty-eight it says, "therefore my beloved brethren, be ye steadfast, unmovable, always abounding in the work of the Lord for as much as ye know that your labor is not in vain in the Lord." Kevin is seeing that now. Kevin is reaping the rewards of being steadfast, unmovable, always abounding in the work of the Lord, always glorifying Him. He is at peace with Jesus. It is well with his soul. I want to ask you today. Is it well with your soul?

"It Is Well With My Soul"
Performed by Praise Team Singers

Amen and glory to God. Thank you Jesus that it can be well with our souls. In the midst of death it can be well with our souls. If it's well with your soul today, you will see Kevin again. What a glorious day it will be when we see Jesus, and we will be reunited with a life well lived.

Father, thank you so much for this time. We thank you for those acts of kindness and love toward the family and towards you. Lord, we just pray that during these days to come that you will strengthen us. I pray that your grace, Lord that your Word says is sufficient and will fill up the souls of this family. I pray that you will give them strength and courage to go on. Lord, I pray that the life that Kevin lived will be a reminder to us daily to live a life for you. Father, we love you and thank you for the hope we have in you. Thank you for this precious time, thank you for your presence in this place, and I pray that it is well with each soul that is here. Thank you for meeting with us this morning. Thank you for Kevin's life, and thank you for the promise that we will see you and him again in Jesus' name I pray. Amen.

As Pastor Craig mentioned, the overcast skies gave way to the brilliance of the morning sun breaking through the clouds. It shone radiantly through the huge glass windows of the mausoleum. In one fleeting moment, I caught the glimpse of an eagle or large hawk as it flew past the window.

Kevin was laid to rest in a beautiful spot in Scenic Memorial Gardens. I said my final good-byes, as I laid my hand on his casket, then gently wiped it with my handkerchief.

December 1, 2006

The service last night was an incredible tribute to Kevin. Thank you so much for sharing his last moments with us. You didn't have to do that. But I know you realize how much he meant to so many people and to share that with everyone was very special. He was blessed to have you for a dad as you were to have him for a son. Please take care of yourself, and I pray all will go well for you in Houston. Please e-mail if you are able while in Houston and keep us posted. I will continue to have your name on our prayer list at Wilkesboro Baptist. Jhonda

Dear Wayne,

I love you! I sat in amazement listening to all the things you and others said about Kevin. I believe God knew when Kevin was placed in your arms for the very first time that he would be a young man "after God's own heart." And I believe He also knew you would love him more than life itself and would be strong and give him all the things Kevin would need to live the life God had planned. God makes no mistakes. Kevin was willing "to let go and let God." If we could only be like that. What a beautiful picture of what God can do for us and with us!

I believe God knew you would hold Kevin dear and go the "extras," and also be comforted when Kevin returned home to His Heavenly Father. You have a son to be so proud of! And Kevin has a Dad he was so proud of, too! God knows your needs. Love … Jill

God works in odd ways at times and I'm sure I'm like you, "Why did He do this to this child?" We wish we could take our children's place, but we can't.

Children are angels that God loans to us until He is ready to bring them home. There is only one good thing about losing a child, and that is that they are in a safe, peaceful, and loving place where they will never be exposed to pain or harm.

The last time I saw Kevin in the clinic, he finally gave me a happy, real smile, and that just brightened my heart. It's a smile I've never forgotten, and I still see it. Love … Suzanne and Sydney

Wayne,

As humans we can not comprehend why bad things happen to good people. Kevin was definitely more than just a "good" person. You did well for him and by him, never doubt that. The battle is over, and Kevin has won the ultimate prize, the gift of eternal life! May God grant you peace. And may we all be able to rejoice for him and someday with him! Godspeed! Denise

December 2, 2006

Dear Wayne,

I love you! I am so glad to be your sister. What a beautiful tribute to Kevin you have shared with us these last two days. It is so clear the bond you two shared. I cry with you and my heart aches for you. I am sad that I was not a more "physical" help for you as you cared for Kevin. But you all have been continually in my prayers and the prayers of my church family.

I believe God, in His great wisdom and love, had a plan for Kevin's life and knew he would need a very special Dad. I believe God knew Kevin would be a young man "after God's own heart," a young man that would give Him glory and honor, a young man of great character, a candle that would burn bright and magnify His Son. For all to be accomplished, Kevin would need to walk in the shadow of cancer. But he did not walk alone. You have been by his side every step of the way, just as God knew you would. You have been strong for him, giving your all. God needed Kevin to have you for his Dad. The arrival of Kevin on December 7, 1986, was all planned. When he arrived, Kevin was God's gift to you and Kathy to hold, protect, love, cherish and "give wings to fly." His life has become a gift to us all.

At the service today (Friday), I felt the presence of God filling the chapel and giving us assurance that Kevin was Home. It felt as if God was saying "I am well pleased." I could sense the presence of Kevin and could see in my mind's eye that huge smile. As the sun shone through the windows and the clouds "rolled," we seemed to catch a glimpse of God's majesty and Kevin's joy. It is an experience I will forever cherish.

I can only imagine the depth of your grief. I pray your spirit will soar and find that peace that surpasses all understanding. Kevin is free from the cancer that bound his body and is now resting in his heavenly father's arms, waiting for the day when he will again see his hero, his Dad.

I love you dearly. I realize just how much I miss you. I pray every day for you. You gave your all and more for your son. Please find comfort in that and in knowing you were a faithful part of the Master's plan. Love always, Jill

Dear Wayne,

I wanted to extend my deepest sympathy to your family with the loss of Kevin. Although I did not get to meet Kevin until recently, I felt like I was able to know him through talking with you. I don't know how to express in words my admiration of you as a father and a person. I can only imagine the time and energy you spent being there for Kevin and never giving up hope for a cure. I hope that I never have to be there for my boys for the same reason as you had to be for Kevin. If I ever get in that situation, you have been the best role model that anyone could have. Your optimism and enduring strength reminds me of the person I should strive to be. My thoughts and prayers are with you and your family. Sincerely ... Todd

Message to Kevin's Special Friends

Hi everyone.

"God gave us memories that we might have roses in December."
—James M. Barrie

The rose was Kevin's favorite flower. Kevin's memorial service was indeed a celebration of his life! Our hearts ache at his absence but rejoice that he is no longer suffering and is with his Heavenly Father. I continue to feel your love and warmth, and it is precious.

Since my pathology report was positive for cancer of the thyroid, I will be flying to Houston tomorrow (Sunday, 12/3) for a four day radioactive iodine treatment. I think the chances of the cancer having spread is minimal. Hopefully, when I return, I can stop living out of a suitcase. I will continue to keep each of you on my Kevin's Special Friends e-mail list for any updates on my condition or on the progress of Kevin's memorial scholarship.

I love and cherish each of you. Please continue to remember me in your daily prayers. Wayne

Thank you so much for sharing the eulogy with us. We will never forget meeting you all at the Astros game. Kevin was a tremendous inspiration to us that night and in the days that followed. We will be praying for your treatments, and that you will have a full recovery. May God richly bless and comfort you in the coming days. Hayes and Marsha

Wayne, just know that you are in my thoughts daily, and I pray that God holds you close and gives you peace. You are a remarkable man, and please know that I respect and cherish our friendship always. I will continue to send good thoughts your way and wish for happier times. Love you, Debbie

I am so sorry for your loss. Kevin was a great kid, and I am glad we got to know him the past six years. I know you tried everything you could to find a cure for him. He will be greatly missed. If you need anything from Dr. Ward or me, just call. Julie

The saying about "it's not what you leave this world with, but rather what you leave with the world" must have been said with Kevin in mind! He's such an inspiration to all of us. He fought a valiant battle and won in so many ways. My prayers and thoughts are with you. Sherry

CHAPTER 12

KEVIN'S LEGACY ... HIS LIGHT STILL SHINES

Parrotia persica
"Persian Ironwood"
Donated by Kenneth Crouse

Dear Wayne,
The "Persian Ironwood" seems like a fitting tribute to Kevin's life here on earth and beyond. To me, it symbolizes uniqueness in its rarity; its beauty and the fact that it blooms at an unexpected time, winter. Yet, its name "Ironwood" symbolizes a resilience or toughness and determination. This tree lives with its feet in the earth, its branches reaching to the heavens, and its leaves receiving the Light from up above. I'm sure Kevin will be proud to have this tree planted in his honor! Ken

In the Light, the presence of God
Forever I am, am I
Constant yearning in You
The Life that never died.
—From Nova Eva

In memory of Kevin and as a place of meditation, Ken and I created this tranquil
memorial garden with the Persian Ironwood as its centerpiece.

Let your light so shine before men, that they may see your good works,
and glorify your Father which is in heaven.
Matthew 5:16

Kevin's passing has left a void in my heart that no one else can fill. That is how it should be. While I mourn his passing, his legacy fills my life and waking hours. I find comfort in knowing that he has transcended this earthly plane and now resides with Jesus Christ, his Savior. The sickness and pain ever present in his earthly realm are not even a memory where he is at this hour. We can rejoice that he has passed from death unto life. No stronger hope lies in my being than the assurance that I will see him, my precious Kevin, again one day. My loss is heaven's gain. Death changes everything. As Christians, it gives us a reason not to fear but to look forward to that glad reunion day. After all, death is an appointment we all will someday keep. Kevin's passing, although bitterly painful, has opened my eyes even wider to the brevity of our time on earth. God has not promised us tomorrow, but He has promised us eternity. We need to be about the Father's business, much as Kevin did, by living each day the best that we can. The Christian life he led continues to guide me. There is a longing for more than what earthly pleasures can offer, a longing for things more spiritual. There is comfort in knowing that no matter what circumstances arise, Kevin has been there, too. And Kevin triumphed over them. His legacy continues to unfold in the lives of those who were changed for the better from knowing him. His light, his legacy, still shines.

The following e-mails are but a small number of those I received. Even today as I read them, they still offer me encouragement, hope, and faith, in the innate goodness of those Kevin and I were blessed to call friends. Indeed, I could have easily added an additional one hundred pages to this book to include just the e-mails, not to mention the cards. God bless each of you for caring!

December 4, 2006

Thank you for the e-mail and for staying in touch. I just read your eulogy, wow. It is very powerful. I really admire your faith and courage. Being the father of a son (Paul, age 4), I can hardly imagine what you've been through. And I am so sorry to hear about your thyroid diagnosis! I pray that your treatment will go well. Know that Kevin's photo in the beautiful plaque you made for me hangs proudly on my

office wall, and I will always remember him. You were a great father to him.
In Christ, Tom

Dear Wayne, Words can't express the way Charlie and I feel. Of course we are celebrating Kevin's new home, but we hold you close in our thoughts and prayers, as you deal with your heavy load. I know it must be so difficult to have made this trip to Houston this weekend without Kevin by your side, but I know that you surely feel the Lord there with you as He has been before. Wayne, at Goshen Baptist Church, my Sunday School class wants you to know that you will continue to remain in our prayers. Of course, just let me know if there is anything at all that we can do, now or in the future. May God bless you, Tiiu

May God bless you, Wayne! You are definitely in our prayers and will continue to be! God obviously used Kevin to bless and encourage many people through his illness. God does work in mysterious ways sometimes. But, He always has a plan even when we do not understand it. I cannot imagine what you have gone through with Kevin and now with what is going on with yourself. God is with you and will stay with you no matter what! (Joshua 1:9) In Christ, Reid

Mr. Triplett,
I am so very sorry to hear about your son. Your loving and effervescent support for him obviously soothed his transition from this world to the next. May you find comfort in knowing that you and your family are in my thoughts and prayers. Best, Nancy D. Perrier, M.D., F.A.C.S.

I just read your eulogy of Kevin's life. It was beautiful, it touched my heart so much, words really can't say how we all grieve for you now. I know Kevin was your life and best friend. I could see it every day I worked with you. Kevin was an exceptional person and you are right, no one's child should go before them, but God knows what's best. Please know that you are in my prayers every day, and I pray that Kevin's scholarship will be bigger than anything we can imagine. God bless you and be with you. Love Sandy

Dear Wayne,

I just wanted to get a short e-mail off to you to tell you that you have been in my thoughts and prayers. I was so sad when I heard about Kevin's passing, but in another way thankful and happy that he would no longer have to endure the pain and affliction he had to deal with his short time on earth.

When I think about people that I admire and respect the most, as I often do, I think about four people. My mom, my dad, my pastor from the church I grew up in, and Kevin. He was such an inspiration to everyone who knew him. While Kevin was a student at West High, there were many days that I would be sitting at my desk thinking about how bad I felt or how major a problem seemed, and then Kevin's face would pop into my mind. It is then when I would realize that I didn't know what sickness was or that the problem was minute compared to what Kevin faced. His desire, determination, and zest for life was an inspiration to me and made me want to dig a little deeper for that strength.

I remember asking Kevin his sophomore year if he would like to be a waitperson at the prom. Of course, I could see the flattery in his face, but he shyly declined. He was so humble. I was so happy his senior year when he was voted Prom King. I remember counting the votes, and Kevin won by a landslide. The other two candidates only had like 17 votes between them, and Kevin had like 82. It was by far the largest margin ever won by a prom king.

I feel very blessed to have known Kevin for the short time he was at West High, and feel like my life is much richer because of the encounters I had with him. I only wish I could have known him longer and had more conversations with him. He was truly an angel on earth and feel our loss is truly Heaven's gain

At a time like this, one doesn't know quite what to say. I can't imagine losing a child, Wayne. Nor can I imagine having to go through what you have had to go through all these years not only with Kevin, but with your own health problems. I truly admire you for everything you have gone through and everything you have done for Kevin.

I hope you don't mind me sharing some of my thoughts with you. I guess, I just wanted you to know how truly fortunate I feel to have known your son. He was definitely a role model for all (kids and adults). I hope that your treatments go well and that you will be able to be at home and cancer free once and for all, soon! I plan to make a donation to the scholarship fund soon. Know you are in my prayers. Take care! Becky

Dear Becky,
Your eloquent words brought me to tears here in Houston and brought comfort to my heart. Thank you for sharing with me the positive impact Kevin made on your life, and for the inspiration he was and is to you. You remain very special to me, and please know that Kevin really cared for you. May God bless you. Love, Wayne

Thanks for the e-mails. Kevin's eulogy sounded absolutely beautiful! You are a strong man and I admire you so much. I would hope that I could do that for someone I loved. I know that your heart is broken and that you are going to miss him so much, but I hope in your time of sadness that you will remember that Kevin is walking, running and jumping on the streets of gold, laughing and shouting with Jesus, and doing everything that was a struggle for him down here. You will have to laugh when you visualize that wonderful sight. Now he is looking down on you and asking God to help you through your time of need. Kevin will always be with you in your heart and in spirit, and he can hold your hand while you are going through some of the same things he did. No one can know any better than he. I wish you the best as you face yet another battle that you will overcome. Hang in there. Please keep in touch! Cheryl

Wayne, My prayers continue to be with you. You are such an inspiration to all parents. My thoughts were with you, and they continue to be with you. How are you doing? I heard you were flying back to Texas for treatments. Is anyone with you? My thoughts and prayers are with you. Take care the best you can. Love ya, Pam at North

My biggest memory was of Kevin telling me about his fellow classmate saying he was "lucky" for he didn't have to go to school while he was in the hospital. This was back in 2000. Kevin told them that there was a teacher at the hospital and he had to go. He had to take a picture of us together to show his classmates. I don't remember what the classmates thought after that. I know that he worked very hard for me and was a wonderful person. You and Kevin gave me a copy of that picture, and I still have it on my desk. Liz

You have been in my thoughts so much. I was sorry to hear about the necessity for you to return to M. D. Anderson, but I surely hope your treatment is effective. Of course, Kevin has been in my thoughts also. The eulogy you delivered certainly reflected the love and devotion you felt for each other. It is so obvious that the son inherited his father's integrity, strength of character, and positive approach to adversity. I realize that you certainly miss him. His life was a most important one, as was the relationship the two of you shared, and I believe that his spirit will remain close to you at all times. You will continue to be on my mind and in my prayers. Please stay in touch. Sincerely, Gayle

December 5, 2006

Thank-you note published in the Millers Creek Baptist Church
Open Door

Dear MCBC Family,
Good-bye can be the saddest word, but not for a Christian like Kevin. He answered the call to come home. His determination and zest for life even while battling cancer endeared him to everyone and led us all to a greater appreciation of life. Thank you for your many acts of kindness and for wrapping us in your love. Hold fast to your cherished memories of Kevin, and he will be close to you forever. "For I reckon that the sufferings of this present time are not worthy to be compared with the glory which shall be revealed in us." Romans 8:18. Take heart, we shall see him again!
We love you. Wayne, Kathy, and the Kevin Triplett Family

Wayne, thank you so much for sending this to us. Kevin was indeed an awesome, spectacular young man. My life is enriched by what little contact I had with both of you. I think Kevin truly used his illness for the glory of God. You and Kathy are both lucky to have had your time with him, and he was definitely lucky to have had you both. I know of no other person who has gone to the lengths that you did to instill hope in a loved one. Even when the doctors gave up, you did not. Above anything else, I sensed that you gave him hope and the ability to be positive through your upbeat demeanor. Quite a wonderful gift and one that not many people receive, even when they live a long life. My husband and I will keep you and your family in our prayers as we ask that you do for us, as my husband goes through treatment for melanoma. One of the Bible verses that is precious to me is Romans 8:18: "For I reckon that the sufferings of this present time are not worthy to be compared with the glory which shall be revealed in us." God bless. Nancy

As expected, we are grieving Kevin's death along with you. You are constantly in our thoughts and prayers. I will never forget speaking to Kevin every morning as I entered my classroom at West High; he usually talked with friends just outside my door. It was an honor to have known him and to know how perseverant he was. Even though I didn't know him all that well, he was truly a remarkable young man, which brings me to another point.

My son has been looking for a long monologue to use in a debate competition. He has searched on-line and read various pieces, but to no avail. When we read Kevin's eulogy, we wondered if you might agree to letting him use it. He would, of course, give an appropriate introduction with a brief description of Kevin and your persistence in his battle with cancer. While we know how very personal this is to you, using it would present yet another opportunity for people all over the state to hear of him. Actually, the North Mock Debate Team competes all over the east from Florida to New York.

If you don't feel compelled to allow him to use the eulogy, we surely understand, but if you feel it is okay, please let us know. We would let you know of local debates in the event that you would like to attend one if you agree to let him use it. As I am writing this, I am hoping that you don't find it inappropriate that we asked. With Deepest Sympathy, The Marcelas

Marsha,

I would be honored for your son to use the eulogy. I think it would create a greater awareness of the plight teens face when dealing with a life-threatening illness. I know he will do well.

Kevin's passing was sudden, since we thought he was at MDA for a tune-up. With so many health complications and issues, it just over-whelmed his cardio-pulmonary systems.

I think of you and Mike often. Please know that I want to continue hearing from you. Kevin loved West High, the staff, and his many friends there, and I am hopeful his memorial scholarship provides other deserving students with needed financial help. Love ... Wayne

Frances forwarded the e-mails you sent to me today. I just finished reading your "tribute" to Kevin. All I can say is, "Wow." I'm attaching one of my most memorable pictures associated with working at the JP. I was so touched and honored a few years ago when Kevin wanted my picture taken with him. Although I did not know him well, I can be certain by the life he lived, that I shall have an opportunity to once again meet with him "on the other side." My prayers are with you and your family at this time. Karin

Wayne, Robert and I were very touched by Kevin's celebration. It made us both feel as though we knew his character and personality. We regret that we did not bring our 15 year old with us. We believe it would have strengthened her spiritually.

We are so sorry to know that your pathology report was returned positive. Prayers are already being sent up on your behalf. We know from your experience with Kevin how important it is that people are running along side of you to encourage you.

Even though lots of years and life have passed since our lives have crossed, you remain very special to me and will always be someone who touched my life. I remember the conversations we had about what we wanted from life. There was no way to know that what you and Kevin have gone through would be a part of that. I do regret that I never had the opportunity to know Kevin or to know Kathy. It seems you are well surrounded by loving family and friends who will help as much as humanly possible during your grieving the loss of Kevin. Please know that you are very much in our hearts and prayers. Dotty and Robert

December 7, 2006

Dear Wayne,

My prayers for you and Kathy have been offered all day as you face Kevin's first birthday with him in heaven. I pray that through your pain you are able to rejoice in his immense reward of celebrating this day with God. I am sure that Kevin is smiling on you today.

Crista and I would like to come visit you when you feel ready. Crista was at Kevin's celebration of life but had to leave when the casket was opened. She did feel strong enough to see Kevin. I was out of the country that whole week, and I am so sorry that I could not be there. You were in my prayers.

Thank you for sending me a copy of the eulogy. Charles and I both wept when we read it. I am so glad that you will be writing a book. You have a real talent, and the book will surely help other children and parents who may be going through similar suffering.

Kevin was and continues to be a blessing to every life he touched. I feel honored and blessed that God allowed me to get to know him if only for a brief time.

Please let me know when we may come to visit you. We love you, Carol and Crista

Happy Birthday Kev! It's the best I'm sure. You're spending it with Christ! Jim

We miss you, dear Kevin. We will some day see you again and be rocking like the old times. R.I.P. Take my breath away

Kevin, you just have no idea how many people you have touched while you were with us here on earth. So many people looked up to you. You were THE nicest and most caring individual I've ever known. The service was great, and I'm so glad that your parents and the rest of your family are dealing with this so well. You will never be forgotten. You will be in our hearts forever and your family will be in our prayers. I fall for (boys)

I'm gonna miss you man. I wish we had of gotten to hang out more, but I will always remember those cool times that you, Michael, and me had when we were kids. I'll see you again someday, brother. Eddie

I just wish that I could have known you better. You have amazing friends here, and we all love you very much. I know you're in heaven where you would want to be. You won't be forgotten. God bless and love, Mae

December 12, 2006

(Thank-you note published in the *Wilkes Journal-Patriot*)

Kevin Wayne Triplett
December 7, 1986–November 27, 2006

Good-bye can be the saddest word, but not for a Christian like
Kevin.
He answered the call to come home. His determination and zest
for life even while battling cancer endeared him to everyone and
led many of us to a greater appreciation of life.

Thank you for your many acts of kindness not only at this difficult
time, but through the nearly seven years which Kevin fought this
disease.

The Kevin W. Triplett Memorial Scholarship has been established
and
will be awarded annually to a deserving West Wilkes High School
senior
who wishes to attend college and may be facing medical or financial
hardships.
It is a fitting legacy honoring Kevin's noble fight against cancer, to
the love he had
for West High, and to the emphasis he placed on the value of an
education.

Hold fast to your cherished memories of Kevin and he will forever
be close to you.
Take heart ... we will see him again!

"For I reckon that the sufferings of this present time are not worthy
to be
compared with the glory which shall be revealed in us." Romans 8:18

We love you.
Wayne, Kathy, and the Kevin W. Triplett Family

December 12, 2006

I pray you are doing well. I have been praying for you (I know it is hard). Thank you for the pictures of Kevin. I have them in front of my computer, and I look at them often. Great memories! May the Lord uphold and strengthen you today. Love you brother. In Christ, Craig

December 18, 2006

Wayne,

I thought I would share this book with you. My dad fought cancer for four years and four months and passed away on July 1, 2006. I found this book and it meant a lot to me. Dr. Kubler-Ross is a medical doctor who has written a number of books. My favorite chapter (or essay) is number three in this book. The book is yours. I hope you find it to be worthwhile reading. Kenneth

On Life After Death
by Elisabeth Kubler-Ross
Essay Three: Life, Death, and Life After Death

I found the book to be a very comforting companion to my bereaved heart.

December 28, 2006

Dear Wayne,

The Cedar Ridge Neighborhood would like you to know that we are all keeping you and your family in our thoughts. In memory of Kevin, the neighborhood will be lighting a luminary at each house on Christmas Eve. Kevin was a special young man who will be greatly missed by our community. If there is anything any of us can do for you, please let us know. You will be in our prayers this holiday season. Cedar Ridge Neighborhood

The glimmering, lone candles at the end of our driveways reminded me of the light that Kevin's life had been to those around him. It was a kind and loving tribute to him.

January 8, 2007

Dear Wayne,

It was good to talk to you tonight. When I sit and think about my life I am amazed that 50 years have passed. I've been your sister for 50 years! It seems you blink and you're "looking back" at the yester-days. I really do miss you. We've never been far apart, but our lives have carried us on different journeys. I tell Sawyer about our times in school when you "looked out" for your little sister. I remember cry-ing, because I took the lamp Moma bought from the "Junk Man" to school and it broke. I came to find you. I remember on the school bus you would not let anyone bother me. I remember how scared I was when Keith hit you in the back of the head with the rock. I remember watching you on stage performing "Dang Me." I remember the day you drove me to the doctor when I passed out in the yard. Fifty years. Imagine that.

And once again you come to my rescue, "looking out" for your little sister. Thank you so much for your love. I know you have had your share of hard times, and I wish I could do something for you. You have my love, always. You won your "little sister's" heart years ago. I know Daddy would be so proud of you and the man you have become. Holding you close in my heart, Jill

January 9, 2007

Hi Terri,

Thank you so much for attending Kevin's memorial service and for your e-mail. It was so wonderful of you guys to make that long trip. I have been wondering how you were doing. I, too, have been thinking about Aaron and Kevin's reunion. What a time they must be having!

As you know it is so difficult just putting one foot in front of the other and carrying on. I took about a month to design and order Kevin's gravestone. I did not want to shut Kathy out of the process, so I have ordered a three space monument with some etchings, photos and quotes of Kevin. We have three burial plots with Kevin in the middle. It will take about four months to get it ... I will send you some photos.

I find myself reading a lot of books (5 or 6) on the afterlife. I will send you a list of titles soon. I am also reading the Bible through (hopefully) this year. Since I live alone, I am befriending Kevin's little dog Taco. He reminds me of Kevin. Of course, I visit Kevin's grave every other day and talk with him. I attend church like Kevin would want me to, and that seems to help. I went to a grief recovery meeting, too.

In a sense, Kevin and I knew that if we couldn't stop the cancer that it would eventually claim him, but we thought our last Houston visit was more of a tune-up, not a good-bye.

Kevin's band did their final concert in honor of him with proceeds going to his scholarship fund. No word yet on how much they raised. I have established his scholarship fund and now need to draw up a student application. Did you do that for Aaron and do you have a copy?

I have ordered and read several books which parents have written on the lives of their deceased children. I have also ordered some book writing software, so I can begin putting my thoughts together to start the book. I hear from Kathy maybe once or twice a week. You may recall seeing her boyfriend in the receiving line.

For the first time in seven years, I am not mixing chemo and researching protocols which is a new feeling, although to have Kevin back, I would do it all over again. In another sense it would be unfair to call him back to a life of suffering and take him away from Aaron, Jesus, and his friends. My challenge is to keep pounding and to look forward to the day when I can and will see him again. Until then, it remains difficult. We should not have had to say good-bye to our kids. We, by nature, are supposed to go first.

Please keep in touch and know that I think of you and your family daily. You mean so much to me, because this bond we share has gone full circle. We can help each other through these difficult times, and that's what friends are for. Thank you for your support through the years. We will see our boys again. Love … Wayne

Thinking about you and your inspirational life adds to my day. You remain in my daily prayers. I treasure the pictures of Kevin and me, as I treasure my memories (although brief) of him. Thank you for the kind note and everything else. Steve

Billie,
These are books I have recently read:

90 Minutes In Heaven ... Piper
Why The Resurrection ... Greg Laurie
A Touch Of His Peace ... Charles Stanley
One Minute After You Die ... Lutzer
Everyday Comfort ... Becton
On Life After Death ... Kubler-Ross
Good Grief ... Westberg
Hope for the Brokenhearted ... Terveen
Confessions of a Grieving Christian ... Ziglar
Pathways to His Presence ... Stanley
Thank you for the gift of knowledge. Your gift has led me to many of the above titles which have brought me much comfort. Keep the faith, and as Kevin always said, Keep Pounding, and Livestrong! Wayne :-)

January 23, 2007

Dear Wayne,

I'm sorry it has taken so long for me to write. I think of you, Kathy, and Kevin, daily. I hope you are doing well. I have thought about your thyroid treatment and hope that cancer is under control.

I wanted to let you know what a blessing your family has been to us. I often think of Kevin and the trials he went through, always with strength and grace. He was truly an inspiration to us all; a living testament of faith. My heart aches that he's no longer here with you.

It has been really tough for me to reconcile myself with God after Aaron's death, but I know the faith both our boys showed is living proof that we will be together again. One of my friends here at work talked to me after Kevin's death, and she said, "Can you imagine what a glorious reunion they had?" No matter how vivid our imagination, we can't come close to the realization of that reunion.

I've also wanted to thank you for including Aaron in Kevin's service. It meant so much to us to know how much he meant to you as well. Let me know how you are both doing. Also, if you are working on that book you thought about. All our love, Terri and Steve

Kevin and I had been involved in the Relay for Life for six years. I was asked to make opening comments at the kick-off for the 2007 campaign, emphasizing Kevin's involvement over the years.

February 6, 2007

Relay for Life Kickoff Notes
Wayne Triplett's Comments

Most of you my age or older remember where you were and what you were doing when pivotal events have taken place in our life times, the assassination of JFK (1963), man landing on the moon (1969), Woodstock (just kidding), Challenger explosion (1986), 9/11 terror attacks (2001). And you remember the most personal event if you are a cancer survivor, your diagnosis of cancer. Kevin's day came in April of 2000.

Kevin and I left Dr. Bennett's office crying. He had said it would take about a year to recover and you may have cancer. Later, at Baptist, Dr. Ward added, "You may lose your leg. It is confirmed to be osteogenic sarcoma or bone cancer. It is rare and only seven kids per million annually in the ten-to-fourteen–year-old age group develop it. There are only two or three occurrences in the general population." Dr. Ward later remarked, "He went in (surgery) a boy but came out a man." It was a life-changing experience and we were never to be the same again.

Our odyssey began in June of 2000 with the allograft (donor bone) surgery which was followed by almost a year of chemotherapy. The Wilkes Relay for Life was only five years old then, still an infant but still walking pretty good.

Kevin wanted to do his part, to be on the team. People like Arnold Lakey and Russell Golds came into our lives to inspire us. We had been involved in the MCES Walk for Friends raising over eleven thousand dollars for the Brenner Children's Hospital in memory of Justin Eller and in honor of Kevin. Fran Cantrell, school nurse, was instrumental in that fundraising. It was a community and school wide endeavor. But we had never raised significant monies as a team before and it was a little scary.

In 2001, Relay for Life was there and so were Kevin's Crusaders raising an astonishing $1200 through gifts and solicitations. Jars with Kevin's picture on it were everywhere. In December 2001, Kevin had a tumor recurrence in his right lung resulting in a resection and four more months of chemotherapy.

In 2002, Relay for Life was there again. Many of you may recall Kevin's passionate keynote address at the event. The allograft failed that year after his Make-A-Wish trip and a prosthetic knee and tibia were surgically implanted.

His banner year came in 2003. He got to carry it with Marsha Sidden. Unfortunately, with tumors still growing, he had an upper right lung lobectomy on December 31.

In 2004, Kevin was involved with his home church's youth praise team and was a member of his church and high school relay teams. The tumors migrated to his mid-chest area and surgery to remove a cancerous paratracheal lymph node was scheduled.

In July 2005, doctors gave up on him saying he had at most a month or two to live. Hospice was called in, but we were not ready to accept the inevitable. Again, he played for his church's relay team sitting in a chair on stage.

The world of alternative medicine was ours for over a month with Kevin taking seventy pills per day. I was able to make a contact with doctors at M. D. Anderson in Houston, Texas, and we flew there for a consultation.

In 2006, Kevin and I were honored to carry the relay banner and make part of the survivors' lap. We made seven flights to M. D. Anderson until Kevin's death there on November 27.

Throughout his struggle Kevin had many cutting edge therapies: inhaled GM-CSF, Gleevec, Avastin, quadramet (samarium 153), chemo + radiation + nuclear medicine. Not only that he had endured multiple surgeries: two leg/knee, three lung, lymph node, three rigid bronchoscopies, crutches eighteen months, two leg casts, two leg braces, one inch elevated right shoe for almost seven years, three pair of crutches, two wheel chairs and one cane. His tumor locations included the leg, brain, chest, lung, mediastinal, shoulder, and sacrum.

Indeed, we considered ourselves fortunate when he was able to celebrate another birthday, Thanksgiving, or Christmas. His faith in God, his church, his music, and band Taking Up Arms, those were his foundation and therapies. He seemed almost invincible. Aware of the constant ups and downs of his medical situation and knowing that he was anchored in his faith, this acceptance gave him an inner peace. There is no doubt in my mind that he is the greatest person I have ever known.

His cancer diagnosis in 2000 meant time to develop a new circle of friends, kids with cancer and a time to become part of a truly great network of friends, Relay for Life. Relay for Life offered Kevin and later me (2005, prostate … 2006, thyroid cancer) something bigger than cancer, a chance to fight with a remarkable team for a most noble cause.

How many of you have perhaps said like me at a funeral home or visitation, "Sorry to say, but this is about the only time I get to see my extended family or old friends. It's a pity we don't get together more often on happier occasions."

Relay for Life mirrors that a little. Each year we renew acquaintances, relive bitter-sweet moments, embrace our old friends and make some new ones. We see the true champions, the survivors. It's so wonderful to see them every year.

Relay for Life has been a rallying point for survivors to network, to check up on each other, and to honor our family and friends (in honor of luminaries) who have been touched by cancer. Relay for Life luminaries are breathtaking when you realize annually that, "I had no idea he or she had cancer." The prevalence of cancer is staggering. The roll call where for a moment in time, when you speak your name, everyone knows that your struggle has endured yet another year and you have reached another milestone.

I became teary-eyed myself last year as Kevin tearfully announced on the microphone, "Kevin Triplett, bone cancer, about six and a half years." Gary York, photographer, captured that moment vividly. Most did not see his grimace as he was overwhelmed with emotion and began to cry as he started the lap. I often wondered what he was thinking at that moment. Lastly, the "in memory of" luminaries, those who fought the good fight who have for a while left our presence, wonderful people like Diane, Jerry, Don, Ray, Becky, Dennis, Joe, Clyde, Justin, Barbara, Chelsie, Max, Walt, Sandy, and Kevin Triplett. Who will add more names to this courageous group? They cannot come to us, but one day we can go to them. There are times and quite frequently, I wish I could make that journey even now.

To everything there is a season, a time and a purpose to everything under the heavens. I believe life is a rehearsal for something even bigger to come. Kevin was wide-eyed just before his passing in that hospital bed in Houston, as if he was glimpsing a most wondrous sight. Life is a test, life is a trust, life here on earth is a temporary assignment.

I've ordered Kevin's monument which should arrive in a few months to Scenic Memorial Gardens. His memorial scholarship is in place at West High and as Arnold, just two years ago presented Kevin with a scholarship, I will be able to present a check for one thousand dollars this year in Kevin's memory to a deserving student who may be battling an illness or is in need of financial support to further his or her education. And then there's the book I hope to begin writing soon about Kevin's battle with cancer over those seven years. Kevin's story didn't end with his passing.

For now we all have work to do, a most noble work. Relay for Life is the single most significant countywide, nationwide, annual event that heightens everyone's awareness of cancer. Relay for Life champions the need to continue the research and it contributes thousands of dollars to fight this enemy, cancer, every year. Last year over $140,000 was raised.

Relay for Life gave Kevin a place to belong, a wonderful circle of caring friends and an important reason among many to never give up and to keep pounding. Kevin often said, "I wish I didn't have cancer, but it has made me appreciate life so much more because of it."

He said, "Fighting cancer has been the roughest battle of my life, but I believe it has brought me closer to God and made me a better person. I think this is God's purpose for my life, to carry on in spite of what has happened to me, to just make the best of difficult days, to make lemonade from lemons." Hard to believe a teenager could have that depth of reflection on the meaning of life isn't it?

He just wanted a normal life, a simplistic life of making music, doing the Lord's work, and enjoying the simple things. He lived a life of inspiration just by being himself, not complaining, taking one day at a time, and that continues to touch many lives.

Thank you for letting Kevin and me be a part of you, of the Relay for Life organization. Thank you for all the good that you will accomplish again this your twelfth year. Set your mark high! You can make this year another banner year in honor of the growing number of survivors and in memory of those who fought the good fight. We owe it to them.

I leave you with two questions: If not us, then who? If not now, then when? Kevin loved the fellowship and of course the meals we shared here in this very room many times in years past. He loved doing his part. In his absence, I'd like to get the fundraising campaign underway by making a contribution on this very special kickoff night in Kevin's memory, a check for $2,000. I think he would be proud that I'm contributing this tonight. Livestrong! Thank you Arnold.

February 24, 2007

Thank you so much for all you do. You are a great and strong man. Many times you and your son have been on my mind over the last couple of years. The loss Sharon and I have had cannot compare to the loss you have experienced. These kind words mean a lot. I have a tremendous amount of admiration for you and your strength. May God bless you. Bergie

As my book began taking shape, I started making inquiries into how to get it published. Karin Clack, reporter at the *Wilkes Journal-Patriot*, had collaborated with Dr. Ben Mathes to write two devotional books, *ROWvotions I* and *II*, emphasizing Rivers of the World, an international exploration and Christian ministry agency. She filled me in on an Internet-based publishing company, iUniverse.com, where authors can self-publish their book(s) with the publisher's assistance. That was all I needed to hear.

I asked Tom and Pastor Craig to contribute the foreword and epilogue respectively for my book. They were honored to do so.

March 4, 2007

Tom,

I hope you are well. I miss the visits Kevin and I made quite frequently to the clinic, and I miss you.

I have ordered Kevin's monument which should arrive by early May. It will be black granite (covering three spaces for Kathy, Kevin and me) and have three etchings of Kevin, six color photos, a scripture quote, and two of Kevin's quotes. In essence, it should be a powerful statement of his tremendous faith. I'll keep you updated.

I have established a scholarship in his memory at his local high school. This spring, and every year thereafter, I will award at least $1,000 to a deserving senior for college expenses.

I began writing my book on Kevin's struggles several weeks ago. I have disciplined myself to write (type) at least four pages (one hour) per night. I am already on page 70. I anticipate perhaps 200 pages and hope to have it finished by early May. It will include an overview of each year of Kevin's struggle and include e-mails sent, messages received, treatment protocols, Kevin's autobiography, and those experiences we had along the way.

I would be honored if you would write the FOREWORD for the book, which is tentatively titled, *This Little Light Of Mine ... The Inspiring Story of Kevin W. Triplett's Battle Against Cancer*. After completing it, I will look for a publisher with proceeds from its sale going to Kevin's scholarship fund.

I wanted to give you plenty of time to consider and hopefully agreeing to write this opening. There is no deadline for you, just whenever you feel so moved. It does not have to be lengthy, just whatever you like and from the heart.

I return to Houston (MDA) in April for a follow-up thyroid scan. I am doing well, although I miss Kevin greatly. You were with us all the way and offered so much encouragement to both of us.

God bless you my friend. Love ... Wayne

Thank you for your thoughtful e-mail. I know you (and Kathy) miss him dearly. I miss him, too. I don't need any time to think about it. I would be deeply honored to write the foreword to your book, which I am glad you're writing. It is comforting to know of his deep faith, and that he is now in heaven, where pain and suffering are no more. I'll be in touch. Warm regards, Tom

Craig,

I hope you are well. I would be honored if you would write the EPILOGUE for the book, which is tentatively titled, *This Little Light Of Mine ... The Inspiring Story of Kevin W. Triplett's Battle Against Cancer*. After completing it, I will look for a publisher with proceeds from its sale going to Kevin's scholarship fund. I am asking Dr. Tom McLean, Kevin's oncologist for seven years, to write the foreword.

Kathy and I would like to help in some way in memory of Kevin. Perhaps you would like a donation for the youth or need some THING we could get in Kevin's memory. We could get a simple plaque made to hang in the Lighthouse or somewhere which might encourage the youth. If you come up with something please let me know.

You were with us all the way and offered so much encouragement to both of us. Kevin loved you so much. God bless you my friend. Livestrong and Keep Pounding! Love ... Wayne

I count it an honor to write the Epilogue for the book. I will be praying and writing. Thanks for the opportunity. Love you! In Christ, Craig

Wayne, thanks for updating me. I miss Kevin everyday. Thanks for all you are doing. I always have said you can do anything. Kevin would be so proud of you. I hope you are feeling well. I am at work. If there is ever anything I can do for you, please let me know. I am here always. Kathy

Wilkes County Schools has traditionally been involved with the Relay for Life with various fundraisers and school teams. Dr. Stephen Laws, superintendent, knew Kevin and I had a unique perspective on cancer from battling it firsthand so many years. He asked that I share my thoughts with our principals to encourage them and their respective schools to become involved in the event.

March 14, 2007

Memo to Wilkes County Schools' Principals

Hi everyone.

All of us can recall significant events in our lives. Many are cherished while some, unfortunately, are tragic. On November 27, 2006, I lost the most important person in my life, my son Kevin, to cancer. My love for him continues to flourish in my heart, even though on many days it is aching. I miss him so much. We shared many of those good times in his nineteen years, but his last seven years were consumed with his battle against the hideous enemy, cancer.

You've read many of my e-mails and know the tremendous battle he put forth. Behind the scenes, he was a tremendous supporter of the Wilkes County Relay for Life. In 2000, after his initial diagnosis, he came up with his own team, Kevin's Crusaders and raised nearly $1,100 for the American Cancer Society. In subsequent years, he was the keynote speaker at the event as well as a member of his school and church relay teams. It was our honor (Kevin and I) to carry the relay banner twice, his last being in August 2006, just three months before his death.

His involvement in this event was his way of helping others. His legacy remains one of selfless giving and helping to raise cancer awareness. Kevin felt strongly that the annual relay was the single most significant, county-wide event to help fight cancer.

On behalf of the Wilkes County Relay for Life steering committee, I challenge each of you to assist in getting your schools involved in this noble cause. Last year, North Wilkesboro Elementary School sponsored their own relay team, the Electrifying Eaglets, and received a plaque as the school team raising the most money.

I encourage each school to:

... form a team with a special name (usually 8 to 10 staff members raising $100 each), or

... sponsor a school-wide "Hat Day" where students pay $1 to wear a hat that day (money for relay).

Teams raising a $1,000 or more will have their team names listed on the back of the official relay T-shirt.

As a cancer survivor, each year at the Relay for Life we renew old acquaintances, relive bitter-sweet moments, embrace old friends, and pay tribute to those who are no longer with us.

This years Relay for Life will take place on June 1 and 2 at Wilkes Community College. Money collected may be turned in to any of the above individuals now through the event. I encourage schools to participate now through mid-May.

Kevin often said, "Fighting cancer has been the roughest battle of my life, but I believe it has brought me closer to God and made me a better person. I think this is God's purpose for my life, to carry on in spite of what has happened to me, to just make the best of difficult days, to make lemonade out of lemons." I can do no less than carry on for a cause we both believed in. Thank you in advance for all the good you will accomplish as your schools support this year's Relay for Life event. Love ... Wayne

It's good to hear your very poignant message. I will do my best to field a team. I hope they find a cure for this ugly disease. My mother is a cancer survivor, I am lucky to still have her. I hope you continue to inspire and lead the charge. You will always have my admiration and respect.

Your friend, John

April 2, 2007

I hope you like it Wayne.
Always
Larisa

I Dream Of You In Heaven

I dream of you in heaven,
My one love for all my life.
Yet as I sit here crying,
I can't control my strife.
You battled long and hard,
Six years you made it through.
Yet now I sit here crying,
For I'm still in love with you.
I never thought this day would come,
You were immortal in my eyes.
So strong in your fight with cancer,
You were the love for all my life.
So here I am alone in bed,
Dreaming of you in a distant land.
Now all I have are faded dreams,
Lost in a sea of memories.
You were the one who took my heart and soul,
Who battled more than most could know,
I know that you are gone Kevin,
But I dream of you in heaven.

Always remembering us, our MDA pediatric and adolescent clinic
family sent us a surprise Easter card greeting.

April 5, 2007

M. D. Anderson Pediatric Clinic
Thoughts of You at Easter

Dear Wayne and Kathy,
Jesus, Easter, and Kevin's pictures remind me of short lives very well
lived. Pete

Thinking of you this Easter and remembering your wonderful Kevin! Peggy

God bless you now and always. Maritza

April 18, 2007

I was honored to be able to attend the MDA quarterly memorial service for pediatric patients who had passed away. Dr. Anderson opened the beautiful ceremony with words of welcome.

M. D. Anderson Children's Cancer Hospital Memorial Service
Dr. Pete Anderson's Comments
From the Heart

We are all just passing through and are temporary visitors here on earth. You, as parents, got to know your children in very meaningful and special ways that few parents ever experience. We have spent extra time together and know what is important.

It was a privilege for us to be a part of that life that we know means so much to you and to your family. It is in this spirit of knowing that we shall all be changed in a twinkling of an eye, that we can find reassurance of better things to come. So, in the grand scheme of things, for all of us it will be "better than expected."

On behalf of all of us at the M. D. Anderson Children's Cancer Hospital, thank you for the gift of allowing us to be a part of your child's life. Your child touched our lives. Thank you for coming.

Dr. Anderson proceeded to light the first Memorial Candle. Hospital officials and family members, including me, spoke and shared our feelings.

The Wake Forest staff remembered Kathy on Mother's Day, knowing it would be a difficult time, especially for her.

May 9, 2007

Dear Kathy.
We wanted you to know that we were thinking of you this Mother's Day.

The Pediatric Oncology Staff (WFUBMC) Tom, Marcia, Nancy, Debby, Diane, Carol, Sharon, Jeff

May 25, 2007

Dear Wayne and Kathy,
I just wanted to let you know that we still often think of Kevin and his guitar playing! I know you must deeply miss him and I want you to know he will never be forgotten. God bless you both … Sandi

I was especially touched by the beautiful tribute poem written by my sister, Jill, and by the card Joe, Kevin's band member and friend, shared with me.

June 18, 2007

My Tribute to Kevin
by Jill Whitman (Wayne's sister)

It's not how long you live, but how you live, that matters most.
It's not how much you get, but how much you give.
It's not if you'll have trials, but that you will.
It's where you place your faith that determines how you live.

There is joy that you have reached your heavenly home
And have traded your cross for a crown.
There is sadness in facing tomorrow
Without you being around.

You lived your life in victory
Because you knew the one in command.
You trusted Him completely
As you walked across life's shifting sands.

Your daily trials were many
More than seemed your share.
You met them all with courage
Even when life seemed so unfair.

You taught me how wonderful and precious
It is to walk with Him.

The one who brings peace in the midst of the storm
And light when our way grows dim.

The way you lived your life
Allowed God's strength and love to abound.
And that brought many others to claim
"I was lost, but now I'm found."

Afraid to die—no.
Ready to die—yes.
Your testimony "It is well with my soul."
"I do not have to guess."

I know that you are safely HOME
You are with the SON.
God is well pleased with the fight you fought
Your battle is now won.

It's not how long you lived, but how you lived, that matters most.
It's not how much you had, but how much you gave.
It's not the trials, but how you faced them.
It's where you placed your faith that made you brave.

Thank you Kevin for all you taught me by your example.

I love you,
Jill

June 20, 2007

Dear Wayne,
Thank you very much for the graduation card and the generous gift of money! I'll be using it towards a new guitar or amp, so don't worry, it'll be put to good use. But anyways, I hope all is well and if there is ever anything you need that I can help with, let me know. Kevin greatly impacted my life, and I believe a good bit of that came from you being a wonderful father and raising him well. I love and respect you very much. Love, Joe

I presented Kevin's scholarship to Tommy Testerman at the West Wilkes High School senior awards program in late May. I was delightfully surprised and deeply moved after reading the card from Tommy and his parents. I knew that Tommy truly deserved the scholarship, and perhaps Kevin was looking out for him.

June 29, 2007

Mr. Triplett,

I'm sorry it has taken me so long to get in touch with you between work, church, and school stuff. I have not had a second to relax. I want you to know, that day at the awards banquet was one of the best days of my life. It's a true honor to get your son's scholarship.

I don't know if you know, but two days after I submitted my application, I was struck in the face with a baseball bat. My nose was broken really bad. I had reconstructive surgery two days before my senior prom. The day I got hit, not one minute before, I had warned my teammates to watch for others. One of my own teammates let go of the bat. Something told me to look up, so I had time to move back so it only got my nose. I have often wondered if Kevin might have been watching over me that night. Thank you for everything, and I'm looking forward to your book. If you ever want to call me, here's my number. Thank you again ... Tommy Lee Testerman

Mr. Triplett,
We both would like to thank you and Kevin's mother for the wonderful gift you have given our son. May God bless you both. Tommy and Vickie Testerman

Kevin's monument finally arrived and was placed on July 4, 2007. I called Pastor Craig the next day and invited him to go with me to see it. He met me there, remaining in his car until I arrived. As Craig approached it, tears came to his eyes. "I miss him so much," he cried. "My, my, it's just beautiful," he said. We looked at the photos and etchings and then read Kevin's quotes on his faith in Jesus Christ. "It will be a lasting testimony for anybody who reads it," said Craig. "It is the most beautiful monument I have ever seen."

"I wanted it to be Kevin's witness from beyond the grave," I cried as I hugged him. "Kevin loved you so much," I said.

"We've got to get the youth out here to see it," he said. "I'm going to bring my family." We had prayer, thanking God for Kevin, for the life he lived, and for his tremendous witness which would endure forever.

July 6, 2007

Wayne,

I think that is the most beautiful monument I have ever seen! Craig said it was unbelievable, and he would have to take me to see it. He was so moved when he came home yesterday and told me about it. What a remarkable testimony of Kevin's life. People, for ages to come, will be able to read about God's wonderful promises and a hope for a better place. Kevin was blessed to have parents like you and Kathy. Your devotion and love for him continues to ring out even today. You continue to honor him and the Lord. May His blessings remain on you. Thanks for sharing these photos. Kim

Kevin spent a lot of time with his grandparents, Ralph and Martha Shew (Pa and Granny), especially during his sickness, and they loved each other dearly. Martha felt moved to contribute her thoughts on her love for him and on his struggles.

July 7, 2007

A Special Message from Martha Shew (Kevin's Granny)

Kevin was my grandson and a great one at that. His grandpa (Ralph) and I kept him a lot during his recovery from surgery and chemotherapy. He struggled with his sickness, but he never lost his faith in the Lord. He knew he had a life threatening disease. Sometimes, I could see the fear in his eyes.

We loved him so much, and we know that he loved us, too, because he told us on many occasions. He asked me to have get-togethers with our family. He enjoyed those special family times, and it meant so much to him when we were all there together.

I'm sure he wondered why cancer struck him. We believe he touched so many lives with his great faith in the Lord through his illness. I believe in the later stages, he knew he was losing the battle. He called me from Houston several days before he passed away saying, "Granny, I'm getting so tired." Every night before I go to bed his words come back to me, "Granny, be glad you're alive. Enjoy life."

He was so special to his grandpa and to me. He still is our bright and shining light, and we hope to meet him again in heaven someday.

Kathy, Kevin's mother, loved him dearly. Her reflections offer a glimpse into the inner anguish she felt at his untimely illness. At the same time, they testify to the ultimate triumph of his spirit.

July 9, 2007

A Special Message from Kathy Triplett (Kevin's Mother)

It is overwhelming writing this and knowing that my Kevin is gone from this life. I miss him everyday.

Kevin's birth changed my life, forever making it sweeter and more precious, while his death is so final. Kevin will always be alive in my heart. I will not let go.

I remember the day Kevin and Wayne went to the doctor and Wayne called telling me it would take a year to get well, but Kevin would probably come through this. "Why?" I asked myself. "I don't understand. Surely not!" I knew something wasn't right. We kept thinking that surely they had made an error in the diagnosis. It must be a misunderstanding. I remember hanging my head as Dr. Ward told Kevin it was cancer. I wanted to protect my son. The doctor told him perhaps later on in life, after this ordeal, he could be sitting on his porch and strumming his guitar. The hope of "someday" seemed enough at that time. Knowing that Kevin could hang on and be alive was comfort enough.

During his many treatments and surgeries, you could not ask for a better patient. He was always willing to try to beat the odds. The chemotherapy made him feel bad. Even though he lost his hair and weight, he still weathered each trial set before him. I don't know how he remained so strong, but he was no quitter.

He loved North Carolina and the Carolina Panthers. I recall him telling people in Houston, "North Carolina is beautiful. You should try to come and see it sometime."

Everyday when I would bring him home, he would ask for the phone to check if anyone had called. Most days, no one had. I thought about asking people to call, but I knew sometimes he did not feel like talking. He also wanted to know if he had mail. With all his pain and suffering, he still tried to carry on with life.

He had a 4-wheeler at one point and enjoyed riding it. In his last months, he would ask for his helmet, goggles, and gloves, and sit on the sofa with his equipment on. I tried to stay behind him, so he would not see me crying, wondering what he was thinking in his head inside the helmet. I knew he would probably never ride again. I was hurting for him. It seemed so unfair. He was always off the scale in height and weight. How could he be struck down with cancer? There was nowhere to go. Be happy with what you have today, because it is all any of us have.

There were so many special things about Kevin. He always thought of others. When he found out he had cancer, the first thing he said was, "It sure is going to be hard on Granny and Pa." He was wise beyond his age. He often told me he felt like an old man. I would tell him he was not old, and that I was sorry he felt that way. It was the disease.

From June 2006 through November 2006, I was with him almost every day. Those days were gifts. In the fall, he would get up and I would bring him a cup of apple cider. He might have to put on a light coat and gloves, but he enjoyed this. We would sit on the porch in the rocking chairs listening to the birds. We just liked being there together. He told me that fall was his favorite time of year. Sometimes we would talk or just be still. He shared with me how he felt, his beliefs, and his values, many of which I carry with me every day. If I felt down he would say, "Mom, if you feel down, do something for someone. That is the best thing to do." If I got aggravated he would say, "Don't get all worked up, Mom."

I will miss being called "mom," Kevin wishing me Merry Christmas, happy birthday, and happy mother's day. I will always be thankful for the blessing he was in my life and the blessing he still is to others. Some parents do not have children, even as long as I had Kevin. As a parent, you always want more for your child. A friend once told me that as long as we are on this earth, there will always be disease, pain, and suffering.

I miss Kevin so much. In his last days, he wondered why he was even here. Sometimes he would say, "Mom, the days end like they begin." He would be coughing, taking medicine, and struggling. He shared with me how life is like a vapor. He would tell me not to worry about him, and that he would be okay. Kevin had grown tired. He wanted to live, but when surgery was not an option, he knew his body could not take much more. His body looked like a body in war with scars down his chest, along his rib cage, and down his leg.

His last night as he lay suffering, he was very restless. The last thing I remember him saying was, "I want to go home."

I miss seeing his phone number light up on my phone and his needing me. I miss the unconditional love a mother has for her son. I could never say enough about my son. The love I have and hold for him is forever and will continue to be with me as long as I live. I will try to take life one day at a time. Kevin is at peace now. No more suffering, no more pills, no more chemo, surgery or radiation, no more doctors telling him there is nothing we can do, just peace forever.

"The most important thing in life is your relationship with God. God has a special plan for everyone.
The greatest decision anyone can make is deciding to trust God's Son Jesus Christ as personal Lord and Savior and repent of their sins."

"As a Christian I try to point people to Jesus. God loves us all and He sent His only Son to die for us,
and He arose from the grave on the third day. Eternity is too long to be wrong. Choose Jesus!"

Kevin's light still shines as his personal quotes grace his monument and proclaim his tremendous faith in Jesus Christ.

My Closing Message to You

The impact of Kevin's life, of anyone's life, is measured not by what we leave this world with, but rather what we leave with this world to enrich the lives of others. I cannot say, "it is finished," because Kevin's legacy lives on. When a loved one dies we have two choices: We can withdraw and choose to be bitter, or take the high road and move forward to answer a higher calling. The latter is the road I have taken.

Kevin left gigantic shoes which no one can fill. His faith, courage, and tremendous will to live while battling cancer touched thousands of lives. His race is run, but the good that he did lingers. His life, his battles against cancer are now an open book, testifying to the impact that Jesus Christ had in his life. Christ sustained him and saw him through to the end. Kevin's mission while on earth was to let others see Jesus in him. Kevin fulfilled that mission. His life was and is a testimony to the awesome power of Jesus Christ in one young man's life. The Comforter was with him. Kevin never walked alone.

The M. D. Anderson Children's Cancer Hospital in Houston, Texas, held a beautiful memorial service in memory of young cancer patients who had recently passed away including Kevin. Dr. Pete Anderson, Kevin's doctor, shared comforting opening comments. Photos of each patient were displayed and candles were lit in their honor. I was able to attend the touching April 2007 ceremony while there for my thyroid recheck. I was given flowers and a pendant created by a cancer patient. Each time I look at my black and blue M. D. Anderson tote bag, I'm reminded of the many times over sixteen months that I packed it full of medicine, tissues, barf bags, and water, hung it over his wheelchair handles, and pushed Kevin nearly a half mile from our hotel room to the clinic.

The 2007 Wilkes Relay for Life was dedicated to the memory of Kevin and Marsha Sidden, and saw its greatest year ever in contributions to fight cancer. I carried the banner in his honor. Kevin had been a team sponsor, a guest speaker, and an inspiration to hundreds of cancer survivors.

Kevin's memorial monument which I designed is truly unique with etchings of Kevin, color photos, scripture, and bears his personal quotes championing his tremendous faith in Jesus Christ. It is a testimony and witness which speaks to anyone walking by and pausing to read.

Kevin loved the youth of his church, and an acrylic podium with an inscription honoring him has been given to the youth ministry for their worship center. It includes an etching of his guitar, which highlights just one of his contributions to worship and service to his Lord.

The Kevin Wayne Triplett Memorial Scholarship has been established, and this past spring a deserving senior at West Wilkes High School was presented a check for one thousand dollars to further his education. It was a touching moment as the young man embraced me and Kevin's mother in appreciation. This scholarship will be given annually with proceeds from the sale of this book benefiting this fund.

Funny how the mind works. I have been pondering the significance of the number seven (7) in Kevin's life. That number is commonly referred to as God's number. Kevin was born on December 7, was diagnosed with cancer in the seventh grade, owned seven guitars, had seven major surgeries, had cancer therapy on the seventh floor at MDA, made seven flights to Houston flying over parts of seven states, battled cancer almost seven years, and passed away on November 27. Coincidence, maybe, but we know that God was at work in his life in a mighty way.

The writing of this book fully establishes the impact Kevin's life had on so many. He just wanted to live a normal life, but when cancer was thrust upon him, he found himself taking on the full armor of Christ to endure his many trials. He never asked for notoriety. It just happened. I knew his story would be an inspiration for others to carry on, even in the face of overwhelming odds.

A gaping hole is left in my life where Kevin once was. His absence at times is heart wrenching, but it has also fueled my desire to pick up the gauntlet Kevin left behind. In passing the torch to me, I must run with it. He is forever with me—in his memorial garden in my front yard; in my visits to his grave; in the quietness of the morning, as I sit in his front porch rocking chair and listen as birds begin their daily ritual of singing; in the music collection he left behind; and, in the changed and enriched lives of those who knew him.

Those touched by Kevin declare the impact of his life on theirs:

"I will never forget him."
"I'll never be half the man Kevin was."
"Kevin's life just makes me want to live for Christ."
"He really inspired me to pattern my life after him."
"What an inspiration he was for me, just keep on going."
"Few people have had an impact on my life like Kevin had."
"You made me want to be a better person and a better Christian."

"Let your light so shine before men, that they may see your good works, and glorify your Father which is in heaven." Matthew 5:16

Kevin said it best as we revisit his "Life's Most Important Things." It is my hope that this book has given you a more personal glimpse into this remarkable young man's life; a glimpse into a life well lived; a glimpse into a life that mattered. I say that with pride as his dad. I say that with conviction, because others have voiced those sentiments as well. Although we grieve in his absence, we rejoice in the realization of his ultimate healing, now that he is with his Savior. I look forward with anticipation to the day I will be reunited with him.

May your life be enriched, may your faith be strengthened, and may you find renewed joy in living, since Kevin passed your way.

Wayne Triplett
Millers Creek, North Carolina
August 2007

Life's most important things

Everyone has got their view on what they think is most important in life. It's sad that some people get so caught up in drugs and alcohol that they miss what is most important in life.

The most important thing in life is your relationship with God. God has a special plan for everyone. The greatest decision anyone can make is deciding to trust God's son Jesus Christ as personal Lord and Savior and repent of their sins.

Another important thing in life is your relationships with others. We should love others even our enemies. We should treat others the way that we want to be treated. When someone does us wrong we should not hold grudges. We should forgive them and love them. It is better to encourage others rather than bring them down.

An education is very important to have in life. Times have radically changed and without a good education it is hard for some people to find a good paying job. I don't always like going to school. I am a senior in High School, and I realize and appreciate more how blessed I am to have had a good education all my life with teachers that care.

Those are three things that I believe are most important in life. They really impacted my life and always will. It's great to be alive. Enjoy life!

"Yesterdays"

by
Switchfoot

Flowers cut and brought inside, black cars in a single line.
Your family in suits and ties and you're free.
The ache I feel inside is where the life has left your eyes.
I'm alone for our last goodbye, but you're free.
I remember you like yesterday, yesterday.
I still can't believe you're gone.
Oh, I remember you like yesterday, yesterday.
And until I'm with you, I'll carry on.

Rev. Craig Church, student pastor, was Kevin's brother in Christ and much more.
I am convinced that Kevin's spiritual strength in great part was due to the guidance,
nurturing, and love shown to him by Pastor Craig.
They talked often and found strength for their journeys in each other.
They loved each other dearly.

EPILOGUE

KEVIN TRIPLETT

What do you think of when you hear the word "courage"? Do you see a para-chutist jumping from an airplane, a circus trainer taming a lion, or do you see an image of a firefighter in the 9/11 attacks? *Merriam-Webster's Dictionary* defines "courage" as bravery and fearlessness. Courage, to me, comes in the form of a nineteen-year-old young man, with a certain disease, facing a certain death, with no uncertainties about life now and life hereafter.

For six full years of my life, courage was synonymous with the name Kevin Triplett. As his youth pastor and friend, I watched the power of defeat crumble as it looked into the face of a young man who knew not cowardice, complaint, or resignation. In the midst of the dreaded disease of cancer, and a sentence of death looming over his life, how could a teenager, a youth, find victory rather than bitterness? It's simple. Kevin was convinced that this life wasn't the end. II Timothy 4:6–8 says, "For I am now ready to be offered and the time of my departure is at hand. I have fought a good fight, I have finished my course, I have kept the faith: Henceforth there is laid up for me a crown of righteousness, which the Lord, the righteous judge, shall give me at that day: and not to me only, but unto all them also that love his appearing."

The life of Jesus was manifested through Kevin. II Corinthians 4:7–10 says, "But we have this treasure in earthen vessels that the excellency of the power may be of God, and not of us. We are troubled on every side, yet not distressed; we are perplexed, but not in despair; persecuted, but not forsaken; cast down, but not destroyed; Always bearing about in the body the dying of the Lord Jesus, that the life also of Jesus might be made manifest in our body." Because of how he lived and died, Kevin showed more people Jesus than we will ever know.

Kevin knew the end was really just the beginning. He had already made the necessary preparations. Jesus Christ was his personal Lord and Savior, his friend, and He could be trusted. On November 27, 2006, Jesus took Kevin by the hand, whispered in his ear "well done," and ushered him into the glories of heaven. Why was there no fear, no apprehension, and no dread? Because, Jesus knows the way home.

Kevin would want me to ask, "Do you know the way?" Jesus said in John 14:6, "I am the way, the truth, and the life. No man cometh to the Father but by me." Kevin not only knew the way, he also pointed the way to others. Kevin Triplett was a life well lived.

Rev. Craig Church
Student Pastor
Millers Creek Baptist Church
Millers Creek, North Carolina
June 2007

Printed in the United States
by Baker & Taylor Publisher Services